The Document Object Model
Processing Structured
Documents

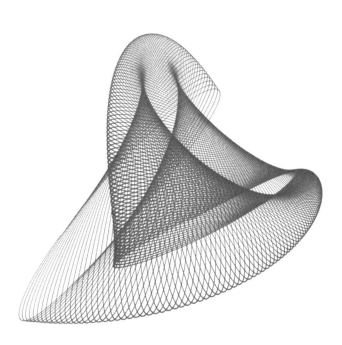

About the Author

Joe Marini has been a professional software engineer for 12 years at companies such as Quark, Inc., mFactory, Macromedia, and Panscopic Corporation. Joe also founded his own software development company, Lepton Technologies, which was acquired by Extensis Corp. in 1997. Joe served as Macromedia's representative to the World Wide Web Consortium's Document Object Model working group from 1999–2000.

In addition to his engineering work, Joe has served as a contributing author on several books, including *Fireworks MX Magic* with Lisa Lopuck and the forthcoming *Beyond Dreamweaver* with Joseph Lowery. Joe is also a regular speaker at various industry conferences on web development and related subjects. Joe works and lives in San Francisco and Lake Tahoe, California with his wife, Stacy, and their dog, Milo.

The Document Object Model: Processing Structured Documents

Joe Marini

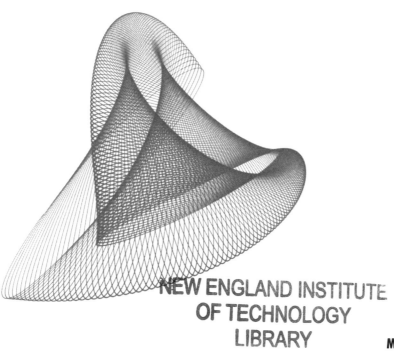

McGraw-Hill/Osborne

New York Chicago San Francisco
Lisbon London Madrid Mexico City Milan
New Delhi San Juan Seoul Singapore Sydney Toronto

4-05

McGraw-Hill/Osborne
2600 Tenth Street
Berkeley, California 94710
U.S.A.

To arrange bulk purchase discounts for sales promotions, premiums, or fund-raisers, please contact **McGraw-Hill/**Osborne at the above address. For information on translations or book distributors outside the U.S.A., please see the International Contact Information page immediately following the index of this book.

The Document Object Model: Processing Structured Documents

1234567890 FGR FGR 0198765432

ISBN 0-07-222436-3

Publisher	Brandon A. Nordin
Vice President & Associate Publisher	Scott Rogers
Acquisitions Editor	Jim Schachterle
Project Editor	Laura Stone
Acquisitions Coordinator	Timothy Madrid
Technical Editor	Andrew Woolridge
Copy Editor	Sally Engelfried
Proofreaders	Linda Medoff, Paul Medoff
Indexer	Jack Lewis
Computer Designers	Carie Abrew, Kelly Stanton-Scott
Illustrators	Lyssa Wald, Michael Mueller
Series Design	Roberta Steele
Cover Series Design	Greg Scott
Cover Illustration	Akira Inoue / Photonica

This book was composed with Corel VENTURA™ Publisher.

To Stacy and Milo,
for their love, patience, and support;
and to my Mom,
for her continual encouragement
and for making it all possible.

Contents at a Glance

Contents

Acknowledgments

Let me say right up front that this is my first full-length book, and I am very grateful to have worked with a wonderful team at McGraw-Hill/Osborne. Most of my writing up until this point had been in pursuit of much smaller-scale projects, and the McGraw-Hill/Osborne team made sure the book went smoothly.

In particular, I want to thank Jim Schachterle for seeing the potential for a book about the Document Object Model, for believing in me, and for getting the project approved. Next, thanks to Timothy Madrid for making sure chapters stayed on schedule, and to Laura Stone for all the editing help and for putting up with all those times I changed my mind about something in mid-stream.

Special thanks go to Andrew Woolridge, my technical editor, whom I've known since the early Dreamweaver days. When I had to find someone with the technical ability to review pages of JavaScript, C++, and Java code, Andrew came through.

I couldn't have completed this book without the help of everyone mentioned above. You hold the completed work of all of us in your hands; I hope it helps you create the next generation of web applications.

Introduction

Web applications have come a long way since the release of Netscape Navigator 2.0, the first web browser to have a scripting language embedded in it. That language, JavaScript, allowed developers for the first time to manipulate their web pages directly in the user's browser. From those humble beginnings arose the Document Object Model, a full-fledged specification of standard methods and properties for working with HTML and XML data.

The need for a standard API for working with these types of documents became clear almost immediately after HTML and XML technologies began to catch on with the Internet development community. The World Wide Web Consortium (W3C) realized that the types of operations needed to work with these documents were common enough that they could be specified in a portable way, allowing different document-processing application vendors to offer a standard interface. This, in turn, allowed developers to focus their energies on building their applications rather than figuring out which browser or platform they would need to port their work to.

With this book, you learn to use the DOM to work with HTML and XML data in a variety of settings, including web browsers, server-side applications, and consumer client applications. The DOM is language independent, so you don't need to worry about learning an unfamiliar programming language. The DOM is also available in most of the web browsers in use today, such as Internet Explorer 5 and later and Netscape Navigator 6 and later (and Mozilla 1.0 and later), so finding a place to test your applications should be easy. You also learn the different ways of manipulating documents and their content, how to provide the user with new kinds of user interfaces, and how to help lighten the server's load by moving some processing to the client.

Who Should Read this Book

Every day, XML and HTML are becoming more and more prevalent in an ever-widening variety of applications. Developers who want to quickly create applications that leverage these technologies can use the Document Object Model to save themselves a lot of time and trouble associated with learning one vendor's proprietary interfaces for working with these kinds of structured documents. In this book, you'll find out how to

▶ Work with the common data types and structures needed to create professional DOM applications

▶ Discover the structure of a document dynamically and navigate its elements

▶ Discover and change any part of a document's content

▶ Build DOM applications that work across multiple browsers and other implementations

▶ Use the browser-based DOM to create entirely new kinds of user interfaces and navigational elements

▶ Offload server-side processing onto the client—for example, sorting data and deriving entirely new data from existing data

▶ Embed XML data in web pages and present it to the user at runtime

▶ Take advantage of common algorithms and processes to avoid reinventing the wheel

▶ Effectively debug DOM applications in browsers and other implementations

How to Use This Book

This book is organized into 12 different chapters in three parts. Part I introduces the DOM, explains some important concepts, and introduces the basic structures that the DOM uses to represent a document. It also introduces the DOM interfaces and reviews their functionalities and purposes. Part II addresses real-world DOM usage, from typical DOM algorithms to the DOM support available in various web browsers and other popular application packages. The subject of debugging DOM-based applications is also covered. Part III examines several practical uses of the DOM and shows examples of how to take advantage of the DOM in your applications, from providing client-side data sorting to performing complex data manipulation directly in the client.

If you aren't already familiar with the DOM or its concepts, then you should read Chapters 1 and 2 for an introduction and high-level overview of the DOM, along with what it specifically does not address and leaves as implementation dependent. Otherwise, you can skip directly to Chapter 3 for a look at how DOM interfaces are used to perform common document operations.

It isn't necessary to have a copy of the W3C DOM specification handy in order to use this book, although you may find it helpful as a reference. You can download a copy in one of many different formats (HTML, PDF, PostScript, etc.) by visiting the W3C on the Web at www.w3.org/DOM.

The different parts of the book are described in detail in the following sections.

Part I: Overview of the W3C Document Object Model

Chapter 1, "Introduction to the DOM," presents a high-level overview of how the DOM is organized and how it came into being. In this chapter you learn the history behind the DOM, the forces shaping its evolution, and the design philosophy that went into making the DOM what it is today.

Chapter 2, "How the DOM Represents Structured Documents," discusses how a DOM implementation represents a structured document to a client application. This chapter introduces basic data types and document structures that all DOM applications need to deal with. It also discusses the DOM document tree and other important theoretical DOM concepts.

Chapter 3 "Navigating and Manipulating Structured Documents," introduces the various DOM Level 1 Core API methods available for inspecting document content, modifying it, and navigating among the document's elements.

Part II: Real-World DOM

Chapter 4, "Algorithms," illustrates some common algorithms encountered when working with the DOM. Read this chapter to learn about basic node traversal, determining the relative positions of nodes, and determining node content.

Chapter 5, "Browsers," examines the current level of DOM support in various browser applications such as Netscape 6, IE 5/6, and Opera 6. This chapter investigates the major differences among the implementations, the proprietary extensions of each, and how to go about creating applications that work across multiple browsers.

Chapter 6, "Applications," explores DOM support in various non-browser applications such as Macromedia Dreamweaver, Apache Xerces, etc. Here we discuss the differences among each, how each evolved, and some common applications.

Chapter 7, "Debugging DOM Applications," illustrates various debugging techniques for working with DOM code in browser and non-browser applications. This chapter examines ways of catching error conditions at runtime, making code easier to debug, and examining document structure at specific points in the application's life.

Part III: Practical Uses of the DOM

Chapter 8, "Providing Automatic Document Navigation," demonstrates common ways of providing the user with navigation aids in a DOM application. In particular, it shows how to build user interface elements that dynamically populate themselves based on document content and how to respond to user events to help a user maintain their place in the document.

Chapter 9, "Dynamic User Interfaces," demonstrates how to make rich, dynamic user interfaces using DOM methods. This chapter covers how to dynamically create and check common form elements in response to user events and how to use HTML elements to create entirely new types of user interface controls.

Chapter 10, "Client Processing of Data-Driven Documents," illustrates some common techniques for document processing on the client side, such as sorting data, reading the contents of a document to derive entirely new data, and performing data calculations on the client.

Chapter 11, "Future Directions for the DOM," looks at the evolution of the DOM and where it is going. Read this chapter to learn about the changes coming up in DOM Level 3, new technologies such as XPath and XSLT, and techniques that have not yet been addressed in the DOM but might be down the road, such as Transaction-based processing.

The appendix, "DOM Core Level 1 API Reference," lists the core modules and interfaces of DOM Level 1, their arguments, and their associated exception types.

Overview of the W3C Document Object Model

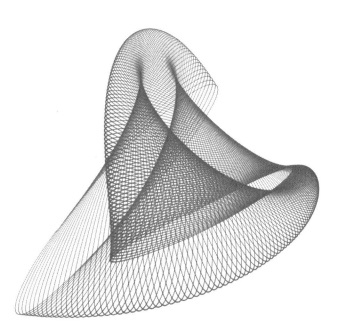

CHAPTER 1

Introduction to the DOM

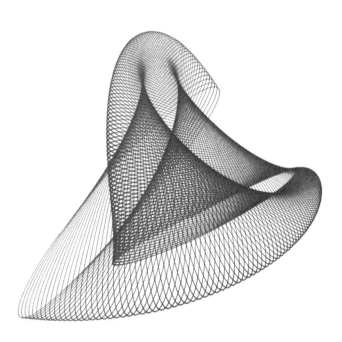

T he Document Object Model specification, published by the World Wide Web Consortium (W3C), represents a significant advancement in the handling of structured documents. The specification provides a standard set of programming interfaces for working with information stored in XML (eXtensible Markup Language), HTML (HyperText Markup Language), and other types of documents containing structured information. Using the DOM application programming interface (API), application programmers can write their code to one common set of methods that will work across various DOM implementations.

The W3C DOM specification is written both for companies who want to implement DOM functionality in their applications and programmers who want to use the DOM programming interfaces to manipulate that information. In this book, we explore the DOM mainly from the programmer's point of view, using the core methods of DOM Level 1 to work with structured documents, along with other parts of the DOM specification where necessary (such as events and Cascading Style Sheets, or CSS). We begin this chapter by examining the philosophy and history of the DOM and taking a look at the different DOM levels of support. Then we cover some important things to remember when reading the W3C DOM specification and general conventions that the specification uses.

What Is the Document Object Model?

Put simply, the W3C Document Object Model, better known as the DOM, is a set of platform- and language-neutral application programming interfaces (APIs) that describe how to access and manipulate information stored in structured XML and HTML documents. It is a recognized and recommended standard published and maintained by the W3C, or World Wide Web Consortium, an organization of member companies dedicated to establishing and promoting standards for the World Wide Web. According to the W3C DOM specification, the term *Document Object Model* was chosen because the DOM is an object model in the traditional object-oriented programming sense: documents are modeled using objects, and the model describes the structure of the document as well as its behavior and the behavior of its objects.

DOM documents are represented by a *tree* structure, with each point in the tree called a *node*, as shown in the following example. Suppose you have a typical HTML document, such as this:

```
<HTML>
<HEAD>
<TITLE>This is a document.</TITLE>
</HEAD>
<BODY>
<B>This is some bold text!</B>
<I>This is some italic text!</I>
</BODY>
</HTML>
```

This HTML code can be represented as a tree structure, as illustrated in Figure 1-1. This figure neatly illustrates the relationship between different tags in the HTML document, much like a family tree. At the top, or *root* of the tree, is the <HTML> tag itself. Underneath the root, the other tags become *children* of the root tag. These child tags can, in turn, have children of their own; for example, the <HEAD> tag is clearly a child of the <HTML> tag; and the <TITLE> tag is, in turn, a child of the <HEAD> tag. Child tags that share the same *parent* tag are said to be *siblings* of each other. The DOM specification uses this type of notation and terminology extensively in its API.

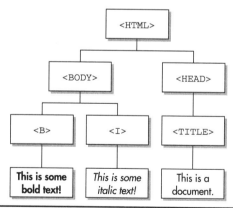

Figure 1-1　*Document tree diagram*

Yet Another Standard?

So why do we need another standard? As the XML language has grown in importance over the past several years, so, too, has the need for a standardized way of accessing the information stored in XML documents. The DOM provides a standard set of methods for adding, removing, changing, and examining a document's elements and for navigating a document's structure. It is important to note that the term *document* is used here in a very broad sense. Even though much of the information that is presented via XML would normally be seen as raw data, XML information is presented as a document, and the DOM can be used to manage this information.

Before the advent of the DOM, companies that wanted to exchange information using XML had to use their own proprietary APIs for getting at the data within these documents; now, vendors can provide a standard set of methods and objects that represent the internal logical structure of their information regardless of its internal representation. In fact, the DOM does not explicitly specify anything regarding how data must be stored internally to an application. Vendors are free to use whatever internal storage mechanism they feel is most appropriate for their data. The DOM attempts only to describe how that data is represented to the outside world from a user of that application's point of view. Content authors can then write to these standard APIs instead of having to learn the proprietary interfaces offered by a large number of different application vendors, which, in turn, enhances and increases the interoperability of the Internet.

The DOM Philosophy

As with any large design project, the DOM Working Group had to choose a reasonable scope for their work, lest the API get out of control and try to accomplish everything. In addition, the group met face-to-face only once every six weeks, so the design had to be modular enough to support collaboration among disparate and remote colleagues. The group also realized early on that there would be a variety of DOM API users, and satisfying them all would be no easy task.

Faced with these realities, the DOM Working Group had to decide on a simple, flexible design philosophy for the DOM specification to succeed in being adopted by vendors. The principles were kept simple and realistic: be open and extensible, make the spec as easy to understand and implement as possible, and stay language and platform neutral.

Design Philosophy

The DOM Working Group, composed of the W3C member companies interested in working together on the DOM specification, decided early on to adhere to a basic philosophy regarding the DOM: specify only what needs to be specified. In other words, focus only on the important parts of document manipulation without worrying about the details of how a program came to be in possession of the document object itself or a host of other platform- and implementation-specific details. The details of the implementation of these and other capabilities were intentionally left to the individual vendor companies, with the understanding that later versions of the DOM would attempt to address them.

In addition, the W3C members realized that platform and language neutrality would play a key part in the DOM's acceptance by application vendors. Thus, the DOM was designed to be used with any programming language; and today there are language bindings for almost every popular language, including Java, JavaScript (ECMAScript), Python, Perl, C/C++, and others. These bindings are available from well-known large companies such as Oracle and IBM, as well as popular open-source movements, such as the Apache Foundation.

The DOM was also designed to be open and extensible; that is, a vendor may add methods and properties outside of those that the DOM specification defines, yet still be considered to be compliant with the DOM spec. Microsoft, for example, provides several Internet Explorer–specific extensions to the DOM API for developers' convenience without breaking compliance with the base DOM specification.

Object-Oriented vs. Flat Views of the DOM Interfaces

The DOM specification takes a couple of different approaches toward specifying interfaces for manipulating XML/HTML documents: a traditional, hierarchical *inheritance* approach, and a simpler, *flattened* approach. The inheritance approach works just like any good object-oriented programmer would expect: there exists a hierarchy of interface classes, with each subclass inheriting the interfaces of its superclass. The flattened approach takes the view that all document manipulation can be accomplished using the Node interface without requiring the programmer to cast a node reference to another type of object.

According to the specification, this decision was made because casting objects from one type to another can be an expensive operation in some programming environments, such as Java and Microsoft's COM. The DOM Working Group realized that the DOM API would be used in performance-critical environments where such operations could have a materially adverse impact on system performance. Thus, the decision was made to allow a significant amount of the DOM's functionality to be used via the Node interface.

Still, the DOM Working Group considers the hierarchical view of the API to be the "primary" view of the DOM, with the added functionality of the Node interface as "extra" functionality that developers can use at their discretion. The spec notes that this leads to some redundancy; for example, even though there is a generic property called `nodeName` on the Node interface, there is still a property called `tagName` on the Element interface. Both of these properties must contain the same value; however, the Working Group considers supporting both as being worthwhile (politics are hard to escape, especially when you're trying to satisfy as many constituencies as the DOM Working Group is).

History of the DOM

Before the DOM became an official W3C specification, the web community had started to develop ways of creating page-based script programs using languages like JavaScript that could be used among different web browsers. This early work led to the development of what was called Dynamic HTML, which was primarily used for such things as richer user interfaces than plain HTML could provide on its own. The origins of Dynamic HTML were in the web browsers, so its development was heavily influenced by the needs of web developers and the capabilities of the browsers themselves. For example, there was no way of dealing with selections of text in a document because the browser was not an editor and didn't need to worry about such things.

When the DOM Working Group was formed at the W3C, application vendors from other domains, such as XML and HTML editors, joined this early group of developers in manipulating documents in different ways. Several of these vendors already had experience with SGML (Standard Generalized Markup Language), an early forerunner of XML and HTML, and this experience helped influence the DOM's development. Many of these vendors had developed their own proprietary interfaces for working with XML and HTML documents to serve their specific needs, such as document editing, and these interfaces have, in turn, also influenced the DOM's evolution.

The DOM on the Client

The DOM got its start on the client side, becoming available around the time of Netscape 2 and Internet Explorer 3. Initially, these early implementations were intended to allow web-scripting programmers to manipulate the contents of web pages, usually for things like animation or richer user interface construction. Thus, these initial advancements in browser capabilities were referred to as Dynamic HTML, the ability to dynamically alter the appearance of HTML code in the browser.

As the browsers improved, so did their APIs for manipulating documents. However, there was no clear standard for doing so, and the programming interfaces for the two main browsers began to diverge. The W3C formed a working group to develop a standard way of working with structured documents, and it released its first recommendation in 1998. Microsoft and Netscape, the two main browser vendors, began working to bring their applications into conformance with the DOM specification; and with the release of Internet Explorer 6 and Netscape Navigator 6, the two companies have achieved complete support for DOM Level 1. Other browser vendors followed, such as Opera, a compact, multiplatform browser, and Konqueror, a popular web browser for the Linux platform.

The DOM on the Server

It wasn't long before companies realized that the benefits of the DOM could be applied on the server side as well as the client side, and DOM implementations began appearing for server-side products as well. One well-known example is the Xerces parser, available from the Apache Foundation, the open-source group responsible for the Apache web server. The Apache team implemented support for the DOM in their Xerces parser, available in Java and C++ source-code versions and additional language bindings for Perl and COM. The Xerces parser can be used for client applications, and also can be used to provide support for parsing and working with structured XML documents on the server.

Levels of the DOM

The DOM is organized into separate levels, each providing its own methods and definitions. These levels define certain capabilities and services that a user of that level can expect from an application that supports the APIs defined in that level. It is tempting to think of the different DOM levels as "versions" of the DOM; however, they are not versions in the true sense of the word. Rather, they define a certain level of functionality that an application provides to its users; a developer who is working with a Level 1–compliant DOM implementation can expect less functionality and features than a Level 2–compliant implementation.

Currently, there are two official DOM levels: Level 1 and Level 2. Each of these levels are W3C Recommendations. The latest level, Level 3, is in working draft form, meaning it has not yet been adopted by the W3C as a formal recommendation. A fourth level, informally referred to as Level 0, is not an official DOM specification or working draft; it refers to the DOM implementations that were provided by the early web browsers such as Netscape 3 and Internet Explorer 3 before the DOM Working Group was formed. These levels have evolved over time, based upon input from the general public, as well as the DOM member companies.

Each level is typically divided into two or more modules. Common to each level is the Core module, which specifies the core methods needed for working with structured documents and objects. The remaining modules focus on more specific features of that particular level. DOM applications may conform to a particular DOM level, or to a specific module within a DOM level. For example, Level 1 of the DOM supports only two modules: XML and HTML. Level 2 increases this support to more than 14 different modules.

NOTE

When discussing the DOM or a particular implementation of the DOM, the term conformance will often pop up. This term is used to describe how much of a particular level or module of the DOM is supported by an implementation. In general, an implementation is said to be conformant to a DOM level if it supports the methods defined in the Core section of that level. DOM implementations may conform to a level of the DOM or even to a particular module within that level.

Level 1

DOM Level 1 was adopted as a W3C Recommendation in October of 1998 (a second edition working draft was published in September of 2000). It is divided into two modules: Core and HTML. The Core module provides a basic set of methods for accessing and manipulating document objects in any structured document, along with a set of extended interfaces for working with XML content. The HTML module provides higher-level interfaces that are used along with those in the Core module for working with HTML documents, though the Core interfaces are usually enough for working with both XML and HTML content.

These two modules provide sufficient functionality for working with parsed XML and HTML documents inside of products that support the API and for populating a skeleton document object using only the provided methods. Creating the document object and saving/loading it to and from persistent storage are left as application-specific operations.

Most applications at the time of this writing support (to varying degrees) most of the methods in Level 1. In particular, the two main browser vendors, Netscape and Microsoft, have implemented almost complete support for DOM Level 1 in Netscape 6 and Internet Explorer 6, respectively. Other applications, such as Macromedia's popular Dreamweaver HTML editing program, support only a subset of the Level 1 API.

Level 2

Level 2 of the DOM was adopted as a W3C Recommendation in November of 2000. Level 2 is divided into 14 distinct modules (Core, XML, HTML, Range, Traversal, CSS, CSS 2, Views, Stylesheets, Events, User Interface Events, Mouse Events, Mutation Events, and HTML Events) and organized into 5 major modules (Core, Views, Events, Style, and Traversal/Range).

DOM Level 2 updated the Core functionality provided by DOM Level 1 with the addition of namespace support, as well as new methods to handle circumstances that Level 1 did not provide explicit support for. For example, DOM Level 1 did not specify a way to create an empty document; DOM Level 2 now includes a method for handling this common case.

In addition to providing fundamental interfaces for handling structured documents, DOM Level 2 stretches its wings a little bit and attempts to address other areas of document handling, such as

▶ **Range**   Specifies methods for working with ranges of content in a parsed DOM document. Though this does not necessarily mean that every range corresponds to a selection of content as made by a GUI user, these selections can be returned to a DOM client application as a range.

▶ **Traversal**   Provides utility interfaces for selectively traversing and filtering a document's content.

▶ **Style/CSS**   Provides base interfaces for supporting any kind of style sheet. When a module provides support for a specific type of style sheet language, it includes interfaces that are derived from these base interfaces. For example, the CSS module provides interfaces that allow programmatic access to CSS constructs from within DOM applications.

▶ **Views**   Provides interfaces that allow documents to have more than one view of the document source. For example, a document may have a view that is computed in real time, such as the application of style sheets, or it may have several views in different browser frames of the same document.

▶ **Events**   Specifies a generic event mechanism for registering event handlers, describing the flow of events in an application and providing event-specific information for the context of each event.

Level 3

Level 3 is still a work in progress and was last issued as a working draft in September of 2001 (though a new draft may have been released by the time you read this). DOM Level 3 further builds on the modules in DOM Levels 1 and 2 and introduces a few new ones:

▶ **Abstract Schemas**   Provides interfaces representing XML abstract schemas, for example, DTDs and XML Schemas.

▶ **Load/Save**   Specifies interfaces for serializing a document to and from persistent storage.

▶ **XPath**   Provides interfaces for using the XPath 1.0 syntax for declaratively locating nodes within a DOM document.

Conventions Used in the DOM Specification

When reading the W3C DOM specification, there are some important issues that you need to keep in mind. First, because the DOM was intended to be used in a multitude of programming environments and implementation languages, the DOM Working Group had to select an interface definition language (IDL) with which to define the interfaces that would lend itself to a language- and platform-independent spec. The Working Group chose to use the OMG (Object Management Group) IDL as specified by version 2.3.1 of the CORBA specification. The OMG IDL is used only as a way of specifying these interfaces and should not be used to infer an association with any particular implementation language. The following is an example of an interface definition using OMG IDL:

```
Interface DOMImplementation {
boolean hasFeature(in DOMString feature, in DOMString version);
// Introduced in DOM Level 2:
DocumentType createDocumentType(in DOMString qualifiedName,
in DOMString publicId, in DOMString systemId)
raises(DOMException);
```

```
// Introduced in DOM Level 2:
Document createDocument(in DOMString namespaceURI,
in DOMString qualifiedName, in DocumentType doctype)
raises(DOMException);
// Introduced in DOM Level 3:
DOMImplementation getInterface(in DOMString feature);
};
```

Second, the interfaces specified in the DOM spec are an abstraction, similar to the way one might use abstract base classes in C++ or interfaces in Java. They are simply a way of describing how to access and manipulate an application's internal representation of a given object. Interfaces—and this is taken directly from the spec—*"do not imply a particular concrete implementation."* Remember, each DOM application is free to maintain whatever internal representation of document objects it feels is best for that application, as long as the interfaces in the DOM spec are respected.

Finally, the DOM is designed to be implemented in any language and avoid implementation dependencies, and the DOM spec particularly calls out four important points relevant to this fact:

1. "Attributes defined in the IDL do not imply concrete objects which must have specific data members."

    In other words, just because the spec specifies an attribute `attr` on interface `intr` does not necessarily mean your code can access it using the code form `intr.Attr`. Many DOM implementations translate this notation to a pair of `setxxx()` and `getxxx()` functions, that is, `intr.getAttr()` and `intr.setAttr()`. Attributes that are read-only will have only a corresponding `get()` function.

2. "DOM applications may provide additional interfaces and objects not found in this specification and still be considered DOM conformant."

    This is important: the DOM was designed to be extensible from the beginning, and the decision was made that application vendors could add their own interfaces to a particular implementation without breaking conformance to the spec. This allows vendors the freedom and flexibility to add convenient, differentiating features to their DOM implementations.

3. "Because we specify interfaces and not the actual objects that are to be created, the DOM cannot know what constructors to call for an implementation."

Basically, the spec is saying here that the objects that are specified by the DOM are implementation specific, and they will only provide interfaces for creating those objects. The DOM spec provides interfaces in the form of `createxxx()` on the Document interface, where *xxx* is the type of document object to be created.

4. "The DOM spec does not specify multithreading mechanisms."

This is pretty self-explanatory. The DOM specification does not specify anything having to do with multithreading or other thread-safety topics. For the moment, this is left up to individual implementations.

What the DOM Isn't

Now that we've spent the better part of the chapter discussing what the DOM is, we'll take a moment and point out a few of the things that the DOM is not (in fact, the actual W3C specification goes out of its way to do pretty much the same thing— perhaps they wanted to avoid any misconceptions of the DOM as early as possible):

▶ The DOM isn't a way of creating programs that are, in the spec's words, "binary compatible," in other words, usable across disparate computer systems without recompiling. Programs that are written using the same language binding will be source-code compatible across platforms, but you can't take a DOM program written for Windows and run it on a Macintosh without recompiling it, for example.

▶ The DOM doesn't describe how to persist objects into XML or HTML, like SOAP (Simple Object Access Protocol) does, for example. It represents documents as a collection of objects.

▶ The DOM isn't a set of specific data structures. It merely describes relationships in a logical fashion. Even though the DOM specification (and this book) will talk about such things as parent-child relationships of objects, they are logical relationships and do not describe any internal representation of objects or data.

▶ The DOM does not describe what information in a document is relevant or how that information is structured; that's what XML Infoset does. The DOM is just an API to this information.

Conclusion

In this chapter, we introduced the basic concepts of the Document Object Model, such as the document tree structure, and we looked at some of the history behind the DOM's origins in SGML and Dynamic HTML. We also examined the different DOM levels and the different types of functionality they provide, along with the different types of DOM implementations available for both the client and server.

In the next chapter, we'll start getting more involved with the DOM's technical side, beginning with a look at how the DOM represents a structured document, along with the different parts of the document as stored by a DOM implementation.

How the DOM Represents Structured Documents

In this chapter, we examine the structure of a DOM document and the various types of objects the DOM uses to represent a document's various parts. We also introduce the core data types and interfaces that the DOM uses to represent information that a DOM application needs to manipulate. In particular, we closely examine the concepts of the document tree structure and the individual document nodes that make up the DOM tree, along with their standard properties and methods. Finally, we take a look at the extended interfaces for manipulating XML content. All of this information will build the foundation necessary for working with documents in later chapters.

This chapter contains a lot of information; if you are so inclined, you can skip ahead to the following chapters and refer back to this one as necessary. It is recommended, though, that you at least familiarize yourself with the material in this chapter before continuing.

Basic DOM Data Types

Every programming interface has basic, atomic data types that are essential to its inner workings, and the DOM is no different. The DOM Working Group had to define some basic data types to represent the information stored inside of a document that could be used and implemented across a variety of languages (both programming and spoken) and platforms. For the most part, they were able to borrow the existing data types from other languages (such as short integers and such), but for more complex types, the committee invented their own. As of DOM Level 2, the basic data types in use by the specification are the DOMString and DOMTimeStamp types.

The DOMString Type

The DOMString type is used to describe a sequence of characters, with each character represented as 16-bit units. It has the following definition in the DOM specification:

```
valuetype DOMString sequence<unsigned short>;
```

According to the DOM spec, DOMStrings are encoded using UTF-16 (which is defined in the Unicode specification). The UTF-16 encoding was selected because it is in wide use in the high-tech industry and it includes support for a wide variety of spoken languages throughout the world.

NOTE

The DOM specification defines the name of the data type to be DOMString, but certain language bindings use names that are different. For example, the Java language uses the String data type to represent DOMStrings because they both happen to be UTF-16 encoded.

DOMStrings are used throughout the DOM specification wherever strings are required. Often, it is necessary to convert a DOMString to a platform-native string type. Some DOM implementations (such as Xerces, for example) provide a method for converting DOMStrings into native character strings. This is purely a convenience provided by the implementation, however; there is no requirement that a DOM implementation provide such a method, and there are no such methods defined in the DOM spec.

The DOMTimeStamp Type

The DOM specification defines the DOMTimeStamp data type as

```
typedef unsigned long long DOMTimeStamp;
```

The DOMTimeStamp is used, according to the spec, to represent a number of milliseconds. It does not specify what the base date is for 0 milliseconds.

NOTE

The DOM specification uses the DOMTimeStamp type, but language bindings may use different types. Java, for example, uses the long type, while the ECMAScript binding uses the Date type.

Handling Errors: The DOMException Interface

One interface that should be introduced right up front is the DOMException interface. DOMExceptions are used by DOM implementations to report error conditions that are, interestingly enough, "exceptional." In other words, the requested operation is impossible to perform for some reason—either the implementation program has become unstable, or there is some logical error in the DOM program that prevents it from continuing. In other nonexceptional cases, specific error codes are returned by interface methods when an error occurs.

The DOMException interface is defined in IDL as

```
exception DOMException {
  unsigned short    code;
};
```

Of course, some languages don't support exceptions. For these particular bindings, an interface's methods may return regular error codes that correspond to the DOM exception that would have been raised otherwise. For specific information on what exceptions are and how they work, you should consult the documentation for your specific language binding. The specific exception codes defined by the DOM are introduced later in this chapter.

The Document Tree Structure

As briefly alluded to in the first chapter, the DOM represents a document using a tree structure. In this section, we take a more in-depth look at the document structure and how the DOM represents the various parts of a document. Let's take another look at the example from Chapter 1. Recall our example code listing:

Listing 2-1 *A typical HTML document*

```
<HTML>
<HEAD>
<TITLE>This is a document.</TITLE>
</HEAD>
<BODY>
<B>This is some bold text!</B>
<I>This is some italic text!</I>
</BODY>
</HTML>
```

For this document, there is a corresponding tree structure that illustrates how the DOM would represent the relationships among the document's elements, as shown in Chapter 1 and repeated here in Figure 2-1.

In fact, the DOM document tree structure can be thought of as a collection of individual subtrees. For example, the branch of the overall tree that begins with the <BODY> tag can be thought of as its own tree within the larger document tree. In a sense, a DOM document can thus be thought of as a collection of trees, or a *grove*. The DOM, of course, doesn't define how the information represented by the tree structure shown in Figure 2-1 is actually implemented for a given DOM implementation; it simply says the information needs to be exposed to the outside world in this way.

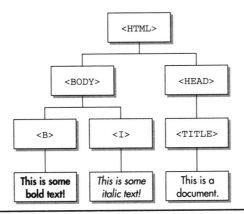

Figure 2-1   *Document tree diagram*

Each box in Figure 2-1 is called a *node* in DOM terminology. A node is an object representation of a particular element in the document's content. Nodes have special names, depending on where they are located in the document tree and what their position is relative to other nodes.

All documents have a *root* node, which is the node located at the base of the tree structure. In Figure 2-1, the root node is the box representing the <HTML> tag. If a node has one or more nodes below it, those nodes are referred to as *child* nodes of the given node, and each of these child nodes is a descendant of its *parent* node. The node represented in the figure by the <HEAD> tag is a child of the <HTML> node, and it in turn, has a child node that represents the <TITLE> tag. This parent-child relationship between nodes is used and referred to extensively throughout the DOM API. Nodes that have no children of their own are called *leaf* nodes, and they are the nodes located at the furthest reaches of the tree. The text nodes that represent the text content of the <B>, <I>, and <TITLE> tags in the figure are leaf nodes.

Continuing with the parent-child relationship metaphor, nodes that share the same parent are called *sibling* nodes. In Figure 2-1, the <BODY> and <HEAD> tags are sibling nodes. If two nodes descend from the same node somewhere in the tree structure, they are said to have a common ancestor node. Figure 2-2 highlights the common ancestor nodes shared by the nodes represented by the <B> and <I> tags, which are the <BODY> and <HTML> tags.

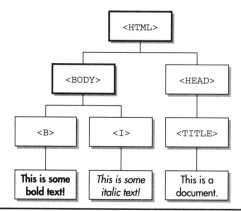

Figure 2-2   *Common ancestor nodes*

Nodes aren't just limited to elements, such as <HEAD> and <TITLE>. Everything in a document is represented as a node, including comments, attributes of elements, text content, XML processing instructions, document type declarations, and so on. If it's in the document, it can be represented as a node.

The DOM API provides several interfaces in the Core module for manipulating nodes and inserting/extracting information to and from nodes. There are also methods provided for determining and changing the relationships between nodes and discovering the type of a particular node.

DOM Node Types

The DOM specification defines 12 different types of nodes that can be contained within a document. Each type of node has a set of related attributes and capabilities associated with it. The following table lists the different types of nodes available as of DOM Level 2 and provides a brief description of each type:

Node Type	Description
Element	Represents an element in an HTML or XML document, which is represented by tags. In Figure 2-1, the <BODY> node is an Element type.
Attribute	Represents an element's attribute. For example, a tag with the syntax <img src="mypicture.jpg"> has an Attribute node named src.

Node Type	Description
Text	Represents the textual content of an element. In Figure 2-1, the `<B>` node has a Text child node that represents the text, "This is bold text!"
CDATASection	Represents a Character Data section in an XML document.
Comment	Represents a comment. Comments are of the form `<!-- comment text -->`
Document	Represents the root node of a document.
DocumentType	Each Document node has a DocumentType node that provides a list of entities defined in the document.
DocumentFragment	Document fragments can be thought of as lightweight or rather minimal Document nodes. They came about because it is common to want to extract just a portion of a document for processing.
ProcessingInstruction	Represents a specific instruction to be used by the document processor. It is used as a way of keeping processor-specific information in the document's content.
Entity	Represents an entity in an XML document.
EntityReference	Represents an entity reference in the document.
Notation	Represents a notation in an XML document. Notations have no parent nodes.

Usually, your DOM programs will only need to manipulate the most important node types, which contain the actual content of the document: Document, Element, Comment, Attribute, CDATA, and Text. The other node types are typically used to describe the format and structure of the information contained in a complex XML document.

NOTE

Specific definitions of each of the node types and their syntax can be found in the W3C XML and HTML specifications; the detailed definition of each of these node types is beyond the scope of this book.

Each node is allowed to have child nodes according to its node type. Some types of nodes are not permitted to contain child nodes at all. The following table lists the types of child nodes that each node type is allowed to have.

Node Type	Allowable Child Node Types
Document	Element (one at most), ProcessingInstruction, Comment, DocumentType
DocumentFragment	Element, ProcessingInstruction, Comment, Text, CDATASection, EntityReference
DocumentType	None
Element	Element, Text, Comment, ProcessingInstruction, CDATASection, EntityReference
Comment	None
Text	None
Attribute	Text, EntityReference
EntityReference	Element, ProcessingInstruction, Comment, Text, CDATASection, EntityReference
Entity	Element, ProcessingInstruction, Comment, Text, CDATASection, EntityReference
CDATASection	None
Notation	None

If a DOM program tries to assign a node as a child of another node that is not allowed to have a child node of the given type, then the DOM implementation will indicate an error condition by raising a DOMException.

The Fundamental Core DOM Interfaces

In this section, we introduce the interfaces that are fundamental to manipulating information inside of a DOM document. We will cover only the interfaces in this section that are related to working with documents that contain HTML and XML content. The next section will cover the extended Core interfaces, which deal with the set of interfaces needed for working with XML-specific document structure elements.

We'll start by taking a look at the specific types of errors that can occur while working with the fundamental interfaces, and then introduce and walk through the basic Node interface. Next, we'll examine some utility interfaces for working with ordered and unordered lists of nodes, and, finally, introduce the interfaces for specific node types. In the next chapter, we'll use these interfaces to manipulate the contents of a DOM document.

DOMException Codes

DOMExceptions were introduced and discussed earlier in this chapter. Table 2-1 lists the current DOMException types, their meanings, and the DOM Level where they were introduced. Each interface can raise one or more of the following DOMException types in the course of working with a document:

Exception Code	Description of Error	DOM Level
INDEX_SIZE_ERR	A specified array index or size is negative, or is larger than the maximum allowed value.	1
DOMSTRING_SIZE_ERR	The given range of text doesn't fit into a DOMString.	1
HIERARCHY_REQUEST_ERR	A node was inserted in a place where that particular node type isn't allowed to be.	1
INUSE_ATTRIBUTE_ERR	An attempt was made to add an attribute that is already in use somewhere else.	1
INVALID_ACCESS_ERR	A particular parameter or operation is not supported by the underlying object.	2
INVALID_CHARACTER_ERR	An invalid or illegal character is specified, such as in a name. The definition of a legal character can be found in production 2 in the W3C XML specification, and the definition of a legal name character can be found in production 5 of the same spec.	1
INVALID_MODIFICATION_ERR	An attempt was made to modify the type of the underlying object.	2
INVALID_STATE_ERR	An attempt was made to use an object that is not, or is no longer, usable.	2
NAMESPACE_ERR	An attempt was made to create or change an object in a way that is incorrect with regard to namespaces.	2

Table 2-1   *DOMExceptions*

Exception Code	Description of Error	DOM Level
NOT_FOUND_ERR	An attempt was made to reference a node in a context where it does not exist.	1
NOT_SUPPORTED_ERR	The DOM implementation does not support the requested type of object or operation.	1
NO_DATA_ALLOWED_ ERR	Data is specified for a node that does not support data	1
NO_MODIFICATION_ ALLOWED_ERR	An attempt was made to modify an object where modifications are not allowed.	1
SYNTAX_ERR	An invalid or illegal string was specified.	2
WRONG_DOCUMENT_ ERR	A node is used in a different document from the one that created it (and the document doesn't support it).	1

Table 2-1   *DOMExceptions* (continued)

Knowledge of how exceptions work is not required to learn how to use the DOM interfaces, though more and more implementations are starting to use them. For the specific DOMExceptions that can be raised by each DOM method, you should refer to the corresponding interface definition for that method in the W3C specification.

The DOM Node Interface

Nodes are a fundamental concept of the DOM (after all, everything in a document is some kind of node), so let's begin by introducing the base interface that provides access to the properties and methods of document nodes. The specific types of nodes, such as Document, Element, and so on, all inherit their methods and properties from the base Node interface.

Following the "everything is a node" part of the DOM's design philosophy, the Node interface contains all of the methods and properties necessary for basic node manipulation, except for creating new nodes. Node creation is handled by the Document interface because all nodes exist only in the context of a containing document.

It is important to note that even though the Node interface exposes methods and properties for dealing with child nodes, not all nodes in a document may be allowed to have child nodes. Calling these methods on a node that does not have child nodes will result in a DOMException being raised.

Some of the properties exposed in the Node interface are put there for the convenience of the developer, such as `nodeName`, `nodeValue`, and `attributes`. These are provided so that the information provided by these properties can be retrieved without having to cast down to the specific node type for a given node. It is common in many types of DOM algorithms to have a list of nodes to process, and it may be time consuming and inelegant to have to first determine the node type before being able to access certain parts of its data. Placing these properties in the base Node interface, even for nodes that don't contain that particular information, simplifies this process.

Some of the information provided in the Node interface may be duplicated in derived interfaces, and the derived interfaces themselves may provide additional information that is specific to that node type. In some cases, the properties in the Node interface may have no meaning for a particular type of node (for example, a Comment node cannot have attributes). In these instances, that particular property returns `null`.

The Node interface has the following IDL definition:

```
interface Node {
  // NodeType
  const unsigned short      ELEMENT_NODE                  = 1;
  const unsigned short      ATTRIBUTE_NODE                = 2;
  const unsigned short      TEXT_NODE                     = 3;
  const unsigned short      CDATA_SECTION_NODE            = 4;
  const unsigned short      ENTITY_REFERENCE_NODE         = 5;
  const unsigned short      ENTITY_NODE                   = 6;
  const unsigned short      PROCESSING_INSTRUCTION_NODE   = 7;
  const unsigned short      COMMENT_NODE                  = 8;
  const unsigned short      DOCUMENT_NODE                 = 9;
  const unsigned short      DOCUMENT_TYPE_NODE            = 10;
  const unsigned short      DOCUMENT_FRAGMENT_NODE        = 11;
  const unsigned short      NOTATION_NODE                 = 12;

  readonly attribute DOMString        nodeName;
           attribute DOMString        nodeValue;
                              // raises(DOMException) on setting
                              // raises(DOMException) on retrieval
```

```
readonly attribute unsigned short    nodeType;
readonly attribute Node              parentNode;
readonly attribute NodeList          childNodes;
readonly attribute Node              firstChild;
readonly attribute Node              lastChild;
readonly attribute Node              previousSibling;
readonly attribute Node              nextSibling;
readonly attribute NamedNodeMap      attributes;
// Modified in DOM Level 2:
readonly attribute Document          ownerDocument;
Node               insertBefore(in Node newChild,
                                 in Node refChild)
                                         raises(DOMException);
Node               replaceChild(in Node newChild,
                                 in Node oldChild)
                                         raises(DOMException);
Node               removeChild(in Node oldChild)
                                         raises(DOMException);
Node               appendChild(in Node newChild)
                                         raises(DOMException);
boolean            hasChildNodes();
Node               cloneNode(in boolean deep);
// Modified in DOM Level 2:
void               normalize();
// Introduced in DOM Level 2:
boolean            isSupported(in DOMString feature,
                               in DOMString version);
// Introduced in DOM Level 2:
readonly attribute DOMString         namespaceURI;
// Introduced in DOM Level 2:
        attribute DOMString          prefix;
                                 // raises(DOMException) on setting

// Introduced in DOM Level 2:
readonly attribute DOMString         localName;
// Introduced in DOM Level 2:
boolean            hasAttributes();
};
```

The first 12 constants defined by the Node interface correspond to the 12 node types that a document can contain. Each node has one of these values stored in its nodeType property, which is read-only: you cannot change the type of a node once it has been created.

The nodeName, nodeValue, and attributes properties have different meanings based upon the node's type. The following table lists the individual meanings of the fields nodeName, nodeValue, and attributes for each particular node type:

Node Type	nodeName	nodeValue	attributes
Document	#document	null	null
Element	Tag name	null	NamedNodeMap
Attr	Attribute name	Attribute value	null
Comment	#comment	Comment text	null
Text	#text	Content of text node	null
CDATASection	#cdata-section	CDATASection content	null
DocumentFragment	#document-fragment	null	null
DocumentType	Name of document type	null	null
Entity	Entity name	null	null
EntityReference	Name of referenced entity	null	null
ProcessingInstruction	Target name	Content excluding the target	null
Notation	Notation name	null	null

The parentNode property refers to the node that is the parent of this node. All nodes with the exception of Attr, Document, DocumentFragment, Entity, and Notation nodes can have parent nodes. If a node has been removed from the document tree or has been newly created but not yet inserted into the document, then this property is null.

The childNodes property contains a list of the nodes that are children of this node. If the node contains no children, then this is an empty list.

The firstChild and lastChild properties represent this node's first and last children, respectively. They are null if there are no such child nodes.

The previousSibling and nextSibling properties refer to the nodes that immediately precede and follow this node. If there are no such nodes, then these properties are null.

The `attributes` property contains a NamedNodeMap structure that represents an unordered collection of the attributes attached to this node if the node is an Element node. It is `null` otherwise.

The `ownerDocument` property contains a reference to the root node of the document that contains this node. If this node is itself a Document node, or is a DocumentType node that is not yet being used by a document, then this property is `null`.

The `namespaceURI` property specifies the namespace URI for this node, or `null` if it is unspecified. For nodes that are not elements or attributes, or any node created with a DOM Level 1 method, this property will be `null`.

The `prefix` property holds the namespace prefix for this node.

The `localName` property returns the local part of the qualified name for this node. This property will always be `null` for nodes that are not elements or attributes, or for any node created with a DOM Level 1 method.

The `insertBefore()` method inserts a new node before the specified child node of this node. It accepts two arguments: `newChild` and `refChild`. The `newChild` argument is the node to be inserted. The `refChild` node specifies the child node to insert the new node before. If `newChild` is a DocumentFragment, then all of its child nodes are inserted before `refChild`. If the `newChild` node is already elsewhere in the tree, it is removed first. The return value is the node being inserted.

The `replaceChild()` method replaces this node's specified child node with a new node. The first argument, `newChild`, is the node that will replace the child node. The second argument, `oldChild`, is the node to be replaced. The function returns the old child node. If `newChild` is a DocumentFragment, then `oldChild` is replaced by all of the DocumentFragment's child nodes.

The `removeChild()` method removes the child node specified by the `oldChild` argument and returns it.

The `appendChild()` method adds a new child node to the end of the list of this node's child nodes and returns the added node. The `newChild` argument is the new child node to be added. If `newChild` already exists in the tree, it is first removed. If `newChild` is a DocumentFragment, then all if its child nodes are added to this node's children.

The `hasChildNodes()` method returns true if this node has child nodes, false otherwise.

The `cloneNode()` method duplicates this node and returns a copy. The duplicated node is not inserted into the tree (it has a `parentNode` of `null`). When an Element node is cloned, all attributes, along with their values, are also copied. This includes attributes that are generated by the XML processor as default attributes. If the `deep` argument is true, then this operation performs a "deep clone," in which all child nodes of this node are also cloned. According to the DOM specification, cloning Document, DocumentType, Entity, and Notation nodes is implementation dependent.

The `normalize()` method removes all empty text nodes and forces adjacent text nodes that are not separated by structure nodes (CDATA, Elements, Comments, and so on) to be joined into single Text nodes. This method is used to ensure that a document's text nodes will be in the same state as if the document had been saved and then reloaded.

The `isSupported()` method tests whether the DOM implementation implements a specific feature that is supported by this node. The feature and version arguments are the same as those passed to the `hasFeature()` method of the DOMImplementation interface.

The `hasAttributes()` method returns true if this node has any elements, false otherwise.

Node Helper Interfaces: NodeList and NamedNodeMap

The Core DOM interfaces provide two "helper" interfaces for working with sets of nodes: NodeList, which implements an interface for accessing a collection of ordered nodes, and NamedNodeMap, which provides support for accessing a collection of nodes by name.

All node references in NodeLists and NamedNodeMaps are "live," which, as defined by the DOM spec, means that the nodes contained in a node collection are directly affected by changes to the node in the document tree. For example, if a particular node is in a certain node collection and that node is somehow changed in the document by another part of the DOM program, then that change is immediately reflected in all NodeLists and NamedNodeMaps that contain a reference to that node.

NodeList

The NodeList interface provides a single method for accessing an ordered list of nodes. The list of nodes in a NodeList is maintained in the order that the nodes are encountered in the document itself. For example, in Listing 2-1, the <HEAD> and <BODY> nodes are both children of the <HTML> node. If you were to obtain the list of child nodes for the <HTML> node, you would receive a NodeList with two elements: one for the <HEAD> node, and one for the <BODY>, in that order.

The NodeList interface contains one property, `length`, which contains the number of elements in the NodeList. The `item()` method accepts a single argument, which is the index in the NodeList of the element to retrieve, and returns the requested Node object.

The NodeList interface has the following IDL definition:

```
interface NodeList {
  Node              item(in unsigned long index);
  readonly attribute unsigned long    length;
};
```

NamedNodeMap

The NamedNodeMap interface provides support for accessing a collection of nodes
by name. NamedNodeMaps do not imply an ordering of the nodes that they contain.
It has the following IDL definition:

```
interface NamedNodeMap {
  Node              getNamedItem(in DOMString name);
  Node              setNamedItem(in Node arg)
                                    raises(DOMException);
  Node              removeNamedItem(in DOMString name)
                                    raises(DOMException);
  Node              item(in unsigned long index);
  readonly attribute unsigned long    length;
  // Introduced in DOM Level 2:
  Node              getNamedItemNS(in DOMString namespaceURI,
                              in DOMString localName);
  // Introduced in DOM Level 2:
  Node              setNamedItemNS(in Node arg)
                                    raises(DOMException);
  // Introduced in DOM Level 2:
  Node              removeNamedItemNS(in DOMString namespaceURI,
                              in DOMString localName)
                                raises(DOMException);
};
```

The NamedNodeMap interface has one property, `length`, which is the number
of elements contained within the NamedNodeMap. The `getNamedItem()` method
returns a node given the node's name. The `setNamedItem()` method adds a node
to the NamedNodeMap with the supplied node name. The `removeNamedItem()`
method removes a node from the list given the node name. The `item()` method allows
the NamedNodeMap to return a node based on an ordinal number, which is the index of
the item in the NamedNodeMap. The other three methods are namespace-aware versions
of the first three methods.

NOTE

Even though the NamedNodeMap interface contains an `item()` *method that will return a node based on an index, it is provided simply to allow the contents of a NamedNodeMap to be enumerated.*

The DOMImplementation Interface

The DOMImplementation interface provides methods that are not dependent upon any single instance of a DOM document. It is up to individual implementations to determine how a DOM program retrieves a DOMImplementation interface. For example, the Netscape and Microsoft browsers provide an implementation object on the document object.

```
interface DOMImplementation {
  boolean              hasFeature(in DOMString feature,
                                  in DOMString version);
  // Introduced in DOM Level 2:
  DocumentType         createDocumentType(in DOMString qualifiedName,
                                  in DOMString publicId,
                                  in DOMString systemId)
                                  raises(DOMException);
  // Introduced in DOM Level 2:
  Document             createDocument(in DOMString namespaceURI,
                                  in DOMString qualifiedName,
                                  in DocumentType doctype)
                                  raises(DOMException);
};
```

The DOMImplementation interface contains no properties. In DOM Level 1, there was only one method, `hasFeature()`, that DOM programs could use to test for the presence of a particular interface or feature. The first argument is a string that contains the name of the DOM module or feature that the program is testing for, and the second argument is a string specifying the level of the feature to test for. If a level is not specified, the method returns true if the implementation supports any level of the requested feature.

DOM Level 1 implementations were free to specify how a DOM program created new documents. In DOM Level 2, the `createDocument()` and `createDocumentType()` methods were added to fill this gap, but only for XML documents. HTML-only implementations do not need to implement these methods and are free to specify how HTML documents are created.

The `createDocument()` method creates a new XML document and accepts three arguments. The first, `namespaceURI`, accepts a namespace URI for the document (see the XML Namespaces specification). This is not required if the following argument, `qualifiedName`, does not specify a namespace prefix. The `qualifiedName` argument is the name of the document, optionally preceded by a namespace name and colon (in which case, the `namespaceURI` argument is not optional). The last argument, `docType`, is the type of document to create, as specified by a DocumentType object.

The `createDocumentType()` method creates an empty DocumentType object and also takes three arguments. The first, `qualifiedName`, is the qualified name of the DocumentType to create. The second and third arguments, `publicID` and `systemID`, specify the public ID and system ID of the DocumentType.

NOTE

Even though this interface has been around since DOM Level 1, many existing implementations do not provide it, including the Netscape and Microsoft web browsers versions 5.0 and earlier. In these cases, it is up to the developer to determine whether a particular implementation exposes the features that a program needs.

The Document Interface

The Document interface represents the entire document, whether it is an HTML or XML document. It serves as the primary gateway to accessing the document's data. In addition to representing the root of the document tree, the Document interface contains the "factory" methods necessary for creating new document objects, such as elements, attributes, Text nodes, comments, and so on. When these factory methods are used to create new document nodes, each node's `ownerDocument` property is set to the document that created it.

The Document interface has the following IDL definition:

```
interface Document : Node {
  readonly attribute DocumentType      doctype;
  readonly attribute DOMImplementation  implementation;
  readonly attribute Element           documentElement;
  Element              createElement(in DOMString tagName)
                                        raises(DOMException);
  DocumentFragment     createDocumentFragment();
  Text                 createTextNode(in DOMString data);
  Comment              createComment(in DOMString data);
  CDATASection         createCDATASection(in DOMString data)
                                        raises(DOMException);
  ProcessingInstruction createProcessingInstruction(
```

```
                        in DOMString target, in DOMString data)
                                    raises(DOMException);
  Attr                 createAttribute(in DOMString name)
                                    raises(DOMException);
  EntityReference      createEntityReference(in DOMString name)
                                    raises(DOMException);
  NodeList             getElementsByTagName(in DOMString tagname);
  // Introduced in DOM Level 2:
  Node                 importNode(in Node importedNode,
                            in boolean deep)
                                    raises(DOMException);
  // Introduced in DOM Level 2:
  Element              createElementNS(in DOMString namespaceURI,
                                in DOMString qualifiedName)
                                    raises(DOMException);
  // Introduced in DOM Level 2:
  Attr                 createAttributeNS(in DOMString namespaceURI,
                                in DOMString qualifiedName)
                                    raises(DOMException);
  // Introduced in DOM Level 2:
  NodeList             getElementsByTagNameNS(in DOMString namespaceURI,
                                    in DOMString localName);
  // Introduced in DOM Level 2:
  Element              getElementById(in DOMString elementId);
};
```

The docType property contains the document's document type declaration. This returns null for all HTML documents and XML documents without a document type declaration. As of DOM Level 2, editing the DocumentType is not supported, though this is planned for the future. In fact, the docType can't be edited in any way whatsoever, including using Node methods like removeNode().

The implementation property refers to the implementation object that handles this particular document. A DOM application can deal with objects created from multiple implementations.

The documentElement property provides direct access to the child node that represents the root element of the document (that is, the <HTML> tag for HTML documents).

The createElement() method creates a new element with the supplied tag name. For example, createElement("IMG") creates a new IMG element, but does not insert it into the document.

The createDocumentFragment() method creates a new, empty DocumentFragment.

The createTextNode() method creates a new Text node. The data argument is the initial text content for the node.

The createComment() method creates a new Comment node. The data argument is the initial text content for the comment.

The createCDATASection() method creates a new CDATASection node. The data argument is the initial text content of the node.

The createProcessingInstruction() method creates a new ProcessingInstruction node and sets the target and data portions of the processing instruction to the values of the target and data arguments.

The createAttribute() method creates a new attribute node with the name supplied in the name argument. The node's initial value is an empty string.

The createEntityReference() method creates a new EntityReference node. If the referenced entity is known, the child list of the EntityReference node is made the same as that of the corresponding Entity node.

The createElementNS() and createAttributeNS() methods are namespace-aware versions of the createElement() and createAttribute() methods. In both cases, the namespaceURI argument specifies the namespace URI of the element or attribute. The qualifiedName argument gives the qualified name of the element or attribute.

The getElementsByTagName() method returns a NodeList containing all of the elements in the document with the same tag name as the tagname argument. The NodeList is ordered by the order in which the Elements were encountered in a preorder traversal of the document tree. If the tagname argument is *, all tags are matched.

The getElementsByTagNameNS() method is a namespace-aware version of the getElementsByTagName() method. It returns a NodeList containing all of the Elements in the document that match the localName and namespaceURI arguments.

The importNode() method imports a node into this document from another document. The node in the source document is not affected in any way: a copy of that node is made before being imported. The returned Node object has no parent node. If the deep argument is true, the entire subtree under the source node is imported as well. This argument has no effect on nodes that cannot have child nodes. Certain types of nodes, such as Documents and DocumentTypes, cannot be imported.

NOTE

There are certain implications of importing nodes based upon the type of node being imported. See the detailed description of the Element interface in the W3C DOM specification for more information.

The getElementByID() method returns the Element whose ID matches the elementID argument. If no element exists with a matching ID, this method returns null.

> **NOTE**
>
> *DOM implementations must state which attributes specify an element's ID. Attributes that are named "ID" are not of type ID unless specifically designated so. If an implementation doesn't know which attributes are of type ID, this method must return* null*. Currently, the major browsers define the attribute named "ID" to be the ID of the element.*

The DocumentFragment Interface

The DocumentFragment interface was added as a "lightweight" way to extract portions of a document and manipulate them without having to populate another whole Document object. The DOM specification notes that a Document object could be used to perform such manipulations; however, documents have the potential to be very heavyweight objects (depending on the implementation) that don't readily lend themselves to such uses. It's natural to want to use a node for something like this and a lightweight object was needed, so the DocumentFragment interface was created.

When DocumentFragments are inserted as child nodes of another node, the children of the DocumentFragment (and not the actual DocumentFragment object) are inserted into the target node.

DocumentFragments are comprised of zero or more child nodes that represent subtrees that define the structure of the document that they are part of. The child nodes of a DocumentFragment do not need to be well-formed XML documents. For example, a DocumentFragment may consist of a single comment node, which does not represent a well-formed HTML or XML document.

The DocumentFragment interface has the following IDL definition:

```
interface DocumentFragment : Node {
};
```

The DocumentFragment interface does not contain any properties or methods other than those it inherits from the Node interface.

The Element Interface

The Element interface represents an element in an HTML or XML document. Elements inherit from the Node interface, so the attributes property of the Node interface can be used to retrieve an element's attributes.

All elements have a `tagName` property, which is the name of the tag they represent. For example, in Listing 2-1, the `<TITLE>` element has a `tagName` of TITLE. In XML, the `tagName` is case preserving because XML is case sensitive. In HTML, the `tagName` is always returned as the canonical uppercase.

In addition, the Element interface provides methods that retrieve attributes both as Attr nodes and simple strings. When working with XML, an attribute value may contain entity references, so Attr objects should be retrieved to examine the possibly complex subtree representing their values. In HTML, however, attributes are always simple strings, so retrieving them as DOMStrings can be done as a convenience.

The Element interface has the following IDL definition:

```
interface Element : Node {
    readonly attribute DOMString        tagName;
    DOMString           getAttribute(in DOMString name);
    void                setAttribute(in DOMString name,
                                in DOMString value)
                                    raises(DOMException);
    void                removeAttribute(in DOMString name)
                                    raises(DOMException);
    Attr                getAttributeNode(in DOMString name);
    Attr                setAttributeNode(in Attr newAttr)
                                    raises(DOMException);
    Attr                removeAttributeNode(in Attr oldAttr)
                                    raises(DOMException);
    NodeList            getElementsByTagName(in DOMString name);
    // Introduced in DOM Level 2:
    DOMString           getAttributeNS(in DOMString namespaceURI,
                                in DOMString localName);
    // Introduced in DOM Level 2:
    void                setAttributeNS(in DOMString namespaceURI,
                                in DOMString qualifiedName,
                                in DOMString value)
                                    raises(DOMException);
    // Introduced in DOM Level 2:
    void                removeAttributeNS(in DOMString namespaceURI,
                                in DOMString localName)
                                    raises(DOMException);
    // Introduced in DOM Level 2:
    Attr                getAttributeNodeNS(in DOMString namespaceURI,
                                in DOMString localName);
    // Introduced in DOM Level 2:
    Attr                setAttributeNodeNS(in Attr newAttr)
```

```
                                          raises(DOMException);
// Introduced in DOM Level 2:
NodeList          getElementsByTagNameNS(in DOMString namespaceURI,
                                         in DOMString localName);
// Introduced in DOM Level 2:
boolean           hasAttribute(in DOMString name);
// Introduced in DOM Level 2:
boolean           hasAttributeNS(in DOMString namespaceURI,
                                 in DOMString localName);
};
```

The tagName property is the name of the element.

The getAttribute() method retrieves an attribute value by name. It returns the Attr value as a string, or the empty string if that attribute does not have a specified or default value.

The setAttribute() method adds a new attribute. If an attribute with that name is already present in the element, its value is changed to be that of the value parameter. This value is a simple string; it is not parsed as it is being set. It has no return value.

The removeAttribute() method removes an attribute by name. If the removed attribute is known to have a default value, an attribute immediately appears containing the default value, as well as the corresponding namespace URI, local name, and prefix when applicable. This function has no return value.

The getAttributeNode() method retrieves an attribute node by name, or returns null if there is no such attribute.

The setAttributeNode() method adds a new attribute node. If an attribute with that name (nodeName) is already present in the element, it is replaced by the new one and the old one is returned; otherwise, null is returned.

The removeAttributeNode() method removes and returns the specified attribute node. If the removed Attr has a default value, it is immediately replaced. The replacing attribute has the same namespace URI and local name, as well as the original prefix, when applicable.

The getElementsByTagName() method returns a NodeList of all descendant Elements with a given tag name, in the order in which they are encountered in a preorder traversal of this Element tree. The name argument specifies the name of the tag to match on. If it is *, all tags are matched.

The hasAttribute() method returns true when an attribute with a given name is specified on this element or has a default value, false otherwise.

The getAttributeNS() method retrieves an attribute value by local name and namespace URI and returns it as a string.

The `getAttributeNodeNS()` method retrieves and returns an Attr node by local name and namespace URI.

The `getElementsByTagNameNS()` method returns a NodeList of all the descendant elements with a given local name and namespace URI in the order in which they are encountered in a preorder traversal of this Element tree.

The `hasAttributeNS()` method returns true when an attribute with a given local name and namespace URI is specified on this element or has a default value, false otherwise.

The `removeAttributeNS()` method removes an attribute by local name and namespace URI. If the removed attribute has a default value, it is immediately replaced. The replacing attribute has the same namespace URI and local name, as well as the original prefix. This method has no return value.

The `setAttributeNS()` method adds a new attribute. If an attribute with the same local name and namespace URI is already present on the element, its prefix is changed to be the prefix part of the qualifiedName, and its value is changed to be the `value` parameter. This value is a simple string; it is not parsed as it is being set. This method has no return value.

The `setAttributeNodeNS()` method adds a new attribute node. If an attribute with that local name and that namespace URI is already present in the element, it is replaced by the new one and the old one is returned; otherwise, `null` is returned.

The Attr Interface

The Attr interface represents an attribute of an Element object. Attr objects inherit from the Node interface; however, they are treated differently than other Nodes in the document. First, they are *not actually child nodes* of the elements that they are attached to, and thus the DOM does not consider them to be part of the Document tree. If you attempt to read the values of the `parentNode`, `previousSibling`, or `nextSibling` properties of an Attr object, they will return `null`. The reason for this is that the DOM considers attributes to be properties of elements rather than having their own, separate identity from the elements they are associated with. The idea is that this should make it easier to implement features such as default attributes for all elements of a certain type.

In addition, because attributes do not have a specific place in the DOM tree, they cannot be immediate child nodes of DocumentFragments, though they can be associated with Elements that are contained in a DocumentFragment.

In XML documents, Attr nodes can have two types of child nodes: Text and EntityReference. Either way, the DOM treats attribute values as simple strings.

The Attr interface has the following IDL definition:

```
interface Attr : Node {
  readonly attribute DOMString        name;
  readonly attribute boolean          specified;
          attribute DOMString         value;
                                    // raises(DOMException) on setting

  // Introduced in DOM Level 2:
  readonly attribute Element          ownerElement;
};
```

The Attr interface extends the Node interface with four properties. The name property holds the name of the attribute. The value property represents the value of the attribute and is returned as a string. When retrieved, entity references are replaced with their values. When the value property is set, a Text node is created with the contents of the supplied string in unparsed form; any characters that an XML parser would recognize as markup are instead treated as literal text.

The specified property reflects whether the attribute was explicitly given a value in the original document. If so, then the value of the specified attribute is true; otherwise, it is false.

In DOM Level 2, the ownerElement property was added, which contains the Element object that this Attr object is attached to, or null if the attribute is not in use by any element.

The CharacterData Interface

You won't find any DOM objects that correspond directly to the CharacterData interface. It functions like an abstract base class and is used to extend the Node interface with methods for accessing character data within a DOM document. The Text and Comment interfaces inherit directly from the CharacterData interface, and the CDATASection interface inherits from it indirectly through the Text interface.

The CharacterData interface has the following IDL definition:

```
interface CharacterData : Node {
          attribute DOMString        data;
                                   // raises(DOMException) on setting
                                   // raises(DOMException) on retrieval

  readonly attribute unsigned long   length;
  DOMString             substringData(in unsigned long offset,
                                      in unsigned long count)
                                          raises(DOMException);
```

```
void                appendData(in DOMString arg)
                                    raises(DOMException);
void                insertData(in unsigned long offset,
                           in DOMString arg)
                                    raises(DOMException);
void                deleteData(in unsigned long offset,
                           in unsigned long count)
                                    raises(DOMException);
void                replaceData(in unsigned long offset,
                           in unsigned long count,
                           in DOMString arg)
                                    raises(DOMException);
};
```

The CharacterData interface contains two properties: data and length. The data property contains the character data of the node that implements this interface. The length property contains the length of the character data, as measured in 16-bit units. The length property may be 0; that is, the node may be empty.

The CharacterData interface provides five methods for working with the character data contained within a node. In the cases where offsets are used as arguments, they are measured using 16-bit character sizes.

The substringData() method extracts a range of character data from within a node. It accepts two arguments, offset and count. The offset argument specifies the 0-based offset into the character data to start extracting data. The count argument specifies the number of characters to extract.

The appendData() method is used to append character data to the end of the node's character data. It accepts one argument, a DOMString to append to the end of the character data.

The insertData() method inserts character data into the node's character data at a specified point. The offset argument is the 0-based character offset at which to insert the data. The arg argument is the DOMString to insert into the node's character data.

The deleteData() method is used to delete a range of character data from the node. The offset argument specifies the offset at which character data should be deleted. The count argument specifies the number of characters to delete from the node.

The replaceData() method replaces a range of characters in the node's data with a string of data. The offset argument specifies the point at which character data should be replaced. The count argument specifies the number of characters that should be replaced. If the sum of the offset and count arguments exceed the length of the character data, all of the characters starting from the offset point until the end of the character data are replaced. The `arg` argument specifies the string that should replace the range of characters in the node's character data.

The Comment Interface

The Comment interface inherits from the CharacterData interface and represents the textual content of an HTML or XML comment, minus the preceding and trailing comment delimiters (the `<!--` and `-->` characters). It does not define any additional properties or methods.

The Comment interface has the following IDL definition:

```
interface Comment : CharacterData {
};
```

The Text Interface

The Text interface inherits from the CharacterData interface and represents the textual content of Element and Attr objects. When a document is first parsed, each contiguous block of text is represented by a single Text node. Text nodes can have adjacent Text nodes, which are created either programmatically or as an indirect result of the user editing the document. There is no way to represent the separation of these nodes in HTML or XML, so there is no way to guarantee that they will persist between editing sessions; the next time the document is loaded, the text will be parsed into one contiguous text node. The Node interface's `normalize()` method can be used to merge adjacent text nodes into a single node.

The Text interface has the following IDL definition:

```
interface Text : CharacterData {
  Text              splitText(in unsigned long offset)
                                  raises(DOMException);
};
```

The Text interface contains a single method, `splitText()`, which takes the Text node and splits it into two nodes starting at the given offset into the text content specified by the `offset` argument and returns a new Text node. When split, the original Text node will contain all the text up to the supplied offset. The new node will contain the text from the offset point until the end of the text content. If the original node has a parent, the new node will be inserted as the next sibling node of the original node. If the supplied `offset` argument is equal to the length of the text of the original node, the new node will have no content.

The Extended Core Interfaces

In this section, we introduce the Extended Core interfaces, which are provided for working specifically with XML documents in addition to the fundamental Core interfaces. The interfaces covered in this section will not be encountered when working purely with HTML documents.

The interfaces within this section are not mandatory for Core compliance, so DOM applications should use the hasFeature() method of the DOMImplementation interface with the arguments XML and 1.0 for DOM Level 1 or 2.0 for DOM Level 2 to determine if these interfaces are available for use.

CDATASection Interface

CDATA sections are used to prevent XML processors from attempting to parse a block of text data as if it were markup. Everything in the CDATA section, between the opening <![CDATA[and the closing]]> sequences, is ignored. The primary purpose of a CDATA section is to include markup text without having to escape each delimiter. CDATA sections cannot be nested within each other.

The CDATASection interface inherits from the CharacterData interface through the Text interface. Adjacent CDATASection nodes are not merged by use of the normalize() method of the Node interface.

The CDATASection interface has the following IDL definition:

```
interface CDATASection : Text {
};
```

DocumentType Interface

Each Document has a docType attribute whose value is either null or a DocumentType object. The DocumentType interface in the DOM Core provides an interface to the list of entities that are defined for the document. Currently, the DOM Level 2 spec does not support the editing of DocumentTypes. This has been left for a future version of the DOM.

The DocumentType interface has the following IDL definition:

```
interface DocumentType : Node {
  readonly attribute DOMString        name;
  readonly attribute NamedNodeMap     entities;
  readonly attribute NamedNodeMap     notations;
  // Introduced in DOM Level 2:
```

```
  readonly attribute DOMString        publicId;
  // Introduced in DOM Level 2:
  readonly attribute DOMString        systemId;
  // Introduced in DOM Level 2:
  readonly attribute DOMString        internalSubset;
};
```

The name property is the name of the DTD; that is, the name immediately following the DOCTYPE keyword.

The entities property is a NamedNodeMap containing the general entities, both external and internal, declared in the DTD.

The notations property is a NamedNodeMap containing the notations declared in the DTD. Duplicates are discarded. Every node in this map also implements the Notation interface. The DOM Level 2 does not support editing notations; therefore, notations cannot be altered in any way.

The publicId property is the public identifier of the external subset.

The systemId property is the system identifier of the external subset.

The internalSubset property is the internal subset as a string.

NOTE

The actual content returned depends on how much information is available to the implementation. This may vary depending on various parameters, including the XML processor used to build the document.

Notation Interface

The Notation interface represents a Notation node in the document. Notation nodes have no parents. A notation either declares, by name, the format of an unparsed entity, or is used for formal declaration of processing instruction targets. See the XML 1.0 specification, sections 4.7 and 2.6, for more detailed information on notations.

The Notation interface has the following IDL definition:

```
interface Notation : Node {
  readonly attribute DOMString        publicId;
  readonly attribute DOMString        systemId;
};
```

The publicID property is the public identifier of this notation. If the public identifier was not specified, this is null.

The `systemID` property is the system identifier of this notation. If the system identifier was not specified, this is `null`.

Entity Interface

This interface represents an entity, either parsed or unparsed, in an XML document. The Entity interface has the following IDL definition:

```
interface Entity : Node {
  readonly attribute DOMString        publicId;
  readonly attribute DOMString        systemId;
  readonly attribute DOMString        notationName;
};
```

The `notationName` property is, for unparsed entities, the name of the notation for the entity. For parsed entities, this is `null`.

The `publicId` property is the public identifier associated with the entity, if specified. If the public identifier was not specified, this is `null`.

The `systemId` property is the system identifier associated with the entity, if specified. If the system identifier was not specified, this is `null`.

EntityReference Interface

The EntityReference interface represents an EntityReference in the document. EntityReference nodes and their descendants are read-only.

The EntityReference interface has the following IDL definition:

```
interface EntityReference : Node {
};
```

ProcessingInstruction Interface

The XML language uses "processing instructions" to send special instructions to the XML processor, which are enclosed by an opening `<?` and a closing `?>` . They specify a target and an instruction to send to the processor. The ProcessingInstruction interface represents these instructions in the DOM.

The ProcessingInstruction interface has the following IDL definition:

```
interface ProcessingInstruction : Node {
  readonly attribute DOMString        target;
          attribute DOMString        data;
                                      // raises(DOMException) on setting
};
```

The `target` property returns the target of this processing instruction. The `data` property contains the data for this processing instruction, from the first nonwhitespace character after the target to the character immediately preceding the closing `?>`.

Conclusion

In this chapter, we introduced the DOM document tree, and you saw how the DOM structures the information contained within a document using DOM nodes. We also introduced some basic DOM data types and interfaces for representing string and time information and handling error conditions. Next, we examined the possible relationships between the nodes of a document and the specific types of nodes available and the information they can contain. Finally, the Core Level 1 DOM interfaces were introduced and examined in-depth to show how each can be used to extract and manipulate information in the document.

In the next chapter, we use the fundamental DOM interfaces introduced in this chapter to create, arrange, and manipulate a DOM document's nodes and content. We also examine some of the ways to extract information from document nodes, and how to use some of the DOM's more advanced utility classes such as NodeIterator and TreeWalker to traverse a document in an ordered fashion.

Navigating and Manipulating Structured Documents

A s discussed in the previous chapter, the DOM API's Node interface provides several methods and properties for working with node information, such as obtaining a node's content, discovering its position with respect to other nodes, and manipulating its child nodes. In this chapter, we'll examine how to use the DOM API's Node interface to inspect, navigate, and manipulate a document's nodes and content. You'll see how properties and methods are used to work with nodes in the context of structured XML and HTML documents. We'll also look at how to handle copying nodes from one document to another, and we'll finish up with an examination of the DOM API's Traversal module, which makes processing documents and parts of documents easier.

Working with Nodes

Structured documents (such as XML and HTML documents) consist of a collection of nodes, so you can use the properties and methods of the Node interface to perform many kinds of common types of document inspection and manipulation. Using the Node interface, you can discover the content of nodes; their positions in the document tree; and the nature of their surroundings, such as their parent, child, and sibling nodes.

Consider the HTML document shown in Listing 3-1.

Listing 3-1   *Sample HTML Document*

```
<HTML>
<HEAD>
<TITLE>Sample Document</TITLE>
<!-- This is a comment -->
</HEAD>
<BODY>
<B>This is bold text</B>
<I>This is italic text</I>
<U>This is underlined text</U>
</BODY>
</HTML>
```

Figure 3-1 shows the corresponding DOM tree structure for this document.

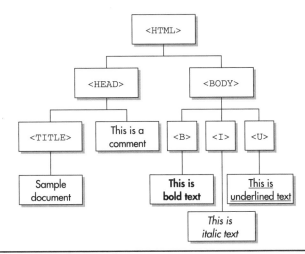

Figure 3-1   *Document tree diagram for Listing 3-1*

This example document contains at least one of each of four types of nodes most commonly found in HTML and XML documents: Document, Element, Text, and Comment. Looking at this document, you can see how the properties of the Node interface are populated for each different type of node. First, however, you need to be able to obtain references to nodes so you can act on them. The Node interface, as well as other specialized functions provided by the DOM API, provides the necessary methods for obtaining references to a document's nodes.

NOTE
The DOM specification defines certain operations as implementation-specific functions, such as obtaining a reference to the Document node. Some implementations, such as web browser–based JavaScript, provide a global "document" object; whereas others (such as Xerces and Macromedia's Dreamweaver) provide API methods for retrieving the document object from the application or parser. You should refer to the documentation for your particular DOM implementation for more information.

A Word About Namespaces

The DOM Level 1 interfaces do not deal with XML namespaces. Namespace support was added in DOM Level 2. According to the W3C DOM Working Group, developers should start using the namespace-aware methods in their new DOM applications; the old, non-namespace-aware methods are left in mainly for backward compatibility and are considered deprecated. However, many DOM implementations do not yet provide support for DOM Level 2, and it technically should still be okay to use the older methods when working with XML documents that do not contain namespaces. For simplicity, this book will use the non-namespace-aware methods because the current versions of most browsers and applications don't yet support DOM Level 2, although any new development that you do using DOM Level 2 should use the namespace-aware methods. More information on XML namespaces can be found at www.w3.org/TR/REC-xml-names/.

Obtaining Object References to Nodes

DOM applications can obtain references to a document's nodes directly by using the properties of the Node interface. Node references can also be obtained by using certain node properties that return nodes and lists of nodes, such as the `childNodes` property of the Node interface; other specialized DOM methods such as `getElementsByTagName()` on the Element interface; and `getElementById()`, provided by the Document interface.

For example, to obtain a reference to the first child node of a document using the properties provided by the Node interface, you would use the following code:

```
var node = document.documentElement.firstChild;
```

NOTE

The previous code is specific to DOM implementations that use a JavaScript implementation binding, such as Microsoft Internet Explorer and Netscape Navigator. Other implementations (such as Xerces) may use slightly different notation to access node properties; see your DOM implementation's documentation for more information.

This line of code would return an object reference to the first child node of the document element; in our example, this would be the element node represented by the `<HEAD>` tag.

As stated previously, you can also use certain DOM methods that return nodes and lists of nodes to obtain node references. For example, the following code fragment will return a NodeList containing all `H1` elements in a document:

```
var h1tags = document.documentElement.getElementsByTagName("H1");
```

The `getElementsByTagName()` method takes a `DOMString` as an argument, which is the type of tag to retrieve. The method scans the document for all tags that match the given tag name and returns them in the order in which those nodes were encountered in the document. You can also obtain a reference to a node by using its ID attribute, if it has one:

```
var theNode = document.getElementById("thenodeid");
```

The ID attribute is an attribute attached to Element nodes that uniquely identify them in a document. Note that the DOM does not enforce this requirement: you can give the same ID to more than one element, but the resulting behavior is undefined, according to the DOM specification.

Node references, including those in NodeList and NamedNodeMap structures, are called "live" references. In other words, changes to a node contained in the document tree will be immediately reflected in all NodeLists and NamedNodeMaps where that node is represented, and vice versa. For example, if a DOM application retrieves a list of the child nodes of a given node and then proceeds to add more child nodes to that node, the presence of the new child nodes will be immediately reflected in the NodeList that was returned previously.

Inspecting Nodes

Using the example document represented by Listing 3-1 and illustrated in Figure 3-1, we can list the properties of the Node interface as they would be populated in a node reference for each of the four node types contained within the document.

Table 3-1 lists the values of the Node interface properties for the Document node.

Because the Document node is the root of the DOM structure, and because documents can have only one Document node, this node has no `ownerDocument`, `previousSibling`, `nextSibling`, or `parentNode`; thus they are all `null`.

Node Property	Value
ownerDocument	null
previousSibling	null
nextSibling	null
parentNode	null
firstChild	Element ("HTML")
lastChild	Element ("HTML")
nodeName	"#document"
nodeValue	null
nodeType	9 (Document node)

Table 3-1 *Node Properties for the Document Node*

In addition, the Node interface specifies that the `nodeValue` of a Document node is also `null`. The Document node has one child, the `HTML` element, which means that the node's `firstChild` and `lastChild` are the same node. The `nodeType` for a Document node is defined to be 9.

Table 3-2 lists the values of the Node properties for the Element node represented by the `<TITLE>` tag.

The `<TITLE>` tag's `ownerDocument` is set to the document that owns this node. It is the first child of the `<HEAD>` tag, so it has no `previousSibling`. Its `nextSibling` property is the Comment node that follows it in the document; and because it is a direct descendant of the `<HEAD>` tag, it has the `HEAD` Element node as its `parentNode`. It has only one child—a Text node—so its `firstChild` and `lastChild` properties are the same. The `nodeName` property reflects the name of the tag that represents the node—in this case, `<TITLE>`. Element nodes, by definition, have no node value, so the `nodeValue` property is set to `null`. The `<TITLE>` tag is an Element node, and its `nodeType` property reflects this with a value of 1.

The `TITLE` node is an Element node, so it has one additional property specified by the Element interface: the `tagName` property, which is the same as `nodeName` (`"TITLE"`).

Table 3-3 lists the values of the Node interface properties for the Comment node.

The Comment node is immediately preceded by the `TITLE` element, causing the `previousSibling` property to contain a reference to the `TITLE` node. There is no node after the comment, which is why the `nextSibling` property is `null`.

Node Property	Value
ownerDocument	Document node
previousSibling	null
nextSibling	Comment node
parentNode	Element node (`"HEAD"`)
firstChild	Text node
lastChild	Text node
nodeName	`"TITLE"`
nodeValue	null
nodeType	1 (Element node)

Table 3-2   *Node Properties for the `<TITLE>` Tag*

Node Property	Value
ownerDocument	Document node
previousSibling	Element node ("TITLE")
nextSibling	null
parentNode	Element node ("HEAD")
firstChild	null
lastChild	null
nodeName	"#comment"
nodeValue	"This is a comment"
nodeType	8 (Comment node)

Table 3-3   *Node Properties for the Comment Node*

Comments do not have child nodes, so the firstChild and lastChild properties are null. Like the <TITLE> tag, the Comment has the <HEAD> tag as its parent (and thus, parentNode contains a reference to the HEAD element node). The nodeName of a Comment is "#comment", and the node's value is the text contained within the comment, not including the comment delimiters (<!-- and -->, respectively). The nodeType for a Comment node is 8.

Comment nodes have additional properties, data and length, which are provided by the CharacterData interface that they derive from. For a Comment node, the data property is the same as the nodeValue property. The length property specifies the number of 16-bit units that comprise the character content of the comment (*not* the number of bytes!).

Table 3-4 lists the values of the Node interface properties for the Text node represented by the text string "This is bold text", which is a child node of the <B> tag.

As with all the other nodes, the Text node's ownerDocument is set to the Document node for this document. The Text node is the only child of the <B> tag, so its previousSibling and nextSibling properties are set to null. Its parent is the <B> tag itself, as indicated by the parentNode property. Text nodes are not allowed to have child nodes, so the firstChild and lastChild properties are both null. The nodeName property for a Text node is defined by the W3C specification to be "#text", and the nodeValue property holds the text content of the node (in this case, "This is bold text"). The nodeType for Text nodes is set to 3.

Node Property	Value
ownerDocument	Document node
previousSibling	null
nextSibling	null
parentNode	Element node ("B")
firstChild	null
lastChild	null
nodeName	"#text"
nodeValue	"This is bold text"
nodeType	3 (Text node)

Table 3-4   *Node Properties for the Text Node*

Like Comment nodes, Text nodes also inherit the data and length properties from the CharacterData interface.

Manipulating Nodes

The Node interface provides all of the necessary methods for modifying the structural order and content of the nodes of a document. The DOM specification states that the firstChild, lastChild, parentNode, previousSibling, and nextSibling properties are read-only, so the only way to change the order of nodes in a document via the Node interface is by using the provided methods— insertBefore(), appendChild(), replaceChild(), and removeChild().

Consider a hypothetical document subtree containing five nodes, as shown in Figure 3-2.

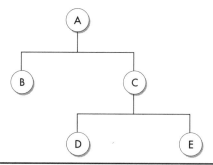

Figure 3-2   *A document subtree*

Let's examine the effects of using the Node interface's node-arranging methods on this subtree.

Adding Nodes

To add new nodes to a node structure, you can use the `insertBefore()` and `appendChild()` methods. The `insertBefore()` method has the following interface definition:

```
Node insertBefore(in Node newChild, in Node refChild)
raises(DOMException);
```

The method takes two arguments: `newChild` and `refChild`. The `newChild` argument is the node to be inserted; `refChild` is the node before which the new node will be inserted. Listing 3-2 illustrates the call necessary to insert a new node F as the first child of node C.

Listing 3-2   *Inserting a new node*

```
// assume that we already have a node F to insert into the tree
nodeC.insertBefore(nodeF, nodeC.firstChild);
```

Figure 3-3 shows the effect this has on the document subtree.

If you specify `null` as the `refChild` argument, the new node is added at the end of the list of children. If the `newChild` node already exists elsewhere in the document, it is first removed from its current location.

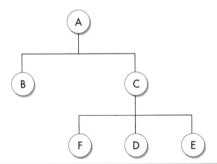

Figure 3-3   *The document subtree after* `insertBefore()`

The appendChild() method takes a new node and adds it to the given node's list of children. It has this interface definition:

```
Node appendChild(in Node newChild)
raises(DOMException);
```

If the child node to be appended already exists somewhere else in the document, it is first removed from that location. This method is functionally equivalent to calling insertBefore(newNode, null). The following code listing illustrates the use of appendChild() to add a new child node F to the end of node B's child list:

```
nodeB.appendChild(nodeF);
```

Figure 3-4 shows the result of this operation on the document subtree from Figure 3-2.

Removing Nodes

The removeChild() method removes a child node from the given parent. It has this interface definition:

```
Node removeChild(in Node oldChild)
raises(DOMException);
```

If the child node itself has child nodes, then they are all removed from the document. The following code listing demonstrates removing the child node C from node A:

```
nodeA.removeChild(nodeC);
```

After removal, the document subtree in Figure 3-2 would look as shown in Figure 3-5.

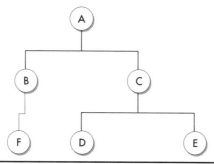

Figure 3-4   *The document subtree after* appendChild()

Figure 3-5   *The document subtree after* `removeChild()`

NOTE

Removing a child from the document tree is not the same as deleting it. The DOM does cover memory management issues, and thus does not specify how to actually delete items from memory.

Replacing Nodes

The `replaceChild()` method replaces one child node with another. It has the following interface definition:

```
Node replaceChild(in Node newChild, in Node oldChild)
raises(DOMException);
```

If the `newChild` argument is a DocumentFragment object, the `oldChild` node is replaced by all of the `newChild` node's children, which are inserted in the same order as they appear under `newChild`. If the `newChild` node already exists somewhere else in the document tree, it is first removed from its current location before being inserted into its new location.

This code snippet demonstrates replacing node D with node B:

```
nodeC.replaceChild(nodeB, nodeD);
```

Figure 3-6 shows the effect of this operation on the document subtree.

Example: Swapping Two Nodes

The DOM API does not directly provide a single method for swapping two nodes in a node structure, but you can perform the operation using the existing methods on the Node interface.

Suppose you have an HTML fragment that looks like this:

```
<OL>
<LI id="node1">List Item A</LI>
<LI id="node2">List Item B</LI>
<LI id="node3">List Item C</LI>
<LI id="node4">List Item D</LI>
</OL>
```

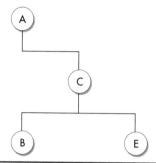

Figure 3-6 *The document subtree after* `replaceChild()`

Figure 3-7 illustrates this HTML fragment's node structure.

To swap the positions of List Item A and List Item B, you can use the following function, written using the JavaScript language binding for the DOM:

```
function swapItems()
{
    // get the element whose id is "node2"
    var theNode = document.getElementById("node2");
    var theParent = theNode.parentNode;
    var tempNode = theNode.previousSibling;

    theParent.removeChild(theNode);
    theParent.insertBefore(theNode, tempNode);
}
```

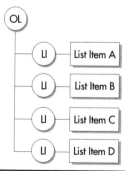

Figure 3-7 *Document structure for ordered list fragment*

The first line of the function retrieves the `LI` node with the ID attribute `"node2"`. You then use the parent of this node to perform the operation of swapping its children. In fact, the call to `removeChild()` is actually superfluous; the node would have been removed anyway by the call to `insertBefore()` because it was already in the tree. The result of this operation is shown in Figure 3-8.

Swapping nodes is actually a common enough operation that Internet Explorer provides a method for it called (appropriately enough) `swapNode()`. It has this interface definition:

```
Node swapNode(in Node refNode)
raises (DOMException);
```

The `swapNode()` method swaps the node from which this method is called with the node specified by the `refNode` argument, which does not need to be a child node. It returns a reference to the node on which this method was invoked. Using the `swapNode()` method, the previous example becomes even simpler:

```
function swapItems()
{
    // get the element whose id is "node2"
    var theNode = document.getElementById("node2");
    var tempNode = theNode.previousSibling;

    theNode.swapNode(tempNode);
}
```

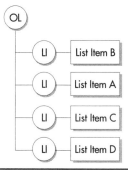

Figure 3-8   *The ordered list fragment after swapping*

Creating New Nodes

Of course, it probably won't be enough for your application to inspect and rearrange existing nodes. At some point, you'll need to create new ones to insert into the document. The DOM provides different ways of doing this. You can create new nodes from scratch or duplicate existing nodes in the document.

Using the Factory Methods

Usually, in most object-oriented programming languages, you create a new object by using the new operator with the type of object you want to create, like this:

```
var obj = new SomeDocumentObject();
```

This doesn't work with the DOM because there are some language bindings that do not support the new operator. To make these cases easier to handle, the DOM uses special methods called *factory methods* that are responsible for creating new nodes. It is then up to the implementation to handle the actual memory management involved with creating these new nodes.

Each type of node has an associated factory method. For example, to create a new Text node, you would write the following code:

```
var newTextNode = document.createTextNode("This is the node content");
```

After a node has been created, it is in a state of limbo; it is not actually inserted into the document tree anywhere but is just sort of floating in space. You need to attach it to the document tree using one of the node manipulation methods discussed earlier, such as appendChild().

Table 3-5 lists the different factory methods that the DOM provides for creating new Document nodes.

Method	Description
Element createElement(in DOMString tagName)	Creates a new Element node of the type supplied by tagName.
DocumentFragment createDocumentFragment()	Creates a new empty DocumentFragment node.
Comment createComment(in DOMString data)	Creates a new Comment node whose content is given by the data argument.

Table 3-5   *Factory Methods for Creating New Document Nodes*

Method	Description
`Text createTextNode(in DOMString data)`	Creates a new Text node whose content is given by the `data` argument.
`CDATASection createCDATASection(in DOMString data)`	Creates a CDATA section whose content is supplied by the `data` argument.
`ProcessingInstruction createProcessingInstruction(in DOMString target, in DOMString data)`	Creates a new ProcessingInstruction node with the given `target` and `data`.
`Attr createAttribute(in DOMString name)`	Creates a new Attr node with the given name.
`EntityReference createEntityReference(in DOMString name)`	Creates a new EntityReference node. The name of the entity to reference is the given name.

Table 3-5   *Factory Methods for Creating New Document Nodes* (continued)

Suppose you want to create a new ordered list structure like the one shown earlier in Figure 3-7, and you want to insert it as the first child of the <BODY> tag. To accomplish this, you need to create each node, set its content, and add the whole thing to the <BODY> tag. The following listing demonstrates the necessary steps to do this.

```
// declare some temporary variables to hold the LI nodes
var newLI, newText;
// create the new ordered list
var newOL = document.createElement("OL");
// now create each new element. Start with List Item A
newLI = document.createElement("LI");
newText = document.createTextNode("List Item A");
// add the text to the LI node
newLI.appendChild(newText);
// add the LI node to the ordered list
newOL.appendChild(newLI);
newLI = document.createElement("LI");
// now do the same for List Item B
newText = document.createTextNode("List Item B");
newLI.appendChild(newText);
newOL.appendChild(newLI);
newLI = document.createElement("LI");
// now do the same for List Item C
```

```
newText = document.createTextNode("List Item C");
newLI.appendChild(newText);
newOL.appendChild(newLI);
newLI = document.createElement("LI");
// now do the same for List Item D
newText = document.createTextNode("List Item D");
newLI.appendChild(newText);
newOL.appendChild(newLI);

// now that the list has been built, insert it as the BODY
// tag's first child. We use the document's getElementsByTagName
// method to get a list of the BODY tags, of which there will
// be only one. We then use the insertBefore() method to insert
// the ordered list into the BODY.
var bodyTag = document.getElementsByTagName("BODY").item(0);
bodyTag.insertBefore(newOL, bodyTag.firstChild);
```

Cloning Existing Nodes

Another way to create new nodes is to clone an existing node using the cloneNode()
method on the Node interface. This will give you a copy of the existing node, optionally
with copies of all of its child nodes.

Using the example document shown in Figure 3-7, you could add new <LI> tags
to the end of the ordered list by using an existing <LI> tag as the template for each
new one. For example, this code listing shows how to clone an existing <LI> tag,
modify it, and add it to the end of the ordered list:

```
var theTemplateNode = document.getElementById("node4");
// make a clone of the node using a deep clone so that we
// get the text node along with the element node
var newNode = theTemplateNode.cloneNode(true);
// now modify the new node's child text node to have the
// data that we want in the new node
newNode.firstChild.data = "List Item E";
// make a new id attribute for it
newNode.setAttribute("id","node5");
// append it to the ordered list
theTemplateNode.parentNode.appendChild(newNode);
```

The code begins by retrieving the node with the ID attribute "node4", which
corresponds to the last <LI> tag. Once you have a reference to that node, you clone
it using a deep clone to make copies of the target node, as well as its child nodes.

Then, you set the content of the child Text node to be the string you want it to have and call `appendChild()` on the original node's parent.

Importing Nodes from Other Documents

Sometimes, DOM programs need to use or operate on nodes from different documents. For example, you might want to copy the information in a node contained in one document into another document. The DOM Level 2 API provides the `importNode()` method for this purpose, which can be found on the Document interface. It has the following interface definition:

```
Node importNode(in Node importedNode, in boolean deep)
raises(DOMException);
```

As its name implies, the `importNode()` method imports a node from another document into the document from which this method is called. The node that is returned from this method call has no parent (that is, its `parentNode` property is set to `null`) until it is inserted into the document tree, but it is owned by the calling document (the one doing the importing). This operation does not change the source node in the target document in any way. It is not removed from the target document's tree—the `importNode()` method makes a copy of the source node, optionally copying all of its child nodes (if the `deep` argument is true).

The node being imported may be entering a document that has a different DTD (Document Type Definition) than the source document from which it came, so the importing process affects different types of nodes in different ways. Table 3-6 lists the different node types and the behavior of imported nodes of that type.

Node Type	Importing Behavior
Element	Attribute nodes of the source element that have their specified property set to true are imported and are attached to the generated element. Default attributes are not copied, though they are automatically assigned to the element if the importing document defines default attributes for this element type. If the `deep` argument is true, all of the element's descendants are copied, and the resulting nodes are assembled into a corresponding document subtree.

Table 3-6 *Imported Node Behavior of Different Node Types*

Node Type	Importing Behavior
Attribute	The Attribute node's ownerElement is set to `null`, and the `specified` flag is set to true. All of the source attribute node's child nodes are also imported, and the resulting nodes are reassembled to form the corresponding attributes subtree. In the case of attributes, the `deep` argument is ignored.
DocumentFragment	If the `deep` argument is false, an empty DocumentFragment node is generated; otherwise, the descendants of the source node are all recursively imported, and the resulting nodes are assembled into the corresponding document subtree.
Text	The `data` and `length` properties are copied from the source node.
CDATA	The `data` and `length` properties are copied from the source node.
Comment	The `data` and `length` properties are copied from the source node.
ProcessingInstruction	The `target` and `data` properties are copied from the source node.
Entity	Entity nodes can be imported. The current version of the DOM specification states that the DocumentType is read-only, however. This may be addressed in a future DOM version. The `publicID`, `systemID`, and `notationName` attributes of the source node are copied on import. If the `deep` argument is true, all of the entity's descendants are copied, and the resulting nodes are assembled into a corresponding document subtree.
EntityReference	The source and destination documents might have defined the entity differently, so only the EntityReference itself is copied, even if the `deep` argument is true. If the importing document defines the entity, its value is assigned.
Notation	Notation nodes can be imported. The current version of the DOM specification states that the DocumentType is read-only, however. This may be addressed in a future DOM version. The `deep` argument is ignored because Notations do not have child nodes. The `publicID` and `systemID` attributes are copied from the source node.
Document	Document nodes cannot be imported.
DocumentType	DocumentType nodes cannot be imported.

Table 3-6   *Imported Node Behavior of Different Node Types* (continued)

Traversing Documents

One of the most common code patterns in DOM applications is document subtree traversal. At some point, somewhere, sometime, your DOM program will need to traverse the document tree structure and process its contents. This can be accomplished in two ways: by using the basic Node interfaces available in DOM Level 1, and by using the more advanced DocumentTraversal interface available in DOM Level 2. In this section, we'll examine both approaches, along with the advantages and disadvantages of each.

Using the Node Interface Properties

The lowly Node interface available in DOM Level 1 provides all of the information and methods that your DOM program needs to traverse the entire structure of a DOM document. You use the properties and methods of the Node interface, such as `firstChild`, `lastChild`, `parentNode`, and so on, to move among the nodes relative to any given node in the tree.

For example, this simple pseudocode listing processes all of the nodes in a document subtree starting with a given node:

```
function processNode(Node n)
{
   doStartNodeProcessing(n);
   for (Node c = n.firstChild(); c != null; c = c.nextSibling())
   {
      processNode(c);
   }
   doEndNodeProcessing(n);
}


function doStartNodeProcessing(Node n)
{
   // Do any processing when a node is first encountered
}


function doEndNodeProcessing(Node n)
{
   // Do any processing when a node is about to be left
}
```

This example, although simplistic, demonstrates a straightforward way of visiting every node underneath a starting node, processing each visited node upon entry and exit of the function. It also has the advantage of being completely implementable under a DOM Level 1 implementation.

Of course, this example also has some drawbacks. First, it visits and processes every node in the subtree whether you want it to or not. There is no way, for example, to only visit nodes that are of a certain type (like elements or comments). You could, of course, add such functionality without too much difficulty:

```
function processNode(Node n)
{
   if (n.nodeType != Node.ELEMENT_NODE)
      return;
   doStartNodeProcessing(n);
   for (Node c = n.firstChild(); c != null; c = c.nextSibling())
   {
      processNode(c);
   }
   doEndNodeProcessing(n);
}
```

Now, you've modified the function so that it only processes Element nodes. It's still not as flexible as it could be, though. For example, you might want to change the types of nodes that you're processing on-the-fly, which means either adding an additional argument to the function header or using a global variable to keep track of what node type you're currently interested in.

However, there are other drawbacks. This example does not allow for stopping; all the nodes are processed one right after the next. It might be useful to be able to stop processing momentarily and then resume later on. To achieve these kinds of requirements, you need to use a more powerful node traversing method, which is where the DOM Level 2 Traversal module comes in.

Using the DOM Level 2 Traversal Module

DOM Level 2 introduced a new module named Traversal. It specifies four interfaces: NodeIterator, NodeFilter, TreeWalker, and DocumentTraversal. The first three interfaces provide robust node traversal functionality over a document's nodes. The DocumentTraversal interface provides the factory methods necessary for creating TreeWalkers and NodeIterators.

Iterators vs. Walkers

NodeIterators and TreeWalkers represent two very different ways of representing a document subtree's set of nodes. NodeIterators present a "flattened" view of the document: the nodes are presented in the order they are encountered in the document, as if they had been laid out one after the other. They present their nodes absent of the hierarchy in the document, so they allow you only to move forward and backward through a list of nodes. TreeWalkers, on the other hand, maintain their representation of the document hierarchy relative to the node that they are currently attached to.

So why use a NodeIterator instead of a TreeWalker (or vice versa)? Generally speaking, NodeIterators are more useful when your DOM application is focused on the *contents* of each node. TreeWalkers are better when your application will *manipulate the structure* of the subtree's nodes.

Logical Views and Physical Views

NodeIterators and TreeWalkers have the ability to present views of the document subtree that may not contain all of the nodes that are actually in the subtree. For example, a NodeIterator or TreeWalker can be told to only visit Element nodes, excluding other node types. The DOM Traversal module specification refers to this as a *logical view.* The actual document subtree independent of the iterator or walker is called the *physical view.* The way this is accomplished is by associating a NodeFilter object with the NodeIterator or TreeWalker. The NodeFilter examines each node and determines whether it should be included in the logical view. NodeFilters are very powerful objects: they can include or exclude nodes based on almost any criteria you can think of, including node type, whether it has or doesn't have certain attributes, what the node's `nodeName` property is, and so on. Figure 3-9 illustrates the difference between a physical view and a logical view of the same document. The document contains several different node types, but the logical view as seen by a certain traversal object contains only Element nodes (shown with bold outlines) because it has chosen to exclude all other node types.

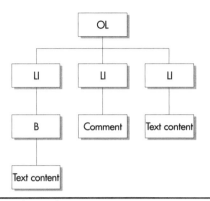

Figure 3-9 *Logical view vs. physical view*

Like other DOM collection objects, NodeIterators and TreeWalkers contain live node references; that is, their logical views will reflect any changes made to the physical subtree that they represent. The key difference between the two, however, is *how* they respond to such changes. NodeIterators will attempt to maintain their location relative to a sequence of nodes when the sequence changes. TreeWalkers will maintain their current location relative to their current node and will stay attached to that node if it moves to a new context due to an external action on the tree by another part of the DOM program. These behaviors will be discussed in more detail later in this chapter.

NodeFilters

NodeFilters are objects that are used to "filter" the node selection process. They can be associated with both NodeIterators and TreeWalkers, but they do not do any node navigation themselves. If a NodeFilter is associated with an iterator or walker, the associated traversal object applies the filter before returning the next node. The filter can decide either to accept or to reject the node. If the node is accepted, the traversal object returns it to the caller. Otherwise, the node is skipped as if it were not there, and the traversal object looks for the next node (this is how the logical view is generated from the physical view).

NodeFilters do not have to perform any node navigation or traversal themselves, so they are easy to write and can be reused among several different traversal objects. The DOM itself does not provide any built-in NodeFilters. You can think of the NodeFilter interface as an "abstract base class" in C++ or an "interface definition" in Java that DOM programs can use as a starting point to build their own filters.

NodeFilters have the following interface definition:

```
interface NodeFilter {
  // Constants returned by acceptNode
  const short              FILTER_ACCEPT                = 1;
  const short              FILTER_REJECT                = 2;
  const short              FILTER_SKIP                  = 3;

  // Constants for whatToShow
  const unsigned long      SHOW_ALL                     = 0xFFFFFFFF;
  const unsigned long      SHOW_ELEMENT                 = 0x00000001;
  const unsigned long      SHOW_ATTRIBUTE               = 0x00000002;
  const unsigned long      SHOW_TEXT                    = 0x00000004;
  const unsigned long      SHOW_CDATA_SECTION           = 0x00000008;
  const unsigned long      SHOW_ENTITY_REFERENCE        = 0x00000010;
  const unsigned long      SHOW_ENTITY                  = 0x00000020;
  const unsigned long      SHOW_PROCESSING_INSTRUCTION  = 0x00000040;
  const unsigned long      SHOW_COMMENT                 = 0x00000080;
  const unsigned long      SHOW_DOCUMENT                = 0x00000100;
  const unsigned long      SHOW_DOCUMENT_TYPE           = 0x00000200;
  const unsigned long      SHOW_DOCUMENT_FRAGMENT       = 0x00000400;
  const unsigned long      SHOW_NOTATION                = 0x00000800;

  short              acceptNode(in Node n);
};
```

The first three constants are returned from a NodeFilter's `acceptNode()` method. If `acceptNode()` returns FILTER_ACCEPT, the navigation methods for a NodeIterator or TreeWalker will return the node. If `acceptNode()` returns FILTER_REJECT, the node is skipped. If the traversal object is a TreeWalker, the child nodes of the given node are also skipped. If `acceptNode()` returns FILTER_SKIP, the node is skipped; but if the traversal object is a TreeWalker, child nodes of the given node will still be considered. NodeIterators treat FILTER_REJECT and FILTER_SKIP the same.

The next 13 constants are used to determine what types of nodes are returned by NodeIterators and TreeWalkers. These constant values and combinations of them can be used as values for the `whatToShow` parameter used in TreeWalkers and NodeIterators, and they represent a bit position in the `whatToShow` parameter. If the corresponding bit position in the `whatToShow` parameter is set to false for the given node type, nodes of that type will be skipped over.

NOTE

The values SHOW_ATTRIBUTE, SHOW_ENTITY, and SHOW_NOTATION are only useful when the NodeIterator or TreeWalker has a node of that type set as its root; attributes, entities, and notations are not considered part of the document tree, and thus will not normally be encountered when traversing it.

The `acceptNode()` method tests whether a given node should be returned by the associated traversal object. It is typically called by NodeIterator and TreeWalker objects under two separate circumstances:

▶ When a traversal method of the NodeIterator or the TreeWalker is executed.

▶ When the node that a NodeIterator is using as its reference node is removed from the tree and a new one must be selected.

NOTE

The exact timing of the two events just described may be different among DOM implementations. The DOM specification explicitly states that NodeFilters should not try to maintain any state information from past invocations because the resulting behavior may not be portable.

Implementing Your Own NodeFilters   The DOM does not provide any built-in NodeFilters. To use a NodeFilter, you must create your own and pass it to a NodeIterator or TreeWalker when it is created. For example, suppose you wanted to create a NodeFilter that only accepted images that have an ALT attribute. A Java implementation of such a filter might look like this:

```
class ImageWithAltFilter implements NodeFilter
{
   short acceptNode(Node theNode)
   {
      // first, see if we're dealing with an element
      if (n.getNodeType() == Node.ELEMENT_NODE)
      {
         // cast the node to an element so we can call
         // getAttributeNode() more easily
         Element el = (Element)theNode;
         if (!el.getNodeName().equals("IMG"))
            return FILTER_SKIP;
         if (el.getAttributeNode("ALT") != null)
            return FILTER_ACCEPT;
```

```
        }
        return FILTER_SKIP;
    }
}
```

To use this filter, you would create it as a new object and pass it to a NodeIterator or TreeWalker, like this:

```
ImageWithAltFilter iwaf = new ImageWithAltFilter();
NodeIterator iterator =
    ((DocumentTraversal)document).createNodeIterator(
            rootNode, NodeFilter.SHOW_ALL, iwaf );
```

Important Notes About NodeFilters   There are some important things to keep in mind when creating and using NodeFilters. The first is that you should avoid writing code for a NodeFilter that can cause exceptions to be thrown. The DOM can't prevent this from happening, so NodeFilter behavior during an exception must be well defined. The DOM specification states that NodeIterators and TreeWalkers do *not* catch exceptions that are thrown by NodeFilters. Instead, they allow the exception to propagate up to the user's application code. For NodeIterators, the nextNode() and previousNode() methods will cause a NodeFilter to execute and will propagate any exceptions that are thrown in the filter. For TreeWalkers, the firstChild(), lastChild(), nextSibling(), previousSibling(), nextNode(), previousNode(), and parentNode() methods will invoke a NodeFilter and propagate any exceptions thrown inside the filter.

The second important thing to remember is that NodeFilters should not modify the contents of a document. Again, the DOM can't prevent this and does not provide any special processing to handle this case, though it goes against the spirit of what NodeFilters are intended to do. It is interesting to note that NodeFilters can still accept a node even if it is removed from the document, which will cause the node to be returned to the caller. The caller might then try to operate on the node, which is no longer in the document tree. This can easily lead to confusing behavior, so the DOM specification urges programmers to leave all tree processing to the code that is outside the filter.

The third thing to remember is that NodeIterators and TreeWalkers apply their whatToShow arguments *before* applying the filter. If a node is skipped over by the whatToShow flag settings, the filter will not be called for the node. The type of behavior that is used to skip over nodes using the whatToShow mask is similar to that of FILTER_SKIP: the node is skipped, but its child nodes will still be considered. This is true even if the associated filter would have returned FILTER_REJECT for the node. To circumvent this behavior, you can set the whatToShow argument to SHOW_ALL and do all your testing inside the filter.

NodeIterators

NodeIterators represent a linear portion of a document. They are created by calling the createNodeIterator() method on the DocumentTraversal interface. They have the following interface definition:

```
interface NodeIterator {
  readonly attribute Node              root;
  readonly attribute unsigned long     whatToShow;
  readonly attribute NodeFilter        filter;
  readonly attribute boolean           expandEntityReferences;
  Node               nextNode() raises(DOMException);
  Node               previousNode() raises(DOMException);
  void               detach();
};
```

The root property contains the root node of this iterator, as specified when the iterator was created. The whatToShow property determines what types of nodes are visible to the iterator. The available values for this property are listed under the NodeFilter interface (discussed earlier in the "NodeFilters" section). The filter property is an optional NodeFilter that can be used to further screen nodes. When both whatToShow and filter are used, the whatToShow property takes precedence. The expandEntityReferences property determines whether the children of EntityReference nodes are visible to the iterator.

The nextNode() method returns the next node in the logical view and advances the position of the iterator to the next node in the logical view. When an iterator is first created, the first call to nextNode() returns the root node. If the iterator is at the end of the node list, nextNode() returns null and the position is not moved. The previousNode() method returns the previous node in the logical view and moves the iterator's position backward in the logical view. If the iterator is at the start of the node list, previousNode() will return null, and the position is not moved. The detach() method "detaches" the iterator from the set of nodes it was iterating over and places the iterator into the INVALID state. Once this method has been called, any further calls to nextNode() or previousNode() will raise an INVALID_STATE_ERR exception.

The nodes in the document subtree represented by a NodeIterator are viewed in *document order*—that is, the order they are encountered in a document when reading from top to bottom.

For example, consider the following XML structure:

```
<node1>
   <node2/>
   <node3/>
   <node4>
      <node5/>
      <node6/>
   </node4>
</node1>
```

Figure 3-10 illustrates the hierarchical view of this fragment.

How Iterators Move Forward and Backward Over Nodes   The following diagram illustrates the linear view of this fragment as seen by a NodeIterator when it is created, with the node represented by node1 as the root. As you can see from the illustration, all notion of document hierarchy has been removed.

NodeIterators have the concept of a "position," which represents the current position of the iterator in the list of nodes with respect to what is called the *reference node,* which is the last node returned. The iterator's position is always before the first node, between two nodes, or after the last node.

The arrow indicates the position of the iterator. In the case of the previous example, after the iterator has just been created with node1 as its root node, the iterator's position is before the first node, which is the current reference node.

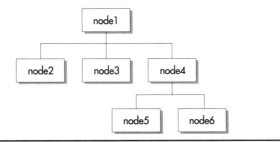

Figure 3-10   *Hierarchical view of XML fragment*

Following a call to `nextNode()`, the iterator returns the next node and then advances the iterator's position—unless the iterator's position is at the end of the list, in which case the return value is `null`. The following example shows the iterator's position after calling `nextNode()`. The position has been advanced, and the reference node has a thick outline.

When `previousNode()` is called, the iterator returns the node immediately before the current position and moves the position backward in the node list—unless the current position is before the first node, in which case the return value is `null`. The next example shows the iterator's position in the node list after calling `previousNode()`.

How NodeIterators Respond to Document Changes   The contents of a document can change while a NodeIterator is active, so it must have a well-defined set of rules that govern its behavior as nodes are added to or removed from the document tree. According to the DOM specification, document changes do not invalidate a NodeIterator. In fact, the only thing that invalidates an iterator is calling its `detach()` method.

To maintain a consistent state, NodeIterators use their reference nodes to determine what happens when the document tree structure changes. Generally speaking, iterators always try to stay "close" to their reference node. Reference nodes are selected based upon whether an iterator's position is before or after its reference node.

If a document tree's changes don't involve the reference node, the iterator doesn't have to worry about anything. Consider the following examples, in which nodes are inserted into and removed from the document tree in Figure 3-10. First, here's a node being inserted into the tree between node2 and node3 when node2 is the reference node:

The iterator always stays close to its reference node, so the insert takes place between the iterator's position and node3.

This next example shows the effect of removing the newly inserted node.

In this case, the reference node is not affected, so there is no change to the iterator or its position.

When the reference node itself is the one being removed from the tree, a new reference node must be selected. The way this is done depends upon the current position of the iterator with respect to the current reference node. Suppose, for example, that node3 is the current reference node, and the iterator's position is between node3 and node4, as in the following example (this is usually what happens when `nextNode()` is called).

If node3 is removed from the document, a new reference node must be selected. Because the iterator's position is currently after the reference node, it will remain so when the new reference node is selected. Node2 is the nearest node that precedes the iterator's position, so it is selected as the new reference node, as illustrated here.

If, on the other hand, the iterator's position is before the current reference node (between node2 and node3), as it would be if `previousNode()` had just been called, and the reference node were removed, the nearest node that is after the iterator's position would be selected as the new reference node. In this case, node4 would become the new reference node, as shown next.

There are two special cases that arise when removing the reference node. The first is when the reference node is the last node in the list and the position is before the node, as shown here, where node6 is the reference node.

In this case, when node6 is removed, the rules state that the new reference node should become the nearest node following the position. However, because there is no next node, the new node becomes the nearest node *preceding* the position (node5), as shown next.

The second special case is when the reference node is the first node in the list and the position is after the reference node, as shown here where node1 is the reference node.

In this case, the rules state that when node1 is removed, the new reference node should be the nearest node preceding the iterator position. Again, there is no node that precedes the position, so the new reference node becomes the node that follows the position (node2), as shown next.

Things get a little trickier when nodes that are outside of the logical view come into play. The reason is this: even though a node may not be included in a NodeIterator's logical view, *it may still become the reference node.* Consider the following example: suppose that node3 is not in the logical view of the document subtree represented by the NodeIterator, and that node4 is the current reference node, as shown here.

If the current iterator position is after the reference node, and the reference node is removed, the *nearest node before the position* becomes the new reference node. This is true regardless of whether the node is actually in the logical view. Thus, if node4 is removed from the subtree, node3 will become the new reference node, as shown next.

Nodes that aren't in the logical view cannot be skipped when choosing a new reference node because the wrong results may occur. For instance, if a new node named node7 that is visible in the logical view was inserted after node3, then the document subtree would look like the following example.

Now, if `previousNode()` is called, node7 will be returned, as would be expected. If node3 had been skipped over and node2 was selected as the new reference node, then the new node would not have been returned as the previous node—which would be incorrect because, as far as the iterator's user was concerned, node7 would have been the previous node had node4 not been removed.

Of course, once the NodeIterator's reference node changes from the node that is not in the logical view, you will not be able to return to it using the NodeIterator's methods because it will be skipped by the `whatToShow` setting or any associated NodeFilter's logic.

TreeWalkers

TreeWalkers, like NodeIterators, allow you to navigate among the nodes of a document subtree. Unlike NodeIterators, however, TreeWalkers preserve the document's tree hierarchy. In fact, using a TreeWalker is almost exactly the same as using the node navigation properties of the base Node interface itself, and the provided methods are analogous to those provided by the Node interface.

One major difference between TreeWalkers and NodeIterators is that TreeWalkers do not have the notion of a position. Instead, TreeWalkers are attached to the node that they are currently operating on. This will be discussed in detail later.

TreeWalkers have the following interface definition:

```
interface TreeWalker {
  readonly attribute Node          root;
  readonly attribute unsigned long whatToShow;
  readonly attribute NodeFilter    filter;
  readonly attribute boolean       expandEntityReferences;
           attribute Node          currentNode;
                              // raises(DOMException) on setting

  Node                 parentNode();
  Node                 firstChild();
  Node                 lastChild();
  Node                 previousSibling();
```

```
  Node               nextSibling();
  Node               previousNode();
  Node               nextNode();
};
```

The root property contains the root node of this iterator, as specified when the iterator was created. The whatToShow property determines what types of nodes are visible to the iterator. The available values for this property are listed under the NodeFilter interface (discussed earlier in the "Node Filters" section). The filter property is an optional NodeFilter that can be used to further screen nodes. When both whatToShow and filter are used, the whatToShow property takes precedence. The expandEntityReferences property determines whether the children of EntityReference nodes are visible to the iterator. The currentNode property is the node at which the TreeWalker is currently positioned.

The parentNode() method returns the closest visible ancestor node of the TreeWalker's current node and sets currentNode to its parent node. If currentNode has no parent node, null is returned and the current node is not changed. The firstChild() method moves the TreeWalker to the first visible child of currentNode and returns the new node. It returns null if currentNode has no visible children and the current node is not changed. The lastChild() method moves the TreeWalker to the last visible child of currentNode and returns the new node. It returns null if currentNode has no visible children and the current node is not changed. The previousSibling() method moves the TreeWalker to the previous sibling of currentNode and returns the new node. It returns null if currentNode has no visible previous sibling and the current node is not changed. The nextSibling() method moves the TreeWalker to the next sibling of currentNode and returns the new node. It returns null if currentNode has no visible next sibling and the current node is not changed. The nextNode() method moves the TreeWalker to the next visible node in document order relative to currentNode and returns the new node. It returns null if currentNode has no next node, or if the search for the next node attempts to step upward from the TreeWalker's root node and retains the current node. The previousNode() method moves the TreeWalker to the previous visible node in document order relative to currentNode, and returns the new node. It returns null if currentNode has no previous node, or if the search for the previous node attempts to step upward from the TreeWalker's root node and retains the current node.

Navigating Documents with TreeWalkers   Let's examine the effects of document traversal using a TreeWalker on the same example document we used earlier for the NodeIterator. Recall that our example document had the structure shown in Figure 3-11.

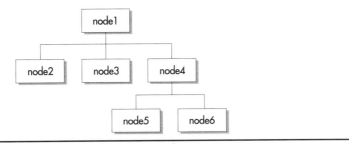

Figure 3-11   *Document structure of the example XML fragment*

Suppose we create a TreeWalker and assign node4 as its root. This also assigns node4 as the current node, as shown in Figure 3-12.

A call to any method that would cause the TreeWalker to step above the root node will return `null`, such as `parentNode()`. Calling `firstChild()` will return node5 and will also set node5 as the new current node. Because node5 has no child nodes, subsequent calls to `firstChild()` will return `null` and leave node5 as the current node.

You can also call methods that allow the TreeWalker to behave like NodeIterator, such as `nextNode()` and `previousNode()`. If node4 is the current node, calling `nextNode()` will return node5. Calling `nextNode()` again will return node6. Calling `previousNode()` will move the TreeWalker back to node5.

Using the TreeWalker interface, we can rewrite the recursive document traversing logic that we wrote earlier using the Node interface methods. The only change we have to make is to ensure that the current node is restored by the processing function because calling TreeWalker navigation methods will change the `currentNode` property. This is easily handled by saving aside the current node at the start of the function and restoring it before the function completes.

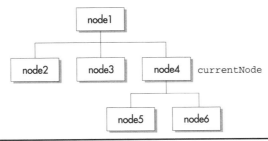

Figure 3-12   *Example document structure with TreeWalker assigned*

```
function processNode(TreeWalker theWalker)
{
   Node theNode = theWalker.getCurrentNode();
   doStartNodeProcessing(theWalker);
   for (Node c = n.firstChild(); c != null; c = c.nextSibling())
   {
      processNode(theWalker);
   }
   doEndNodeProcessing(theWalker);
   theWalker.setCurrentNode(theNode);
}
```

The major advantage of using the TreeWalker over the regular Node interface in this example is that you can associate a NodeFilter with the TreeWalker to filter out unwanted nodes while keeping the same function that iterates over the document. In fact, you could use the same processing function over and over with different TreeWalkers to obtain different results.

NOTE

It is important to recognize that the logical view of a document represented by a TreeWalker may be a completely different structure from the physical view itself. For example, a TreeWalker that only accepts Comment nodes would present all visible Comment nodes as siblings of each other, without any parent node.

How TreeWalkers Respond to Document Changes   TreeWalker must deal with document structural changes just like NodeIterators do, but they do so in a different manner. TreeWalkers are actually attached to their current node, so there does not need to be any logic that selects a new node when the current node is removed from the document tree or moved elsewhere within the tree. For this reason, TreeWalkers are never invalidated like NodeIterators are.

Recall our example document from Figure 3-12, where node4 is the root node of a TreeWalker. Suppose that node5 is the current node. If node5 were removed from the document (via the `removeChild()` method of the Node interface, for example), the TreeWalker would go with it and remain valid, even though the current node is no longer part of the document tree. If node5 had child nodes, you would still be able to navigate through them using the TreeWalker's methods, but you would not be able to navigate outside of node5 because it no longer has any parent node or siblings.

Suppose, further, that we were to add node5 back into the document, this time outside of the subtree represented by node4, which is still the root node. For example, adding node5 between node2 and node3 would make node5 a child of node1. The TreeWalker would still be valid, and, in fact, calling `parentNode()` on it would return node1, which is outside of the root node represented by node4. This would result in a document structure represented by Figure 3-13.

This is perfectly valid, and the TreeWalker can deal with such situations. If the TreeWalker were to somehow navigate back into the subtree represented by node4, the TreeWalker's logic would then prevent it from navigating back outside of the root node again.

If the TreeWalker is being used with a filter, it gets slightly more complicated because moving the current node or explicitly selecting a new one can cause the TreeWalker to have a current node that would otherwise have been rejected or skipped by the filter's logic. In this case, the DOM specification refers to the current node as a "transient" member of the logical view. According to the specification, you can navigate off of this node just as if it had been visible, but you will not be able to navigate back to it unless the conditions of the filter's logic or the TreeWalker's `whatToShow` parameter changes. If the current node somehow becomes a part of the document subtree that would otherwise have been rejected entirely by the filtering logic (that is, as if FILTER_REJECT had been returned for the subtree's root node), then all of the nodes in that subtree are transient members of the logical view. The TreeWalker will navigate through the subtree as if its root node had only been skipped instead of rejected, until the TreeWalker navigates above it. Then, normal filtering will apply.

For instance, suppose that, in our example document, node1 was set as the root node of the TreeWalker, node3 is the current node, and node4 represents a subtree that would be rejected entirely by the TreeWalker. If node3 is somehow inserted into the subtree represented by node4, the TreeWalker will navigate around inside the node4 subtree until the navigation takes the TreeWalker above node4. From then on, node4 and all its child nodes will be skipped.

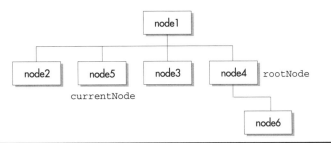

Figure 3-13 *TreeWalker example where* `currentNode` *is outside of root*

Conclusion

In this chapter, we examined the properties and methods of the Node interface that allow us to get references to, inspect, modify, and rearrange a document's nodes. We also saw how to create new nodes in a document, how to move nodes between documents, and how to traverse a document's set of nodes for processing using the Node interface. Finally, we took a look at the Traversal module of DOM Level 2, which can be used for advanced node processing.

This chapter brings us to the end of Part I, in which we introduce the DOM API, its concepts and history, and some basic knowledge of how to use the API to manipulate documents. In the next section, Part II, we'll begin taking a look at how the DOM is used in the real world, including common algorithms, the DOM support available in today's browsers and applications, and some tips and tools for debugging your DOM application code.

Real-World DOM

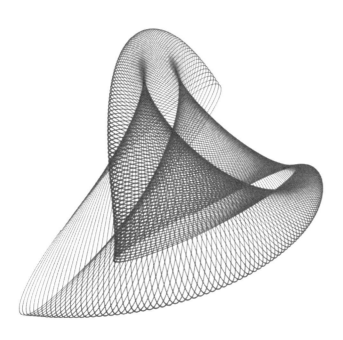

Algorithms

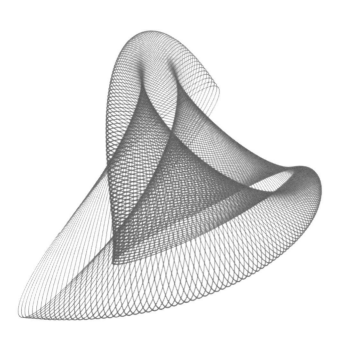

Part I introduced the DOM; discussed its concepts, design, theory, and origins; and introduced the main interfaces of the DOM application programming interface (API). It also explored how the DOM API can be used to examine and manipulate the information in HTML and XML documents.

In Part II, we take a look at how the DOM is used in the real world (hence the title of the section). This chapter introduces and dissects several common algorithms and code patterns that appear regularly when using the DOM to process the information in structured documents.

DOM Algorithms

When using the DOM API, it soon becomes clear that there are certain types of document processing algorithms that you need to use over and over again. Common algorithms include

▶ Determining whether a node is contained within another node

▶ Determining whether a node has a sibling of a certain type

▶ Finding a node based on the value of an attribute

▶ Processing the children of a node

These algorithms can be readily used in your own DOM code or modified slightly to suit a related but different purpose. Let's start by discussing two different types of DOM algorithms: position based and content based. Position-based DOM algorithms are best when you are more interested in the *position* of nodes within a document than the node's actual contents; content-based algorithms are best when you are more concerned with the *contents* of nodes.

For example, determining whether a given node is contained within another node is an example of a position-based algorithm; you are trying to discover whether a node occupies a particular place in the DOM tree. Determining whether a node contains another node is an example of a content-based algorithm; you are more concerned about the contents of a node.

Basic Node Traversal Algorithms

Before we cover the position- and content-based algorithms, we first take a look at some basic node traversing algorithms that will be used later on. These examples will only use the DOM Level 1 Node interface; traversal using the Traversal interface is not presented here. For more information on the Traversal interface, see Chapter 3.

The DOM document structure is organized as a tree, so there are two ways to traverse nodes: depth first and breadth first. The depth-first algorithm visits nodes starting at the root node of a subtree and recursively processing each child node of the root node. Based upon where you place the processing logic within the recursive function, the algorithm processes either parent or child nodes first. The node traversal algorithm we introduced in Chapter 3 was an example of a depth-first traversal. Recall the code listing

```
processNode(Node n)
{
   doStartNodeProcessing(n);
   for (Node c = n.firstChild(); c != null; c = c.nextSibling())
   {
      processNode(c);
   }
   doEndNodeProcessing(n);
}
```

In this listing, parent nodes are processed first (by the `doStartNode Processing()` function); then child nodes are processed. Depth-first traversals follow the pattern shown in Figure 4-1.

The dotted arrows show the order in which the nodes are visited. In this example, the nodes are visited in the order A, B, D, E, C, F, G.

Breadth-first node traversal visits each child node of a given parent before processing any other child nodes of the children of that parent. If that sounds confusing, Figure 4-2 should clear things up.

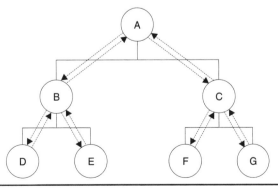

Figure 4-1 *Depth-first node traversal*

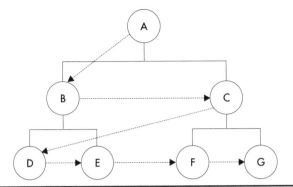

Figure 4-2   *Breadth-first node traversal*

The code for processing nodes breadth first is slightly different from the depth-first algorithm because all of the child nodes at the current level need to be processed before moving to the next level down. The following code listing shows one possible example of breadth-first processing that processes each branch of a tree separately:

```
processNode(Node n)
{
    doStartNodeProcessing(n);
    if (n.hasChildNodes())
    {
        for (Node c = n.firstChild(); c != null; c = c.nextSibling())
        {
            // do child node processing in here
        }
        for (Node c = n.firstChild(); c != null; c = c.nextSibling())
        {
            // now move to the next level for this parent
            processNode(c);
        }
    }
    doEndNodeProcessing(n);
}
```

The dotted arrows show the order in which the nodes are visited. In this example, the nodes are visited in the order A, B, C, D, E, F, G.

There is no real logic-related advantage to using breadth-first over depth-first, or vice versa, even though the breadth-first algorithm suffers from a performance disadvantage because it iterates over the child nodes of a given node twice. Your application should use the algorithm that is most appropriate to solving your specific traversal problem.

Position-Based Algorithms

Position-based algorithms work by examining the locations of nodes within a given DOM document; the contents of the node are secondary (if considered at all). Two common position-based algorithms are determining whether a node has an ancestor node of a particular type and determining whether a node has a sibling of a particular type.

Determining Whether a Node Has an Ancestor of a Given Type

Suppose your program needs to determine whether a node is contained within another node. For example, in HTML, image tags can be contained within anchor tags, which allows them to serve as hyperlinks to other URLs, as in the following:

```
<a href="http://your.url.here.com"><img src="myimage.jpg"></a>
```

If your application needs to treat a node differently depending on whether it is contained by another type of node, you can use the algorithm in the following code listing to determine if a node has a particular ancestor:

```
Boolean isContainedBy(Node n, DOMString nodeName)
{
   Node testNode;
   testNode = n.getParentNode();
   while (testNode)
   {
      if (testNode.getNodeName().equals(nodeName))
         return true;
      testNode = testNode.getParentNode();
   }
   return false;
}
```

This function starts with a given node and traverses up the DOM tree, examining each node to see if the given node is contained by the node with the given name. If the current parent node does not match the criteria, set the `testNode` to the current parent node and repeat the loop. To see how this works, consider the sample document tree represented by Figure 4-3.

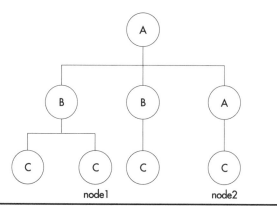

Figure 4-3   *Sample document tree*

Suppose you had a reference to the C node labeled node1 and wanted to see if the node was contained within a B node. You would call the function `isContainedBy()` like this:

```
Boolean bHasBParent = isContainedBy(node1, "B");
```

In this case, the function would return true because node1 is contained by a B node. If the same call were made on the C node labeled node2, the function would return false.

This example could easily be modified to see if a node was contained by a parent of a particular node type (such as Element), with particular attributes, and so on. For instance, to change this example to see if a node is contained within a particular type, you would change the `nodeName` argument from a DOMString to a short integer representing the node type. The part of the function where the test is done would be changed to check the node type instead of the node name, like this:

```
if (testNode.getNodeName().equals(nodeName))
    return true;
```

Then you would call this function like this:

```
var bHasBParent = isContainedBy(node1, Node.ELEMENT_NODE);
```

Determining Whether a Node Has a Sibling of a Given Type

Determining whether a node has a sibling of a particular type is similar to the previous example of determining whether it has a particular parent. You simply use the `previousSibling` and `nextSibling` properties of the Node interface. This code listing shows one way of accomplishing this:

```
Boolean hasSiblingWithNodeName(Node n, DOMString nodeName)
{
   Node testNode;
   // first check the previous siblings
   testNode = n.getPreviousSibling()
   while (testNode)
   {
      if (testNode.getNodeName().equals(nodeName))
         return true;
         testNode = testNode.getPreviousSibling();
   }
   // now check the following siblings
   testNode = n.getNextSibling()
   while (testNode)
   {
      if (testNode.getNodeName().equals(nodeName))
         return true;
      testNode = testNode.getNextSibling()
   }
   return false;
}
```

Again, just like the previous algorithm, this one could easily be modified to see if a node had a sibling node of a particular node type (such as Element), with particular attributes, and so on.

Content-Based Algorithms

Whereas position-based algorthms focus on the location of a node within a document, content-based algorithms focus on the actual content of the nodes and their attributes. Some of the more common content-based algorithms are determining whether a given node contains another particular node, retrieving nodes based upon their type (text, element, and so on), and finding a node with a particular attribute value.

Determining Whether a Node Contains Another Node

This example is the opposite of the example presented previously, where we determined whether a given node was contained within another node. Here, we determine whether a particular node contains another node. For example, in the document represented in Figure 4-4, which contains all element nodes, you can check to see if the node labeled node1 contains a node of type D.

To accomplish this algorithm, use the depth-first node traversal algorithm presented earlier to examine all child nodes under the given source node. The following code listing will determine whether a node contains another node with a given node name:

```
Boolean containsNode(Node n, DOMString nodeName)
{
    Boolean bFound = false;
    if (n.getNodeName().equals(nodeName))
        return true;

    for (Node c = n.firstChild();
         c != null && !bFound;
         c = c.nextSibling())
    {
        bFound = containsNode(c, nodeName);
    }
    return bFound;
}
```

The `containsNode()` function first examines the given node to see if it matches the node name that you are looking for. If so, the function returns true, and you're done. If not, you recursively process each child node to see if it matches the supplied node

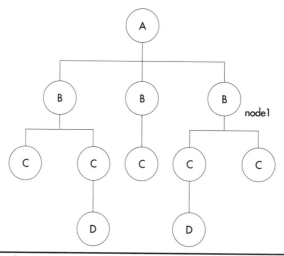

Figure 4-4   *Sample document structure containing only Element nodes*

name, and you continue this until either the name has been found or there are no more children of the node to search. To call this function in order to solve our stated problem, you would write

```
Boolean bContainsDNode = containsNode(node1, "D");
```

In this case, the function returns true because the tree does in fact contain a D node. To see if node1 contained any text nodes, you would write

```
Boolean bContainsDNode = containsNode(node1, "#text");
```

in which case, the function would return false because there are no text nodes.

This example could be modified slightly to determine whether a node contains another specific node and not just a node of a given type. To do this, the containsNode() method would need to accept a node as its second argument instead of a DOMString. The following code illustrates this:

```
Boolean containsNode(Node source, Node theNode)
{
   Boolean bFound = false;
   if (source == theNode)
      return true;

   for (Node c = source.firstChild();
        c != null && !bFound;
        c = c.nextSibling())
   {
      bFound = containsNode(c, theNode);
   }
   return bFound;
}
```

Better Versions of Node Interfaces: Retrieving Relative Nodes by Type

The Node interface provides properties for retrieving the first and last child node of a given node and for returning its previous and next sibling nodes. Using a bit of logic similar to that in the first example, you can make methods that are "smart" about the types of nodes they return.

For example, to write methods for returning the first and last child nodes of a particular node type, you can write functions named getFirstChildOfType() and getLastChildOfType(). The getFirstChildOfType() method returns the first child of a node with the given node type and can be implemented by the following code listing:

```
Node getFirstChildOfType(Node n, short nodeType)
{
   Node testNode = null;
   Boolean bFound = false;
   testNode = n.getFirstChild();
   while (testNode)
   {
      if (testNode.getNodeType() == nodeType)
         return testNode;
      else
         testNode = testNode.getNextSibling();
   }
   return null;
}
```

The algorithm works by first retrieving the first child node of node *n* and checking if its nodeType is the same as the requested nodeType. If so, then the node is returned. Otherwise, you move through each following sibling node until there are no more sibling nodes or a matching node has been found. If no matching node is found, the function returns `null`. Calling this function would look like the following:

```
Node n = getFirstChildOfType(theNode, Node.TEXT_NODE);
```

The matching code for `getLastChildOfType()` is almost exactly the same, with two exceptions: the function begins by retrieving the last child of the given node, and it moves backward through the sibling nodes using `previousSibling()`. The following code snippet shows the changes to the function:

```
Node getLastChildOfType(Node n, const unsigned short nodeType)
{
   Node testNode = null;
   Boolean bFound = false;
   testNode = n.getLastChild();
   while (testNode)
   {
      if (testNode.getNodeType() == nodeType)
         return testNode;
      else
         testNode = testNode.getPreviousSibling();
```

```
    }
    return null;
}
```

To use this code to find the last child Comment node for a given node, you would call the function like this:

```
Node n = getLastChildOfType(theNode, Node.COMMENT_NODE);
```

The implementations of the `getPreviousSiblingByType()` and `getNextSiblingByType()` are both very similar to the preceding two algorithms and are left as exercises for the reader.

Finding a Node by Attribute Value

Sometimes it is especially useful to be able to find a node given an attribute value. For example, your DOM application might be interested in retrieving an image tag (`"IMG"`) with a specific value for the SRC attribute, or maybe your application tags a node with a special attribute to denote some kind of state that the node is in.

This is substantially similar to the `containsNode()` example, except that in this case you are looking for a specific attribute value. The following code listing shows how to find a node that has a specific attribute attached to it.

```
Node getElementByAttributeValue(Node n, DOMString attName,
                                DOMString attVal)
{
    Node theNode = null;
    // if this node matches the given attribute name and value,
    // the we can return it.
    if (n.getNodeType() == Node.ELEMENT_NODE)
    {
        if ((Element)n).getAttribute(attName).equals(attVal))
            return n;
    }

    // otherwise process all of the child nodes.
    for (Node c = n.firstChild();
         c != null && !theNode;
         c = c.nextSibling())
    {
        theNode = getElementByAttributeValue (c, attName, attVal);
    }
    return theNode;
}
```

The major difference between this example and `containsNode()` is that you are always checking for Element nodes because they are the only nodes that can have attributes. If the test shows that the supplied argument "n" is in fact an element node, you know that you can call `getAttribute()` on it, which will return an empty string if the attribute is not present. Then you check to see if the value of the attribute matches what you are looking for.

To find out if a document contains an element that has an attribute with a given name, you can call this function with the document's `documentElement` as the first argument:

```
Node theNode = getElementByAttributeValue(document.documentElement,
                                          "myattr", "myattrvalue");
```

This example can be enhanced to return a list of nodes that have a given attribute value by combining the logic from `getElementByAttributeValue()` and the depth-first processing code from earlier in this chapter. The resulting function, `getElementsByAttributeValue()`, can be written in Java as

```
Vector getElementsByAttributeValue(Node n, DOMString attName,
                                   DOMString attVal)
{
    Vector theNodes = new Vector();
    addNodesToList(n, theNodes, attName, attVal);
    return theNodes;
}


addNodesToList(Node n, Vector v, DOMString attName, DOMString attVal)
{
    // if this node matches the given attribute name and value,
    // then add it to the list of nodes.
    if (n.getNodeType() == Node.ELEMENT_NODE)
    {
        if (((Element)n).getAttribute(attName).equals(attVal))
            v.add(n);
    }
    // now recursively process all of the node's child nodes
    for (Node c = n.firstChild(); c != null; c = c.nextSibling())
    {
        addNodesToList (c, v, attName, attVal);
    }
}
```

The `addNodesToList()` method performs almost the same function as the original `getElementByAttributeValue()` method, except that instead of simply returning the first matching node, it adds the node to a list and keeps going.

Conclusion

In this chapter, we introduced some of the basic node processing algorithms that commonly appear in DOM applications. We first covered the basic depth-first and breadth-first node traversal algorithms and discussed their differences. Next, we introduced and discussed position-based and content-based algorithms, and you saw examples of each. In particular, we examined algorithms that showed how to tell if a node is contained within another node, how to see if a node contains another node, and how to retrieve lists of nodes based upon node types and attribute values.

In the next chapter, we'll take a look at the DOM implementations provided by the more popular web browsers in use today, such as Internet Explorer 6, Netscape 6, and Opera 6.

Browsers

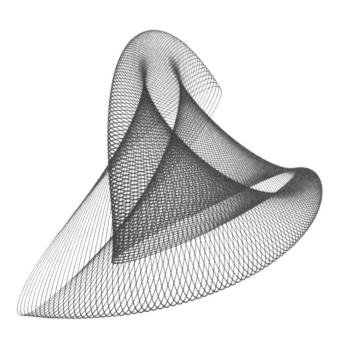

Modern DOM had its beginnings in the web browser, going back to Netscape 2 and Internet Explorer 3. In those days, the DOM was not an official specification, and the various browser vendors added functionality to their browsers to fit their needs using their own proprietary interfaces. This, of course, made it very difficult to create web pages that would work across multiple browsers, which was supposed to be one of the main selling points of the Web.

The situation has (thankfully) changed rather significantly since then. The latest generation of browsers (6) from Microsoft, Netscape, and Opera Software incorporates the most complete support for the W3C DOM standards available to date. Although still not perfect, it is now much easier today to create web pages that will work in multiple browsers than it was even a couple of years ago. In this chapter, we review the DOM support of the latest releases of the major web browsers, take a look at some examples of browser-based DOM usage, and discuss some of their quirks and special features as they relate to the DOM.

DOM Support in the Major Browsers

Perhaps the most logical place to start examining the DOM's real-world support is today's major web browsers. With Netscape 2 and Internet Explorer 3's initial implementations of the JavaScript programming languages, web authors could give their pages some added interactivity. Developers could dynamically change the contents of documents, cause an image to point to a new source URL, check the contents of forms, and more, all by writing some simple script code and tweaking the right properties of an HTML tag or two. Later browser versions allowed layers to be moved around the screen over a certain time period, providing simple animation effects. This was powerful, heady stuff at the time, though it was certainly limited. Not all of the properties of a given page could be manipulated, and some browsers offered more control than others (although sometimes they came from the same vendor!). Even if you could technically accomplish everything you needed to, very often you had to write special-case code all over the place to handle the inevitable differences between the various browsers that might visit the page.

Today's browsers have come a long way since then. Using the DOM API, it is now possible to dynamically change the appearance of almost any part of a web page, from the style sheets to the actual structure and content of the page itself. In addition, because the DOM provides a standard set of interfaces for doing so, the need for special case code is often greatly reduced (though not yet completely eliminated). This allows for the building of more complex, engaging user interfaces, as well as enhanced document processing programs that work across multiple DOM-compliant browsers.

In this chapter, we will examine the DOM support of the major web browsers available today: Microsoft Internet Explorer 6, Netscape Navigator 6, and Opera 6. All the major browsers available today support at least some of the W3C DOM specification. Microsoft Internet Explorer 6 and Netscape 6.*x* provide the most comprehensive support. Opera 6 supports some of the more important DOM API methods but does not yet provide a full implementation. Although the majority of the code examples in this chapter will work in all three of the major browsers, some will not; those that do not will be noted.

Microsoft Internet Explorer 6

With the introduction of Internet Explorer 6, Microsoft provides full support for DOM Level 1 in its flagship web browsing application. Internet Explorer 6 provides full support for the Core and HTML interfaces of DOM Level 1, along with CSS (Cascading Style Sheets) 1. In addition, IE6 supports the DOM Level 2 method `getElementById()`, along with several nonstandard properties and methods for developers' convenience that are not included in the W3C specification for DOM Level 1.

Internet Explorer 6 fully supports the DOM Level 1 interfaces, so scripts can take full advantage of the DOM's capabilities, including creating page elements dynamically at runtime, discovering and changing the structure and content of a page, and modifying a page's appearance through style sheets.

Netscape Navigator 6.*x*

The venerable Navigator web browser produced by Netscape (now a part of America Online) received a hefty amount of DOM support in its latest revision (as of this writing, 6.2.1), which is based upon the open-source Mozilla project. This latest version of the Netscape browser provides full support for DOM Level 1 and part of DOM Level 2, including the DOM 2 Events module.

Scripts can take advantage of the DOM's capabilities in Netscape Navigator just as they would in Internet Explorer. Scripts can discover the structure and content of pages and make changes to a page's content at runtime. In addition, because Navigator supports the DOM Level 2 Events module, script developers can attach event listeners to page elements (more on this later).

Opera 6

The Opera browser, made by the Norwegian company Opera Software, does not yet (as of version 6) provide full support for the W3C DOM. However, according to the company's website (www.opera.com), they are working on providing support for DOM Level 1, along with many other public Internet standards.

Using Opera's current (as of this writing) DOM implementation, applications cannot currently modify the structure of the document or dynamically create new page elements at runtime. They can, however, examine the document structure and discover its contents. Opera 6's support for DOM methods and properties is currently as follows.

On the document object:

▶ `getElementsByTagName()`

▶ `getElementById()`

▶ `getElementsByName()`

On HTML elements:

▶ `getElementsByTagName()`

▶ `contains()`

▶ `parentNode`

Most of the examples in this chapter will work with Opera 6, except where specifically noted.

Using the DOM in a Browser Environment

The browsers discussed in this chapter use JavaScript as their native programming language, and each provides a JavaScript language binding for the DOM in its implementation of the W3C DOM specification. Scripts do not have to do anything special to start using the DOM methods and structures provided by these browsers—they are an inherent part of the JavaScript namespace within the browser and can be used in any script.

Obtaining a Reference to the Document

Scripts do not need to do anything special to obtain a reference to the document. The JavaScript DOM binding provides a `document` keyword that represents the document object of the document in the current browser window. Browser scripts are always run in the context of being embedded in a document, so there is always a current document to refer to. Scripts use this keyword to operate on the document itself and obtain references to its child nodes.

For example, consider the following code snippet, which will display the title of the document in an alert box when a form button is clicked:

```
<HTML>
<HEAD>
<TITLE>The DOM Explorer Page</TITLE>
<SCRIPT LANGUAGE="JavaScript">
function buttonClick()
{
     // "document" is a global keyword that refers to the document
     // "title" is a property of the DOM1 HTMLDocument interface
     alert(document.title);
}
</SCRIPT>
</HEAD>
<BODY BGCOLOR="#FFFFFF">
<H1>The DOM Explorer</H1>
<FORM NAME="form1" METHOD="post" ACTION="">
     <INPUT TYPE="BUTTON" NAME="Button" VALUE="Button"
      onClick="buttonClick()">
</FORM>
</BODY>
</HTML>
```

When the button is clicked, an alert displaying the title of the document appears, as shown next.

Getting a little more fancy, you can use the code that follows to see the values of the basic node properties `nodeName`, `nodeValue`, and `nodeType` of the document object.

NOTE

This code example does not work in Opera 6.

```
<HTML>
<HEAD>
<TITLE>The DOM Explorer Page</TITLE>
<SCRIPT LANGUAGE="JavaScript">
function buttonClick()
{
     // "title" is a property of the DOM1 HTMLDocument interface
     alert("Document Node Properties: " + document.nodeName + ", " +
           document.nodeValue + ", " + document.nodeType);
}
</SCRIPT>
</HEAD>
<BODY BGCOLOR="#FFFFFF">
<H1>The DOM Explorer</H1>
<FORM NAME="form1" METHOD="post" ACTION="">
     <INPUT TYPE="BUTTON" NAME="Button" VALUE="Button" onClick="buttonClick()">
</FORM>
</BODY>
</HTML>
```

Now when the button is clicked, an alert will appear showing the document's `nodeName` (#document), `nodeValue` (null), and `nodeType` (9).

Examining the Structure and Content of a Page

Using the DOM methods, a browser script can obtain information about the structure of a web page and discover the types of content in it. Usually, this is accomplished

in one of two ways or a combination of both. The first is by using the
DOM methods `Getelementsbytagname()`, `Getelementbyid()`, and
`Getelementsbyname()`. The `getElementsByTagName()` method is
part of Core DOM Level 1, the `getElementById()` method is part of
Core DOM Level 2 (although it is supported by most current browsers), and
`getElementsByName()` is part of HTML DOM Level 1. The second way is
to use the properties `firstChild`, `lastChild`, `childNodes`, and so on,
which are part of the DOM Level 1 Node interface. Because none of the current
major browsers implement the NodeIterator or TreeWalker interfaces, they can't
be used to navigate the document.

Examining Single Nodes

To obtain a reference to a single node in the document tree using the Node interface
properties, you can chain as many of the Node interface's child accessor properties
together as you need to build a path to the desired node. For example, consider the
following document:

```
<HTML>
<HEAD>
<TITLE>Sample Document</TITLE>
</HEAD>
<BODY>
<P>Paragraph 1</P>
<P>Paragraph 2</P>
<P>Paragraph 3</P>
</BODY>
</HTML>
```

NOTE

Opera 6 does not support the `firstChild`, `lastChild`, `previousSibling`,
or `nextSibling` *properties, so the next three examples will not work in Opera 6.*

To obtain a reference to the `<P>` tag that defines paragraph 1, the code snippet
that follows can be used.

```
var oPara1 = document.documentElement.lastChild.firstChild;
```

The `lastChild` node of the document element is the `<BODY>` tag (the
`firstChild` would be the `<HEAD>`), whose `firstChild` node is the `<P>` tag

that defines paragraph 1. Similarly, to refer to the <P> tag that defines paragraph 2, you simply need to ask for the first paragraph node's next sibling:

```
var n = document.documentElement.lastChild.firstChild.nextSibling;
```

The first child node of the paragraph 1 node is a text node containing the text data "Paragraph 1." The following code snippet displays an alert containing the text inside the Paragraph 1 node:

```
alert(document.documentElement.lastChild.firstChild.firstChild.data);
```

Alternatively, the childNodes array can be used to access the same information:

```
alert(document.documentElement.childNodes[1].childNodes[0].
    childNodes[0].data);
```

If each of the paragraph nodes had unique ID attributes, the getElementById() method could be used to obtain a reference to each node in a straightforward fashion without having to use the Node interface properties. For example, consider this modified version of the document:

```
<HTML>
<HEAD>
<TITLE>Sample Document</TITLE>
</HEAD>
<BODY>
<P ID="para1">Paragraph 1</P>
<P ID="para2">Paragraph 2</P>
<P ID="para3">Paragraph 3</P>
</BODY>
</HTML>
```

Each of the paragraph nodes has now been assigned a unique ID attribute. To obtain a reference to the first paragraph, the getElementById() method can be used:

```
var oPara1 = document.getElementById("para1");
```

Obtaining a List of Nodes Using getElementsByTagName()

Recall from Chapter 2 that the getElementsByTagName() method returns a NodeList containing the nodes that match the given tag name. For example, the following code snippet will obtain a reference to the <BODY> tag:

```
var oBody = document.getElementsByTagName("BODY").item(0);
```

There is only one <BODY> tag in an HTML document, so it will always be the first element in the NodeList, which is item(0).

This method is useful when you want to process an entire list of a document's tags of a particular type. For example, to find out which <IMG> tags in a particular page do not have an ALT attribute defined (which is necessary for screen readers to be able to read a representation of a picture to sight-impaired users), you can use the following code:

```
<HTML>
<HEAD>
<TITLE>Image Alt Test</ TITLE >
<SCRIPT LANGUAGE="JavaScript">
function checkAltTags()
{
      var oImgList = document.getElementsByTagName("img");
      var i=0;

      if (oImgList.length > 0)
      {
            for (i=0; i<oImgList.length; i++)
            {
                  var altText = oImgList.item(i).getAttribute("alt");
                  if (altText == "")
                        alert("Image: " + oImgList.item(i).src +
                              " has no ALT attribute!");
            }
      }
}
</SCRIPT>
</HEAD>
<BODY>
<IMG src="image1.gif" border="0" alt="My First Image">
<IMG src="image2.gif" border="0" alt="My Second Image">
<IMG src="image3.gif" border="0" alt="My Third Image">
<IMG src="image4.gif" border="0">
<P>
<INPUT TYPE="button" NAME="button" VALUE="Check ALT Tags"
      onClick="checkAltTags()">
</P>
</BODY>
</HTML>
```

When the Check ALT Tags button is clicked, the `checkAltTags()` function retrieves a list of <IMG> tags in the document using `getElementsByTagName()`. It then uses the `getAttribute()` method to see if each element has an ALT attribute. If it finds an <IMG> tag with no ALT attribute, an alert is displayed containing the name of the image. In this example, the fourth image tag has no ALT attribute, so it will be flagged by the code.

NOTE

Most browsers will let you retrieve the content of an attribute by referring to the attribute's name as a property of a tag (that is, `document.title` or `image.src`). However, using the `getAttribute()` method is more flexible and is more likely to work across multiple DOM implementations, not just web browsers. In addition, some browsers may not properly register custom user-defined attributes as properties of a node, so this notation may not work in those circumstances. To be safe, portable, and in tune with the specification, always use `getAttribute()`.

Creating and Modifying Page Elements

Creating and modifying document elements in a web browser dynamically is relatively straightforward using the DOM. Once you have obtained a reference to the node or list of nodes that you want to modify, you can use the DOM to change attributes, rearrange nodes, or change their content.

Modifying Document Nodes

To modify an attribute associated with a page element, you can use the `setAttribute()` and `removeAttribute()` methods. For example, the following code allows the user to set the background color of the document by clicking one of three buttons:

```
<HTML>
<HEAD>
<TITLE>Untitled</TITLE>
<SCRIPT>
function setBackground(backColor)
{
   var oBody = document.getElementsByTagName("BODY").item(0);
   if (backColor == "")
     oBody.removeAttribute("bgColor");
   else
     oBody.setAttribute("bgColor",backColor);
}
```

```
</SCRIPT>
</HEAD>
<BODY BGCOLOR="#FF0000">
<INPUT TYPE="button" VALUE="Black" onClick="setBackground('Black')">
<INPUT TYPE="button" VALUE="White " onClick="setBackground('White')">
<INPUT TYPE="button" VALUE="Blue " onClick="setBackground('Blue')">
<INPUT TYPE="button" VALUE="Default " onClick="setBackground('')">
</BODY>
</HTML>
```

When one of the buttons representing a color is clicked, the background of the page is changed to that color by setting the BGCOLOR attribute of the <BODY> tag. If the Default Background button is clicked, the color of the page is set to whatever the default for the browser is—in effect, the BGCOLOR attribute is removed from the <BODY> tag.

Similarly, block-level items, such as paragraphs and other elements, can be modified by changing attributes. For example, to change the alignment of a paragraph, a script only needs to set its align attribute, as shown in the following example:

```
<HTML>
<HEAD>
<TITLE>Align Example</TITLE>
</HEAD>
<BODY>
<P ID="para1">Paragraph 1</P>
<P>
<A HREF="#" ONCLICK="document.getElementById('para1').setAttribute(
    'align','left')">Align Left</A>
<A HREF="#" ONCLICK="document.getElementById('para1').setAttribute(
    'align','center')">Align Center</A>
<A HREF="#" ONCLICK="document.getElementById('para1').setAttribute(
    'align','right')">Align Right</A>
</P>
</BODY>
</HTML>
```

This code uses the getElementById() method to retrieve the paragraph node whose ID attribute is para1. When each link is clicked, the align attribute of the paragraph node is set to left, right, or center. The results are updated immediately in the browser.

In addition to modifying the appearance of a page or its nodes, the content of the nodes themselves can be changed. This is accomplished by changing the `data` property of a given text node. The following code is the same as the previous example, but the code has been updated to change the text of the paragraph node with ID para1. Because the first child of the paragraph node is a text node, changing its `data` property will update the text content.

```
<HTML>
<HEAD>
<TITLE>Untitled</TITLE>
</HEAD>
<BODY>
<P ID="para1">Click on a link!</P>
<P>
<A HREF="#"
ONCLICK="document.getElementById('para1').firstChild.data=
 'You clicked link 1'">Link 1</A>
<A HREF="#"
ONCLICK="document.getElementById('para1').firstChild.data=
 'You clicked link 2'">Link 2</A>
<A HREF="#"
ONCLICK="document.getElementById('para1').firstChild.data=
 'You clicked link 3'">Link 3</A>
</P>
</BODY>
</HTML>
```

Creating and Removing Document Nodes

Creating nodes at runtime is accomplished by using the DOM's factory methods for creating nodes: the various `create()` methods of the Document interface, such as `createElement()`, `createTextNode()`, and so on. Each of these methods creates a new type of node. For example, the following code creates new paragraph nodes and appends them to the end of the document's <BODY> tag:

```
<HTML>
<HEAD>
<TITLE>Creating New Nodes</TITLE>
<SCRIPT>
var pCounter = 1;
function addParagraph()
{
```

```
var oBody = document.getElementsByTagName("BODY").item(0);
var oParaNode = document.createElement("P");
var oParaText = document.createTextNode("Paragraph #" + pCounter++);
oParaNode.appendChild(oParaText);
oBody.appendChild(oParaNode);
}

function removeParagraph()
{
     var oBody = document.getElementsByTagName("BODY").item(0);
     oBody.removeChild(oBody.lastChild);
}
</SCRIPT>
</HEAD>
<BODY>
<A HREF="#" ONCLICK="addParagraph()">Add New Paragraph</A>
<A HREF="#" ONCLICK="removeParagraph()">Remove Last Paragraph</A>
</BODY>
</HTML>
```

When the Add New Paragraph Node link is clicked, a new paragraph node is created as an element by a call to `createElement()`. The text content for each paragraph is created separately as a text node by calling `createTextNode()`, which is then appended to the paragraph node as a child of the paragraph. Then the whole thing is appended to the document's `<BODY>` tag.

When the Remove Last Paragraph Node link is clicked, the last child node of the `<BODY>` tag is removed.

Using this technique, you can create some fairly complex documents entirely using the DOM. The code that follows creates an HTML Table dynamically using the DOM methods.

NOTE

This code will only work in Netscape Navigator 6.x and Internet Explorer. Opera 6 does not yet support dynamically creating page elements.

```
<HTML>
<HEAD>
<TITLE>Create Table</TITLE>
<SCRIPT>
function createTable()
{
```

```
var i=0, j=0;
var oBody = document.getElementsByTagName("BODY").item(0);

// create the TABLE, THEAD, and TBODY tags
var oTableNode = document.createElement("TABLE");
var oTableHead = document.createElement("THEAD");
var oTableBody = document.createElement("TBODY");

oTableNode.appendChild(oTableHead);
oTableNode.appendChild(oTableBody);

// for the THEAD, create one row that spans two columns
// and place a label in it indicating it is the header
var oTableHeadRow = document.createElement("TR");
var oTableHeadTH = document.createElement("TH");
oTableHeadTH.setAttribute("colspan","2");
// create the text
var oTableRowText = document.createTextNode(
                            "This is the table header");
// add the text to the table row
oTableHeadTH.appendChild(oTableRowText);
oTableHeadRow.appendChild(oTableHeadTH);
// add the TR to the THEAD
oTableHead.appendChild(oTableHeadRow);

// Now build the table
var oTR;
var oTD;
// build the table two rows by two columns
for (i=0; i<2; i++)
{
     // create the row
     oTR = document.createElement("TR");
     for (j=0; j<2; j++)
     {
          // create each column
          oTD = document.createElement("TD");
          oTD.appendChild(document.createTextNode(
                    "This is table cell " + i + "," + j));
          oTR.appendChild(oTD);
     }
```

```
        oTableBody.appendChild(oTR);
    }
    // set the table's border to 2 and the width to 75%
    oTableNode.setAttribute("border","2");
    oTableNode.setAttribute("width","75%");

    // Finally, add the table to the document
    oBody.appendChild(oTableNode);
}
</SCRIPT>
</HEAD>
<BODY>
<A HREF="#" ONCLICK="createTable()">Create An HTML Table</A>
</BODY>
</HTML>
```

Figures 5-1 and 5-2 show the results of this function in both Netscape 6 and Internet Explorer 6.

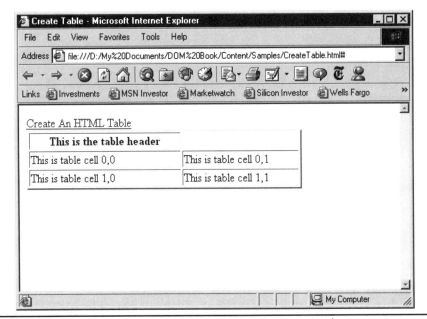

Figure 5-1   *Results of dynamic table creation script in Internet Explorer 6*

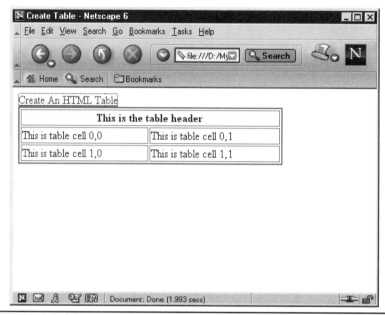

Figure 5-2   *Results of dynamic table creation script in Netscape 6*

Handling Events with the DOM Level 2 Events Interface

One of the modules introduced in DOM Level 2 is the Events module, which specifies a method for handling events within DOM documents. Events are generated as the user performs certain actions within a document (such as mouse clicks, key presses, and so on) and when the browser itself performs certain actions (a page has finished loading, and so on). These events can be processed by a DOM application using an Events module–aware browser to provide a high degree of interactivity.

The event models built into earlier browser versions used event handlers that were attached to elements as attributes, as shown in this code snippet, which handles the click event for an anchor tag:

```
<A HREF="#" ONCLICK="alert('I was clicked!')">Click me!</A>
```

However, using this method becomes awkward when more than one event handler for a given event needs to be attached to an element, or when event handlers need to be attached to and removed from elements dynamically. In addition, it isn't possible to attach event handlers to non-Element nodes using this type of model because only Elements can have attributes.

The DOM Level 2 Event model takes care of these and other event features that DOM applications can use in an Events module–compliant browser. In this section, we introduce the DOM Level 2 Events interface and illustrate how it can be used to provide advanced interactivity in your web pages.

NOTE

Currently, only Netscape Navigator 6.x implements the DOM Level 2 Events interface. Internet Explorer has a similar event model but does not follow the W3C standard.

How Events Flow Through a Document

The term *event flow* is used to describe the process by which an event originates in a particular implementation of the DOM and travels through the document. Using the DOM methods, events can be handled in different ways: either locally at the element where the event originates, or higher up in the document tree at one of the element's ancestors.

Every event has an associated event target. This target is usually a particular node in the document at which the event originates. In addition, each event target may have one or more event listeners, which are triggered when an event is fired for the target. Figure 5-3 illustrates how an incoming event is processed by a target's event listeners.

There are two directions in which an event may flow in the document tree: up or down. The direction in which an event flows is dictated by what type of event listeners are registered for a given event. An event listener may designate itself as using event capture, in which case it will be the recipient of events before any of its descendants. This is how an event can flow downward in the document tree. Some types of events trigger listeners on their targets and then move upward through the

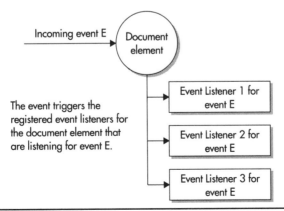

Figure 5-3 *An event triggering an event target's listeners*

document tree to each successive parent target. These types of events are called *bubbling* events because they bubble upward through the document like bubbles of air in water. Figure 5-4 illustrates these two different directions of event flow in a sample document tree.

Suppose that node D was clicked by the user, and that nodes A, B, and D each have two event listeners for the click: one using event capture and one not using capture. Node A will receive the first event and trigger its capture-based event listener (point 1 in the figure). Next, node B will trigger its capture-based event listener (point 2). Finally, node D will trigger its event listener (point 3). At this point, the event will "bubble" back up through the document tree, triggering event listeners on nodes that are not using event capture—first on node D (point 4), then on node B (point 5), and finally back up to node A (point 6).

The EventTarget and EventListener Interfaces

The DOM Level 2 EventTarget interface has the following IDL definition:

```
interface EventTarget {
void addEventListener(in DOMString type, in EventListener listener,
                      in boolean useCapture);
void removeEventListener(in DOMString type, in EventListener listener,
                      in boolean useCapture);
boolean dispatchEvent(in Event evt) raises(EventException);
};
```

 Represents each node's event listener

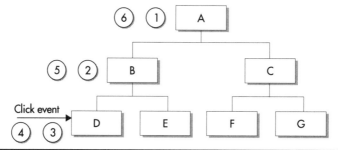

Figure 5-4   *Event flow in a document tree*

The addEventListener() method attaches an EventListener (discussed shortly) to a particular event target (usually a node in the document). The type argument specifies the type of event that the listener handles (see the DOM2 Events module specification for a list of event types). The listener argument is the particular EventListener that will handle the events. In the JavaScript DOM implementation, this is a function that takes a single argument (an Event object). The useCapture argument specifies whether this listener should use event capture when listening for events. If it is true, the event target for this listener will receive events of the type for which it is registered before any of its descendants in the document tree. If a listener is added while an event target is already processing an event, it will not be triggered by the current event. Adding identical event listeners will cause the duplicate listener to be discarded.

NOTE

A node that has an event handler registered for an event using capture and another event handler that is not using capture for the same event is considered to have two separate handlers, even though they are for the same event.

The removeListener() method removes a listener from an event target. Note that in order to remove a listener, you must provide the type, listener, and useCapture arguments that were all used when the listener was registered. This is because the type alone is not enough to uniquely identify the listener. Listeners can be registered for the same event type but with different settings for useCapture, and each listener is considered to be separate and distinct.

The dispatchEvent() method allows a DOM application to manually dispatch events into the event model. These manually dispatched events will have the same types of bubbling and/or capture behavior as events that are generated normally by the implementation.

The EventListener interface is specified as

```
interface EventListener {
  void handleEvent(in Event evt);
};
```

The EventListener interface has just one method, handleEvent(), which takes an Event as its only parameter.

You'll see how the methods of the EventTarget and EventListener interfaces are actually used later in the section. First, there's a bit more theory to cover.

Event Phases

There are three phases that a DOM event can be in: the Event Capture phase, the At Target phase, and the Event Bubbling phase.

When an event is being handled by an EventListener that is using event capture, the event is in the Event Capture phase. Each EventListener that is registered for an event will get first crack at an event before the event target on which it is registered if the EventListener is using event capture (its `useCapture` argument was set to true when it was attached to the target).

When an event is being handled by an EventListener that is attached to the actual target of the event, then the event is in the At Target phase.

If this event is specified as a bubbling event, the event begins to bubble back up the document tree hierarchy all the way to the Document node itself.

NOTE

According to the DOM spec, when an event begins to bubble, the chain of event targets from the original event target to the top of the tree is determined before the event is actually dispatched. If the structure of the document tree changes while the event is bubbling, the event follows the path of the initial state of the tree. Also, not all types of events bubble (for example, focus events). Refer to the DOM2 Events module specification for a list of events that bubble.

The Event Interface

All events in the DOM Events specification have the Event interface as their base interface. The Event interface has the following interface definition:

```
interface Event {

  // PhaseType
  const unsigned short CAPTURING_PHASE = 1;
  const unsigned short AT_TARGET = 2;
  const unsigned short BUBBLING_PHASE = 3;

  readonly attribute DOMString        type;
  readonly attribute EventTarget      target;
  readonly attribute EventTarget      currentTarget;
  readonly attribute unsigned short   eventPhase;
  readonly attribute boolean          bubbles;
  readonly attribute boolean          cancelable;
  readonly attribute DOMTimeStamp     timeStamp;
  void stopPropagation();
```

```
  void preventDefault();
  void initEvent(in DOMString eventTypeArg, in boolean canBubbleArg,
                 in boolean cancelableArg);
};
```

The `type` property specifies the type of the event (click, mouseover, and so on). The `target` property specifies the event target of this event—the node that the event was originally sent to. The `currentTarget` property is the event target that is currently processing the event. The `eventPhase` property indicates the phase that the event is currently in (capture, at target, or bubbling). The `cancelable` property indicates whether the event can have its default action prevented (i.e., whether it is possible to stop the implementation from taking the default action associated with this event). If this property is true, the `preventDefault()` method (discussed shortly) can be called on this event. The `timeStamp` property indicates the time, in milliseconds, that the event was created. This property may not be available for all events on all systems. If it is not available, it will be set to 0.

The `stopPropagation()` method stops the event from propagating to the next event target. This works for events in all event phases. When this method is called, all of the EventListeners for the current event target will complete, but the event will not travel to any more event targets.

The `preventDefault()` method will prevent the DOM implementation from taking any default action associated with this event type. This method can only be called if the `cancelable` property is true. This method can be called for an event in any event phase.

The `initEvent()` method is called to initialize an event that was created directly by the DOM application. If your application creates its own events, it can initialize them using this method.

How DOM Applications Handle Events

As stated earlier, DOM applications handle events by attaching event listeners to document nodes. Consider the following example document, which uses pre-DOM, attribute-based event handlers to handle events:

```
<HTML>
<HEAD>
<TITLE>Old-Style Events Example</TITLE>
</HEAD>
<BODY>
<A HREF="#" ONMOUSEOVER="this.style.fontWeight='bold'"
```

```
ONMOUSEOUT="this.style.fontWeight='normal'">Link One</A>
<A HREF="#" ONMOUSEOVER="this.style.fontWeight='bold'"
ONMOUSEOUT="this.style.fontWeight='normal'">Link Two</A>
</BODY>
</HTML>
```

When the user moves the mouse over the links in this document, the links become bold. To accomplish the same thing using DOM 2 event listeners, the code would look like this:

```
<HTML>
<HEAD>
<TITLE>DOM Events Example</TITLE>
</HEAD>
<BODY>
<A HREF="#" ID="link1">Link One</A>
<A HREF="#" ID="link2">Link Two</A>
<SCRIPT>
function makeBold(evt)
{
      evt.currentTarget.style.fontWeight='bold';
}

function makeNormal(evt)
{
      evt.currentTarget.style.fontWeight='normal';
}

document.getElementById("link1").addEventListener("mouseover",makeBold,false);
document.getElementById("link1").addEventListener("mouseout",makeNormal,false)

document.getElementById("link2").addEventListener("mouseover",makeBold,false);
document.getElementById("link2").addEventListener("mouseout",makeNormal,false)
</SCRIPT>
</BODY>
</HTML>
```

Instead of attaching onClick handlers to the anchor tags, each tag has two event listeners registered that listen for mouseover and mouseout events. The listeners are registered by the calls to addEventListener(). Each event listener function can be attached to more than one target. When one of these events occurs for a given target, the corresponding event handler will be called, and the link will be made bold or normal, depending upon the event.

So, why do the handlers use evt.currentTarget instead of evt.target? It's because events are always targeted at the most deeply nested nodes in the tree. In this case, that would be the text nodes that represent the text strings "link1" and "link2". However, that's not what you want—you want the <A> tags to have their styles changed. The event's target property will be set to the original target of the event, which is the text node for the anchor tag. The mouseover event is a bubbling event, so you can just wait for it to bubble up to the <A> tag's event listener and then operate on it using currentTarget, which, at this point, will be set to the <A> tag's node.

Getting a little more sophisticated, we can demonstrate the use of event capture and bubbling with the following code listing:

```
<HTML>
<HEAD>
<TITLE>Capture, At Target, and Bubbling Demo</TITLE>
</HEAD>
<BODY>
<UL ID="List1">
     <LI>List item 1</LI>
     <LI>List item 2</LI>
     <LI>List item 3</LI>
     <UL ID="List2">
          <LI>List item 4</LI>
          <LI ID="item5">List item 5</LI>
          <LI>List item 6</LI>
     </UL>
</UL>
<TEXTAREA ID="output" NAME="textfield" ROWS="5" COLS="75"></TEXTAREA>
<A HREF="#" ONCLICK="document.getElementById('output').value='';">
Clear Entries</A>
<SCRIPT>
function clickListener(evt)
{
     var outStr;
     outStr = "Event Target: ";
     if (evt.target.tagName)
          outStr += evt.target.tagName + "; ";
     else
          outStr += "(text node); ";

     outStr += "Current Target: ";
     if (evt.currentTarget.tagName)
     {
          outStr += evt.currentTarget.tagName +
               "(" + evt.currentTarget.getAttribute("ID") +
               ")" + "; ";
     }
```

```
        else
            outStr += "(text node); ";

        if (evt.eventPhase == 1)
            outStr += "Capture phase\n";
        else if (evt.eventPhase == 2)
            outStr += "At Target phase\n";
        else if (evt.eventPhase == 3)
            outStr += "Bubbling phase\n";

        document.getElementById("output").value += outStr;
}

document.getElementById("List1").addEventListener("click",
    clickListener,true);
document.getElementById("List1").addEventListener("click",
    clickListener,false);
document.getElementById("List2").addEventListener("click",
    clickListener,true);
document.getElementById("List2").addEventListener("click",
    clickListener,false);
document.getElementById("item5").addEventListener("click",
    clickListener,true);
document.getElementById("item5").addEventListener("click",
    clickListener,false);
</SCRIPT>
</BODY>
</HTML>
```

This document contains two unordered lists at the top of the <BODY> section, one of which is embedded inside the other. There are three nodes in particular that we are interested in, all given ID attributes: List1, List2, and item5. Note that there are two calls to addEventListener() for each of the event targets. This is to register a handler for event capture, as well as a noncapture handler. Each time a click event is triggered on one of the listeners, the code records some information about it and displays it in the text area.

When you run this example in Netscape 6.*x* and click the list item List Item 5, there will be six events triggered. The first three will be the capture-style event handlers trapping the events on their child nodes, starting at the top of the document: List1, List2, and item5. The next three will be the click event as it bubbles upward through the tree: `item5`, `List2`, and `List1`. Because the event is directed at the text node for the List Item 5 that is the child node of the corresponding `<LI>` list item, there will be no at target phase displayed. However, if you click the little bullet circle next to the text, the target of the event will be the `<LI>` tag itself, and the at target phase will be reflected in the textarea.

Using regular, noncapture-style event handlers is relatively straightforward because they handle an event directly on a target. So, when is it useful to employ a capture-style event handler? Consider the following example:

```
<HTML>
<HEAD>
<TITLE>Event Capture Demo</TITLE>
</HEAD>
<BODY>
<UL ID="List1">
      <LI>List item 1</LI>
      <LI>List item 2</LI>
      <LI>List item 3</LI>
      <LI>List item 4</LI>
      <LI>List item 5</LI>
</UL>
<SCRIPT>
var oSelectedNode = null;
function listListener(evt)
{
      var targetNode = evt.target;

      if (oSelectedNode)
      {
            oSelectedNode.style.color = "Black";
            oSelectedNode.style.fontWeight = "normal";
            oSelectedNode = null;
      }

      // is it a text node? If so, set targetNode to the parent
      if (targetNode.nodeType == 3)
            targetNode = targetNode.parentNode;

      if (targetNode.tagName)
      {
            if (targetNode.tagName == "LI")
            {
                  targetNode.style.color = "Red";
                  targetNode.style.fontWeight = "Bold";
```

```
                oSelectedNode = targetNode;
            }
        }
    }
}

document.getElementById("List1").addEventListener("click",listListener,true);
</SCRIPT>
</BODY>
</HTML>
```

In this example, there is one unordered list (ID "List1"). One capture-style event listener is registered on the list itself. If you view this example in Netscape 6.*x* and click the list items, you'll notice that each one you click turns bold and red. If one was already red, it turns back to normal and black, and the new one turns bold and red.

The secret to this behavior is that the single event listener is handling click events for all of the list's child nodes because, as a capture-style listener, the parent <UL> node is getting first crack at the event. This is why the handler is registered on the list and not the individual items. The handler determines which node was clicked and whether it was the text node for the list item or the list item itself, and it handles highlighting the item by changing its associated style. Note that if you add new list items to the list, even programmatically using the DOM, they will all inherit the same behavior from the event listener on the list.

Using capture-style event listeners is a very powerful way of assigning the same behavior to a node's group of child nodes. With this technique, the child nodes can all be made to exhibit the same behavior without having to attach event listeners to each one.

How Event Listeners Interact with Old-Style Listeners

Prior to the DOM Level 2 Events specification, event listeners were registered using attributes on the intended event target. Because all of the current browsers still allow this technique to provide backward compatibility, there has to be a way for the two to coexist.

According to the DOM Level 2 Events specification, DOM implementations can view the setting of an event handler attribute on an element as analogous to creating and registering an event listener on that element, with the `useCapture` argument defaulting to false. In other words,

```
someElement.onmouseover = myEventFunction;
```

is the same as

```
someElement.addEventListener("mouseover", myEventFunction, false);
```

If an existing event handler attribute is changed, it is analogous to removing the old event listener and attaching a new event listener.

When using event handler attributes, there is no way for an event listener that has been registered via an attribute on an element to obtain event-related context information, such as the current target or event phase.

Internet Explorer–Specific Methods and Properties

Unlike Netscape, Internet Explorer adds dozens of proprietary properties and methods to its version of the DOM API that are not specified by the W3C. In this section, we review some of the more important and interesting methods and properties and demonstrate their usage. A word to the wise here: using nonstandard properties and methods will make your code less portable, so you should use them only when you are sure that users of your application will be using a particular browser or when there is no other way to accomplish a particular programming task. In general, it is usually preferable to stick to the standard methods. A complete list of IE-specific properties and methods can be found on the Microsoft website http://msdn.microsoft.com.

Internet Explorer–Specific Properties

Two of the more important and powerful proprietary properties that Internet Explorer adds to its implementation of the DOM are `innerHTML` and `outerHTML`. Though not a part of the W3C DOM standard, they are very useful and can be used to perform a wide range of operations on document nodes.

Essentially, these two properties provide access to the inner and outer HTML of the node upon which these properties are used. The inner HTML of a node is the HTML code contained between the closing bracket (>) of the opening tag and the opening bracket (<) of the closing tag. The outer HTML of a node is the code between the opening bracket of the opening tag and the closing bracket of the closing tag. For example, consider the HTML tag for a document's title:

```
<TITLE>This Is My Document Title</TITLE>
```

The `innerHTML` property of the title node would be `This Is My Document Title`—the content between the closing bracket of the `<TITLE>` tag and the opening bracket of the closing `</TITLE>` tag. The `outerHTML` of the title node would be `<TITLE>This Is My Document Title </TITLE>`, as illustrated in Figure 5-5.

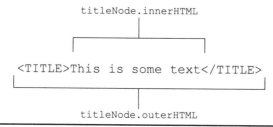

Figure 5-5   *The* `outerHTML` *and* `innerHTML` *properties*

Each of these properties is both readable and writable, which means you can alter any portion of the HTML of a document by setting the appropriate property on a node. For example, suppose your HTML document contained the following code snippet:

```
<P ID="para1">This is some text</P>
```

To make the text inside the `<P>` tag bold, you could use the following code:

```
var pNode = document.getElementById("para1");
pNode.innerHTML = "<B>" + pNode.innerHTML + "</B>";
```

This code surrounds the `<P>` node's existing `innerHTML` (`This is some text`) with opening and closing `<B>` tags and places the result (`<B>This is some text</B>`) back into the `innerHTML` of the node.

NOTE

Netscape Navigator 6 adds support for Internet Explorer's `innerHTML` property. Scripts can use the `innerHTML` property just as they would in Internet Explorer. Curiously, Netscape 6 does not support the `outerHTML` property—attempts to access it return "undefined."

Internet Explorer–Specific Methods

Internet Explorer 6 adds dozens of methods that are not a part of the DOM standard, but they are useful to developers who are working within an IE-only environment or who are willing to sacrifice some code portability in exchange for the convenience or added features that they provide. In most cases, the functionality provided by one of these methods can be implemented in other browsers by using existing DOM methods. Some of the more useful methods that Internet Explorer adds are `contains()`, `swapNode()`, `applyElement()`, and `replaceNode()`. A full list of methods can be found on the Microsoft Developer Network site at http://msdn.microsoft.com/.

The `contains()` method can be used to determine whether one node contains another node. It returns true if the node on which it is called contains another specific node, false otherwise. Its syntax is

```
var bContainsNode = node.contains(anotherNode);
```

The `swapNode()` method swaps the position of the node upon which this method is called with the node represented by the argument to the function. Its syntax is

```
var oNode = oElement.swapNode(oAnotherElement);
```

The `swapNode()` method returns a reference to the element upon which the method was called.

The `applyElement()` method makes the element upon which the function is called either the parent or child of another element. Its syntax is

```
oElement = oObj.applyElement(oTarget [,sWhere]);
```

The `oTarget` argument is the element that becomes either the parent or child of `oObj`. The `sWhere` argument is a string that indicates how the object is to be applied. A value of outside, which is the default, indicates that the `oTarget` element is to become the parent of `oObj`. A value of inside indicates that `oTarget` is to become a child of `oObj`. The function returns a reference to the applied element.

The `replaceNode()` method is very similar to the Node interface's `replaceChild()` method, but it replaces the node upon which it is called, not a child of the node. For example, this code snippet replaces a node with a new node:

```
node.replaceNode(newNode);
```

It is functionally equivalent to writing

```
node.parentNode.replaceChild(node, newNode);
```

The `replaceNode()` method returns a reference to the node that was replaced.

Browser Quirks

Although the latest versions of the browsers do an admirable job of implementing the DOM standard, a few quirks are worth mentioning so you can avoid or deal with them in your browser-based DOM applications.

Internet Explorer

Some of Internet Explorer's more notable DOM-related quirks:

▶ Versions prior to 6 don't support `createAttribute()`, `getAttributeNode()`, or `setAttributeNode()`. You must use the `getAttribute()` and `setAttribute()` methods instead.

▶ Versions prior to 6 don't support the `normalize()` method of the Node interface.

▶ If you call `getAttribute('style')` on an Element, the return value will be an object, not a string. You can get the content by using `getAttribute('style').cssText`.

▶ Calling `getAttribute('class')` on an Element returns `null`, even if a class attribute has been defined.

Netscape Navigator

Netscape Navigator's more notable DOM quirks are

▶ Newline characters are treated as individual text nodes. This may cause your DOM applications that expect child nodes of a certain type to always be in a particular location to fail because a newline character in the source text may be treated as a text node. Always check node types before operating on them to make sure that what you have is what you think you have (this is true for all browsers).

▶ Versions of Navigator prior to 6.1 have event capturing problems when clicking on a text node contained within a DIV. The event will not properly be captured by the `<DIV>` element.

▶ Navigator 6 doesn't provide backward compatibility for old DHTML constructs (like document.layers).

Conclusion

In this chapter, we examined the DOM support provided by the major web browsers in use today from four different vendors. In particular, we discussed the support provided by Internet Explorer 6, Netscape Navigator 6, and Opera 6. Of these, Internet Explorer and Netscape 6 have the most complete support for the DOM specification, whereas Opera currently has the least support.

Both Internet Explorer and Netscape Navigator contain some proprietary methods and properties, and have a few quirks in their implementations. Each browser, however, has come a long way from the 3.0 and 4.0 days, when scripts that had to work in both browsers could require radically different code to obtain the same result. Using the DOM specification, scripts can be much more uniform now and reuse much of the same code, though, in some cases, browser-specific code will still be needed.

In the next chapter, we'll examine the DOM support provided by some nonbrowser applications.

CHAPTER 6

Applications

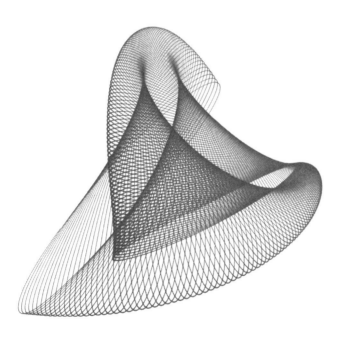

U ntil recently, support for the Document Object Model was mostly limited to web browsers. However, with interest in XML growing by leaps and bounds every day, it has become clear that there is a need for developers to be able to process XML and other structured documents in many more places than has been the tradition. As a result, DOM support is being added to an increasing number of applications and with good reason: its standard way of manipulating information in all kinds of structured documents flattens the learning curve, promotes code reuse, and reduces development time.

In the previous chapter, we explored the DOM support provided by the major web browsers available today (Internet Explorer, Netscape Navigator, and Opera Software's Opera) using their native JavaScript language bindings. In this chapter, we'll take a look at how the DOM is supported and accessed in several popular application packages, both standalone and embedded.

DOM Implementations Aren't Just for Browsers

Although the DOM traces its origins to the web browser, it is useful in many applications in which a web browser is not the ideal implementation form factor. Developers are beginning to realize the advantages of having a common way to manipulate structured information, and DOM support has started showing up in more and more non-browser-based applications. After all, the DOM essentially gives developers a standard way of manipulating all kinds of data that fits a structured hierarchy, and many applications have a common need to do so.

Consider one of the most simple, ubiquitous, yet commonly overlooked examples: storing preferences or common configuration information for an application. Most applications have some sort of configuration data that they store in a persistent state. This information is often manipulated in response to the user's changes and needs to be accessed in a variety of places throughout the application. Because this kind of information is almost always stored in a well-defined, structured format (such as categories, settings, and values) it is a perfect candidate for using the DOM to manage it. Major and minor categories for the configuration settings can be represented by XML tags, and the individual settings themselves can be represented by XML tags, tag attributes, or a combination of both. Changing, adding, and removing settings requires simply calling the right DOM APIs to modify the given nodes.

Some of the more popular nonbrowser DOM implementations available today can be found for both client- and server-based applications. Some of these implementations are available as standalone libraries that can be integrated into an application, whereas others are available as embedded implementations intended for use by application plug-ins and extensions.

In this chapter, we will examine the DOM implementations in products developed by the Apache Software Foundation (the Xerces parser), Microsoft (MSXML), and Macromedia (Dreamweaver).

Standalone vs. Embedded DOM Implementations

Standalone DOM implementations are not tied to or embedded within a larger application, such as a web browser. These implementations are usually provided as statically or dynamically linked libraries that can be used by applications that need to work with structured information, and there are several such standalone DOM implementations available today. Most are freely downloadable and can be integrated into a development project for zero or limited cost. Two of the more popular packages available are the Apache Software Foundation's Xerces parser and Microsoft's MSXML parser. Each of these parser packages provides comprehensive support for the W3C DOM Level 1 Core specification. In the case of Xerces, DOM Level 2 support is also provided.

Embedded implementations, on the other hand, are much more like browser implementations because the DOM architecture is hosted and exposed by the application. In this case, the DOM is usually accessed through the hosting application's extensibility architecture, which may be implemented in one or more languages, such as C++, Java, JavaScript, Perl, and so on. There are several such applications available that expose a DOM to their extensions, such as Macromedia's Dreamweaver HTML authoring application.

The Apache Xerces Parser

The Apache Foundation's Xerces Parser, commonly known as Xerces (named for the Blue Xerces butterfly), is available as a free download from the Apache Software Foundation's website (see the following section for specifics). Xerces is an XML parser that follows the DOM Level 2 specification and can be integrated into applications that need to manipulate structured information. It is available in both C++ and Java implementations. In addition to the core DOM APIs, Xerces provides several useful utility classes for working with XML documents and data, such as transcoding utilities to convert Unicode documents to local machine code and formatting XML output.

In this section, we'll examine Xerces' support for the DOM and take a look at how common DOM operations are accomplished using the Xerces API.

Where to Get Xerces

Xerces can be downloaded directly from the Apache XML website, located at http://xml.apache.org/xerces-c/ (for the C++ version, Xerces-C) and http://xml.apache.org/xerces-j/ (for the Java version, Xerces-J). As of this writing, Xerces-J is at version 1.4.4, while Xerces-C is at version 1.7.0.

Xerces can be downloaded in either source-code form or a binaries-only distribution. Prebuilt binaries are available for several platforms, including Windows, Macintosh, and several variants of the Unix operating system, such as Linux and Solaris. The Xerces parser is also available as part of the Apache Xalan download, another open-source package available from the Apache Foundation. Xalan is an XSLT processing engine that uses Xerces as its XML parser. When you download and install Xalan from the Apache Xalan website (http://xml.apache.org/xalan/), Xerces is installed automatically.

Whether you should use the Java or C++ version of Xerces depends on the application you have in mind. If you're writing an application that will be used in a server environment, the Java version is probably the better choice. If your application is on the client side and is a shrink-wrapped, commercially available application or is using a client user interface library such as MFC, the C++ version is probably the right way to go. Because there are several references available that use Java in their examples, this section will focus on the C++ version (though each version, of course, provides excellent support for Level 2 of the DOM specification). If you're not a C++ programmer, don't worry: one of the really nice things about Xerces C++ is that it is very similar to the Java version in both design and use. Converting Xerces Java code to use C++, and vice versa, is a straightforward process.

NOTE

This section will focus only on the current, official Xerces-C DOM classes. The Xerces-C team is in the process of creating a new interface to the Xerces-C API called IDOM; this interface is still experimental and will therefore not be covered here. The Xerces distribution contains some information on this API and some related example code, and interested developers should look there for further information on IDOM.

Installing Xerces

When downloading Xerces, you get to choose whether to install the entire Xerces project, complete with source code, or only the binary distribution files. If you're not planning on making any modifications to the source code or building the library for a platform that is not supported by the binary distributions, downloading and using the binary distribution package for your platform is probably the best way to go. However, you'll need the source code if you want to build your application for a platform that is not supported by the standard Xerces download.

Once you've downloaded Xerces, you will need to unpack the archive file to re-create the Xerces folder structure. Figures 6-1 and 6-2 show the Xerces folder structures for the Windows version of the source code and binary distribution packages.

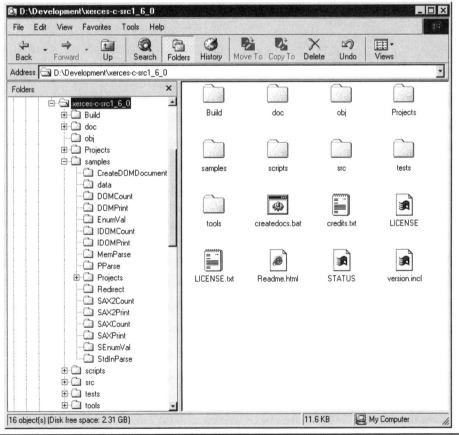

Figure 6-1   *The Xerces source distribution folder hierarchy for Windows*

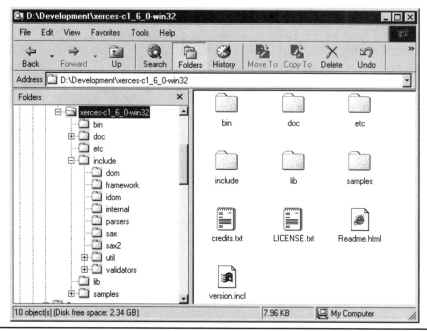

Figure 6-2   *The Xerces binary distribution folder hierarchy for Windows*

Among the directories created by the Xerces unpacking process, those that you will most likely be interested in are doc, Projects, samples, and src. If you're using the binary distribution, you won't have the Projects and src directories; instead, you'll see include and lib.

In the source distribution, the Build directory contains the executable versions of the sample applications, as well as the debug and release builds of the Xerces DLLs. This directory isn't included in the source distribution installer; it is built by the compiler when the source code is compiled. For the binary distribution package, the bin directory contains the executable DLLs and sample applications, and the lib directory contains the Xerces import libraries that your application links to.

By default, the Xerces library is built as a dynamic link library (DLL) on Windows. This is so that if more than one application needs to use it, each application can use the one copy of the implementation rather than bloating the code by including a statically linked copy in each version.

The doc directory contains the Xerces documentation. The documentation is available in XML, HTML, and PDF formats (except the API documentation, which is available only in HTML).

The Projects directory contains the various projects needed to build the Xerces library for the various platforms on which it is supported. Inside this folder, the Win32 directory contains the project files for VisualC++ 6.0 for building the Windows version of the library. The MacOS folder contains the project files for Metrowerks' CodeWarrior IDE and Apple ProjectBuilder for MacOS X.

The samples folder contains the source code and makefiles for all of the sample projects that ship with Xerces. There are sample projects showing how to parse files, parse memory buffers, install custom error handlers, create documents, and so on. There is also a data directory that contains some XML and DTD files to use with the sample projects.

The src folder contains the Xerces source code implementation and header files (for the binary distribution package, these files are in the include folder). You won't usually need to view the contents of this folder unless you are making changes to Xerces itself. However, you will need to include this directory in your source code via an `#include` statement in order to compile your application because this is where the compiler will expect to find the declarations for all of the DOM and related utility classes.

Getting to Know the API

The Xerces API documentation is available in both the source-code and binary distributions. When the Xerces library is installed, the API documentation can be found inside the apiDocs folder, which is located inside the doc folder. Whereas the rest of the Xerces documentation is available in XML, HTML, and PDF formats, the documentation for the programming interfaces is currently available only in HTML form. There is a brief programming guide available; the file \doc\html\program.html describes some general characteristics of programming Xerces. This information can also be found in the PDF and XML documentation.

The API documentation provided with Xerces is mostly reference material gathered from the various source code header files and does not provide much detail on the usage of the various classes. Thankfully, Xerces ships with a number of useful examples, and you should familiarize yourself with them before attempting you build your first application. Table 6-1 lists the sample applications that ship with the Xerces distribution and what they demonstrate.

One of the major differences between the Java and C++ APIs are the DOM class names. In the C++ version of the API, the various DOM class names are prefixed with DOM_. For example, the Document class becomes DOM_Document, the Node class becomes DOM_Node, and so on. According to the Xerces documentation, this

Sample Project	Description
CreateDOMDocument	Uses the DOM API to create a new document and add elements to it
DOMCount	Parses an XML file and counts the number of elements in it
DOMPrint	Parses and prints the contents of an XML file
SAXCount	Uses the SAX (Simple API for XML) interface to parse an XML file and count its elements
SAXPrint	Uses the SAX interface to parse an XML file and print its contents
MemParse	Demonstrates parsing an XML file that is stored in a memory buffer
Redirect	Shows how to use the EntityResolver class to redirect the parser to an external DTD file
Pparse	Demonstrates the technique of *progressive parsing,* in which an input stream is parsed a piece at a time
StdInParse	Parses an XML file that is read from standard input
EnumVal	Illustrates how to enumerate the values defined in a DTD Grammar
SenumVal	Same as EnumVal, but enumerates values defined in a Schema Grammar
SAX2Count	Uses the SAX2 interface to parse an XML file and count its elements
SAX2Print	Uses the SAX2 interface to parse an XML file and print its contents
IDOMCount	Demonstrates parsing an XML file and counting its elements using the new, experimental IDOM interfaces
IDOMPrint	Uses the experimental IDOM interfaces to parse and print the contents of an XML file

Table 6-1   *The Xerces Sample Applications*

is done to avoid collisions with existing code that might try to use the same class names, either in the application or some other third-party libraries that the application is using. This could have been avoided using C++ namespaces, of course, but the Xerces documentation notes that there are still several C++ compilers that do not yet use namespaces. If you are so inclined, you could always use `typedef` declarations to rename the C++ classes to be the same as their Java counterparts, such as

```
typedef DOM_Document Document;
typedef DOM_Node Node;
typedef DOM_Element Element;
```

This technique may be particularly useful to developers converting a body of existing Xerces Java code to C++.

Aside from the class name differences, programming Xerces in C++ is very similar to programming Xerces in Java, and a great deal of effort went into making the two as similar as possible. Most of the memory management is done automatically behind the scenes by the library, and the built-in DOM classes are implemented using object reference counting. For the most part, your code will not have to do any explicit object deletion. For this reason, there are some important points you need to keep in mind when writing Xerces C++ applications:

▶ Always create DOM classes as local variables on the stack, or as member variables of another class. Do *not* try to create them on the heap using `new()` or `malloc()` because this will cause the internal automatic memory management mechanism to become confused and will most likely lead to objects not being freed correctly. In other words, do this:

```
DOM_Document myNode =
theDOMImpl.createDocument(0,"root",DOM_DocumentType());
```

Not this:

```
DOM_Document *myDocument = new DOM_Document();
```

▶ The public DOM classes can be copied via the assignment operator (=), passed as function parameters, and returned from functions by value, just as they can be in Java.

▶ You should not try to subclass the public DOM classes (for example, DOM_Node, DOM_Document, DOM_Attr, and so on). In practice, this is almost never necessary anyway. If you need to attach application-specific data to a DOM document tree, the DOM_Node class provides a "user data" field that your application can use to store this data. You'll see an example of this later in the chapter in the "Using the Node's userData Field" section.

NOTE

In Xerces-C, the `DOMString` == operator checks to see whether two DOMString variables refer to the same object in memory, not whether they contain the same content. This follows the Java model of equality testing, and the DOM classes also use it. To see if two DOMStrings contain the same characters, your code should call the `equals()` method on one of the strings and pass the other as the argument to the function.

Using Xerces

In order to use the Xerces-C library, your application needs to link in the appropriate import libraries that are built from the source distribution, depending on whether you are building in debug mode or release mode. For the debug version of Xerces, this is the xerces-c_1D.lib file. For the release version, your application will link to the xerces-c_1.lib file. If you are using the prebuilt binary distribution package, these libraries are stored in the lib folder. For the source distribution package, the libraries are stored in the Build folder. No other third-party libraries are needed.

In this section, we'll examine how some common uses of the DOM are accomplished using the Xerces-C interfaces.

Initializing and Terminating the Parser

Before the Xerces API can be used to process structured documents, it needs to be initialized by the application. This only needs to be done once per instance of the application, although it is safe to initialize and terminate the library as much as you like. (Note that this is different from previous versions of Xerces, which only allowed the library to be initialized and terminated once per process.)

To initialize the Xerces library, your application needs to call `XMLPlatformUtils::Initialize()`. To shut down Xerces, your application calls `XMLPlatformUtils::Terminate()`. These are static methods in the XMLPlatformUtils class. The following code snippet illustrates how to do this:

```
try
{
    XMLPlatformUtils::Initialize();
}
catch(const XMLException& toCatch)
{
    char *pErrMsg = XMLString::transcode(toCatch.getMessage());
    cerr << "Error during Xerces-C Initialization: " << pErrMsg;
    delete pErrMsg;
}
```

The call to `Initialize()` in the try block will attempt to initialize the Xerces library. If anything goes wrong, the method will throw an XMLException, which is handled inside the catch block. In this example, the code simply prints an error message. This type of initialization only needs to be done once, unless your application initializes and terminates Xerces as needed (although this shouldn't be necessary). If your application is using a framework such as MFC, the previous code could be called from within your application's `InitInstance()` method override.

Assuming everything goes well, the Xerces library will now be initialized and can be used in your application. After your application has finished using the Xerces library, it needs to release the library by calling the `Terminate()` method, as shown here:

```
XMLPlatformUtils::Terminate();
```

Again, if your application is using a framework such as MFC, this code would be called from your application's `ExitInstance()` method.

Creating a New Document

Once the Xerces library has been initialized, your application can start using it to create and/or process documents. To create a new document, your code calls the `createDocument()` method on the DOMImplementation interface. For example, the following code snippet creates a new, empty document with a root element named rootnode:

```
// declare an instance of the DOM Implementation class
DOM_DOMImplementation impl;

// create a document with no namespaceURI, a document root element
// named "root", and the default DocumentType
DOM_Document doc = impl.createDocument(0,"root",DOM_DocumentType());
```

Once the document is created, you can add elements to it or manipulate it in other ways using the DOM interfaces.

Creating Document Content

Once you create a new document, you can add new document objects to it. The following code snippet builds a "Hello World" document containing a comment, a *hello* element, and a text string, assuming that the document has already been created as in the example above and is stored in a variable named doc.

```
// retrieve the document element from a DOM_Document
// object variable "doc"
DOM_Element theRoot = doc.getDocumentElement();

// create the comment node and append it to the document
DOM_Comment theComment = doc.createComment("This is a comment");
theRoot.appendChild(theComment);

// now create the hello element. This will contain our text string
DOM_Element helloNode = doc.createElement("hello");
theRoot.appendChild(helloNode);

// Finally, create the text string and append it to the hello element
DOM_Text theTextStr = doc.createTextNode("Hello World!");
helloNode.appendChild(theTextStr);
```

This code creates three objects: a comment, an element, and a text node, and appends them to a document object named doc (assuming the code has earlier either created this document or retrieved it from somewhere else, like the parser).

Parsing a Document File

Documents are not always created in memory from scratch. The much more common case is one where you have a document stored in persistent memory, such as on disk, and you want to load and parse it to build a DOM structure. There is no standard way of accomplishing this in the DOM API under Levels 1 or 2, so each implementation is free to provide its own methods for doing this.

The way Xerces accomplishes this task is by providing a class called *InputSource*. An InputSource specifies a source of data, whether it is a file, memory buffer, URL, and so on. The Xerces library reads data from the InputSource and constructs a DOM from it. In addition to specifying a source of data, the Xerces parser allows the application to set a variety of parser configuration options that are used when the file is parsed, such as whether to use validation, whether to use namespaces, what kind of error handler to use, and so on. The Xerces library provides InputSource-derived classes for files, memory buffers, URLs, and standard input. You will never use the InputSource class directly; your application will make use of one of the derived classes, depending on the source of the data.

This process is illustrated here:

```
LocalFileInputSource *theSource; // input source for the file
// define some default options for the parser
DOMParser::ValSchemes valScheme = DOMParser::Val_Auto;
bool bNamespaces = false;
bool bSchema = false;

// create the parser (ok to use new() here because
// DOMParser is not a DOM_ class)
DOMParser* parser = new DOMParser;
// set the parser options
parser->setValidationScheme(valScheme);
parser->setDoNamespaces(bNamespaces);
parser->setDoSchema(bSchema);

// parse the file
theSource = new LocalFileInputSource("myfile.xml");
try
{
   parser->parse(theSource);
```

```
}
catch (const XMLException& toCatch)
{
   // handle the XMLException
}
catch (const DOM_DOMException& toCatch)
{
   // handle the DOMException
}
catch (...)
{
   // handle all other kinds of exceptions, like memory exceptions
}

// get the document from the parser
DOM_Document doc = parser->getDocument();

// perform any document operations

delete theSource; // deallocate the memory we allocated earlier
delete parser;
```

In this example, some local variables are first declared that will store the input source for the document and some parsing options. In particular, the valScheme variable is set to the constant value `DOMParser::ValAuto`, which means perform automatic validation if a DTD is present in the file. Other possible values are `ValNever`, which means never validate; and `ValAlways`, which means always validate. The `bNamespaces` and `bSchema` variables are each set to false, indicating that you do not want the parser to handle namespaces or schemas.

Next, a DOMParser object is created on the heap. This is okay to do here because DOMParser is not a DOM class, but a utility class provided by Xerces that parses an InputSource and builds a DOM_Document. After the parser is created, the various options are set by calling the `setValidationScheme`, `setDoNamespaces`, and `setDoSchema` methods.

A LocalFileInputSource, which is one of the InputSource-derived classes, is created on the application heap, along with the path to the file to parse (hard-coded here to `"myfile.xml"`). Once everything is ready, the parser's `parse()` method is called, which reads the input source and creates a document. This method can throw exceptions, so you need to surround the call with a `try-catch` block to catch any exceptions that arise. There are two specific handlers for DOM_DOMExceptions (which means there's something wrong with the document tree) and an XMLException, which means there's something wrong with the XML code.

Assuming the parser was able to parse the source data, you can retrieve the document by calling the parser's `getDocument()` method, which will return a DOM_Document. At this point, you can use DOM methods to manipulate the document.

For a more complete example of file parsing, see the DOMCount example in the Xerces samples directory.

Parsing a Document in Memory

Parsing a document that is stored in memory is not much different from parsing a document stored on disk; you simply need to provide a different kind of InputSource. In this case, you need to use a MemBufInputSource. We can adapt the earlier example of parsing a file to using a MemBufInputSource pretty easily, as shown in this example:

```
static const char* gBuf = "\
<?xml version='1.0'?>\n\
<rootNode>\n\
    <childNode>value</childNode>\n\
</rootNode>\
";

static const char*  gMemBufId = "someID";

 // define some default options for the parser
DOMParser::ValSchemes valScheme = DOMParser::Val_Auto;
bool bNamespaces = false;
bool bSchema = false;

MemBufInputSource* mbIS = new MemBufInputSource (
        (const XMLByte*)gBuf,
        strlen(gBuf),
        gMemBufId,
        false);

// create the parser (ok to use new() here because
// DOMParser is not a DOM_ class)
DOMParser* parser = new DOMParser;
// set the parser options
parser->setValidationScheme(valScheme);
```

```
parser->setDoNamespaces(bNamespaces);
parser->setDoSchema(bSchema);

// parse the file
try
{
   parser->parse(*mbIS);
}
catch (const XMLException& toCatch)
{
   // handle the XMLException
}
catch (const DOM_DOMException& toCatch)
{
   // handle the DOMException
}
catch (...)
{
   // handle all other kinds of exceptions, like memory exceptions
}

// get the document from the parser
DOM_Document doc = parser->getDocument();

// perform any document operations

delete mbIS; // deallocate the memory we allocated earlier
delete parser;
```

For a complete example of memory buffer parsing, see the MemParse example in the Xerces samples directory.

Serializing a Document

In addition to loading documents from various input sources, your application may find it necessary to save the internal representation of the document to persistent storage. This is slightly more involved than loading a document because Xerces does not provide classes for serializing a document. One way to do it is to use the stream classes provided by the operating system and provide your own overrides of the << operator to stream out the different node types. An actual working example of this technique is too long to list here; however, the DOMPrint example in the Xerces samples folder provides a complete working example of how this is done.

Useful String Utilities

The Xerces library provides some useful string utilities that almost all DOM applications need to use from time to time. For example, the Xerces parser stores documents using 16-bit characters because this is how Unicode is implemented. Unfortunately, most operating systems or existing applications do not work directly with Unicode, so it may be necessary to first transcode Xerces strings to the machine's local code page before operating on them. This can be accomplished in two primary ways: by calling the DOMString class's `transcode()` method or by using the static `XMLString::transcode` method.

The DOMString class provides a method for transcoding Unicode strings to the local machine code page. It allocates and returns a native C character pointer (`char *`), which can then be passed to C and C++ library methods, such as `strlen()`, `strcpy()`, or other native OS methods requiring C strings. For example, to convert a DOMString returned from a call to `getAttribute` to a C string, you could use code that looks like this:

```
// get the myAttr attribute
DOMString dsAttr = someElement.getAttribute("myAttr");

// convert the DOMString to a C string
char *p = dsAttr.transcode(); // NOTE -- this call allocates memory!
// call some C library method that takes a char *
int len = strlen(p);
// when finished, it is your responsibility to delete the pointer
delete [] p;
```

Note that the call to `transcode()` allocates memory, so it is your responsibility to deallocate the returned string pointer when you have finished with it.

NOTE

If you are building for Windows, you must make sure that you are using the same runtime model as the Xerces-C library when you deallocate memory that was allocated by Xerces. For example, if you are using the debug version of the Xerces DLL, you must make sure that you are linking against the debug version of the C runtime library, or the OS may throw an exception.

The other option is to use the `XMLString::transcode` method. This is useful when you don't have a DOMString, but you do have a sequence of XMLCh characters, which are defined to be 16 bits wide. There are four methods provided for transcoding strings: two sets of two functions for transcoding between XMLCh strings and 8-bit char * strings. Within each set, there is one function that returns a newly allocated string and one that takes the address of a previously allocated string.

For example, the following code takes an XMLCh string and transcodes it to a char *:

```
XMLCh *pXMLStr;
char *p;
// transcode the XML string to a char *
p = XMLString::transcode(pXMLStr);
```

As in the previous example, the returned char * must be deallocated by the caller.

The XMLString class provides a number of other utility functions for working with 16-bit XML strings, such as comparison, substrings, searching, hashing functions, and so on. It isn't intended to be a full replacement for other string classes, such as MFC's CString, but it does contain most of the common methods needed for manipulating 16-bit strings. For more information on XMLString, see the Xerces API documentation on the XMLString class.

Transcoding an Entire Document

The Xerces parser stores its internal representation of the document content using Unicode characters, so it may be necessary to first transcode the document to the local machine code before saving it or handing it off to another application, such as a text editor. The Xerces library provides several built-in transcoders to assist in this process.

To transcode an entire document, your application needs to make use of the transcoding services provided by Xerces by following these general steps:

1. *Allocate the output buffer.* Your application should allocate a buffer to store the resulting transcoded text. This need not be large enough to hold the entire file because the transcoding engine can process slices of the document.

2. *Create a transcoder object.* The XMLPlatformUtils class contains a member variable called fgTransService, which is an object that represents the XML transcoding service. To create a new transcoder, your application calls this object's `makeNewTranscoderFor` method with the type of encoding to transcode for.

3. *Decide how unrepresentable characters will be handled.* The Unicode character set can represent thousands of characters, so some of them may not be representable in the target character set. Your application needs to indicate to the transcoder what to do when one of these characters is encountered. The transcoder can either replace the character with the default character for the target character set, which is guaranteed to be legal, or throw an exception.

4. *Call the* `transcodeTo` *method.* Once the transcoder has been allocated, your application calls the `transcodeTo` method as many times as it needs to process all of the document's content.

The following code illustrates the transcoding process. In this example, the document is being transcoded to the UTF-8 encoding.

```
XMLCh *psDocument; // pointer to XML string for the document
char *psOutString; // pointer to a char *, the output string
// if the transcoder cannot be created, this variable will contain
// the code indicating the reason for failure. The list of constants
// can be found in the API docs under the XMLTransService section.
XMLTransService::Codes failReason;
unsigned int charsProcessed; // the number of characters processed
unsigned int charsWritten; // number of chars placed in output buffer

psOutString = new char[1024]; // allocate the output buffer

// assume that the psDocument pointer contains the document source

XMLTranscoder *pTransCoder;
pTransCoder = XMLPlatformUtils::fgTransService->makeNewTranscoderFor(
    "UTF-8", // the target character set
    failReason, // holds the result code
    1024 // size of the buffer
    );

// now call the transcodeTo method until
// all characters have been processed
unsigned int charsLeft = XMLString::stringLen(psDocument);
while (charsLeft)
{
    charsWritten = pTransCoder->transcodeTo(
        psDocument, // the string to transcode
        charsLeft > 1024 ? 1024 : charsLeft, // number of characters to process
        (XMLByte *)psOutString, // the output buffer
        1024, // size of the output buffer
        charsProcessed, // returns with number of source chars processed
        XMLTranscoder::UnRep_RepChar // replace illegal chars with default char
    ;)
    // write out the buffer
    . . . (buffer output code goes here)
    // subtract off the number of chars left
    charsLeft -= charsProcessed;
}
delete [] psOutString;
```

Using the Node's userData Field

Occasionally, it is useful to store some application-specific data with a particular document node, or perhaps the entire document. For example, your application may display some data in a user interface that is associated with a particular node, and it may be inefficient to regenerate the data each time you want to display it.

The DOM_Node class cannot be subclassed, so the Xerces library provides a separate mechanism for storing application-defined data with document nodes. Each node has a property named userData, which can be accessed using the Xerces API methods `setUserData()` and `getUserData()`. Note, however, that the memory pointed to by the userData field is not automatically deleted for you when the node is deleted. It is your application's responsibility to delete any memory pointed to by this field.

This code shows how to set and retrieve the userData field:

```
DOM_Node myNode;
typedef struct {
    int someValue;
    char *someString;
} myStruct, *myStructPtr;

// make a new myStruct and give it some values
// NOTE: your responsibility to delete!
myStructPtr theData = new myStruct;
theData->someValue = 5;
theData->someString = new char[10];
strcpy(theData->someString, "hello");

// set the user data field
// assume we somehow got a Node from the document
myNode.setUserData(theData);

// later on, we can retrieve it
theData = (myStructPtr)myNode.getUserData();
delete [] theData->someString;
delete theData;
```

NOTE

The DOM method `cloneNode()` *does not clone the data pointer associated with the userData field. The Xerces FAQ has an in-depth discussion of why this decision was made, but the upshot is that if you want to clone the userData pointer along with the node, you will have to write your own wrapper interface that performs the cloning operation.*

It should be noted that the userData field is considered an experimental part of the Xerces DOM API, and it may disappear in future versions. The new DOM Level 3 specification, although not yet final, is considering a mechanism that would be more flexible than the current userData implementation in Xerces (more on this in Chapter 11).

Where to Get More Information About Xerces

The Xerces website is a good source for information, providing quality documentation along with a maintained FAQ and several good example projects to use as starting points for your own projects. In addition, the Xerces parser is supported by a community of knowledgeable developers on the xerces-c-dev and xerces-j-dev mailing lists who are always willing to help new developers. Before posting a question to the mailing list, however, make sure you read the FAQ—many of the most commonly asked questions are already answered there, and it will save you a lot of time (and embarrassment) if you can find an answer to your question there first.

The Microsoft MSXML Parser

The MSXML parser is Microsoft's implementation of the Core DOM Level 1 interfaces, along with a collection of Microsoft-specific extension APIs. MSXML version 4 also provides support for XML Schema (XSD), XPath 1.0, the SAX2 API (an alternative to DOM processing), and XSLT 1.0.

Where to Get MSXML4

You can download MSXML4 from the Microsoft Developer Network website at http://msdn.microsoft.com. Go to the MSDN Downloads | Web Development | XML Web Services area, and you will find installers for the current version of MSXML in a variety of languages, along with the redistributable files necessary to include with your application so it can use the MSXML library.

Installing MSXML4

When MSXML4 is installed on the user's computer, it is installed in what Microsoft calls *side-by-side* mode, in which any previous existing version of MSXML is left untouched. This prevents introduction of incompatibilities with previous versions; different versions of the Microsoft Windows operating system and Microsoft Internet Explorer are released with different versions of MSXML.

The MSXML4 SDK installation creates an MSXML 4.0 directory on the computer's hard drive containing three directories: doc, inc, and lib. The doc directory contains the MSXML4 SDK documentation in a standard WinHelp file. The inc folder contains the MSXML header files that contain the necessary DOM definitions, and the lib folder contains the import library that your application must link to in order to use the MSXML4 DLL.

Getting to Know the API

The MSXML API prefixes the DOM class names with IXMLDOM. Thus, the Document interface becomes IXMLDOMDocument, Element becomes IXMLDOMElement, and so on. Most of the names are direct matches, with a few exceptions (for example, the MSXML parser names the Attr interface IXMLDOMAttribute).

Using the MSXML DOM interfaces is relatively straightforward, assuming that you are familiar with the things you need to do to work with COM interfaces, such as using VARIANT data types, checking HRESULT return values from functions, and using BSTRs instead of regular strings.

The documentation provided with the MSXML SDK is fairly complete and well documented, although a little light on sample code snippets. This is compounded by the unfortunate fact that, unlike the Xerces distribution, the MSXML SDK installer does not install any example code to learn from. It takes some searching, but it is possible to find some sample code on the MSDN site under the Web and Internet Samples Home page at (http://msdn.microsoft.com/downloads/samples/internet/default.asp). There is a separate section under XML for downloading XML-related sample code, whether you are using C++, Visual Basic, ASP, .NET, or JScript.

This section, like the Xerces one preceding it, will focus on C++, although the concepts illustrated here are easily portable across other language binding implementations.

Using MSXML4

To use MSXML4, your application needs to initialize the COM interfaces for the application's thread, obtain the appropriate MSXML interfaces, and call the desired DOM methods. In this section, we will examine how some common DOM operations are performed using the MSXML library. This section assumes that you are familiar with Microsoft's COM specification and using COM classes. If you are not familiar with COM, you should still be able to follow along. A full tutorial on COM is beyond the scope of this chapter and book; more information on COM is available on the MSDN site and from several third-party books on the subject.

Initializing the Parser

Nothing special needs to be done to initialize the MSXML parser outside of initializing the COM system, which must be done before you can call any COM methods. To initialize COM and begin using the MSXML parser DOM classes, your application calls the `CoInitialize()` method like this:

```
CoInitialize();
```

For each successful call to `CoInitialize()`, your application must call the `CoUninitialize()` method to close the COM library and free any resources that it is maintaining. The call to `CoUninitialize()` looks like this:

```
CoUninitialize();
```

Creating a Document

Creating a new DOM Document in MSXML is accomplished in two steps. First, you must retrieve the class ID (CLSID) of the COM class you wish to create, which in this case is the class ID for DOMDocument. Next, you call `CoCreateInstance()` to create an instance of the class. For example, the code to create a new, empty DOM Document can be written as

```
// Get the CLSID for the MSXML4 DOMDocument
CLSID CLSID_DOMDocument40;
HRESULT hr;
hr = CLSIDFromProgID(OLESTR("Msxml2.DOMDocument.4.0"), &CLSID_DOMDocument40);

// now create a new instance of the document
IXMLDOMDocument *pDocument = NULL;
hr = CoCreateInstance(CLSID_DOMDocument40, // Class of object to create
            NULL, // pointer to Iunknow interface. Leave as NULL
            CLSCTX_INPROC_SERVER, // context for the newly created object
            IID_IXMLDOMDocument2, // ID of the interface being requested
            (LPVOID *)&pDocument // receives the new document
    );
```

After the call to `CoCreateInstance()`, the returned DOM document in the pDocument pointer is empty and ready to receive content.

Adding Content to Documents

Once you have obtained a pointer to the DOMDocument interface, you can use it to add new document objects to the document. The MSXML parser provides the standard DOM interfaces needed to create the various types of document elements. For example, to add elements to the newly created document in the previous example, the following code could be used:

```
BSTR sNodeName = NULL;
IXMLDOMElement *pElem = NULL;
IXMLDOMNode *pNode;
IXMLDOMText *pText;

// new node named "rootNode"
sNodeName = ::SysAllocString("rootNode");
pDocument->createElement(sNodeName, &pElem);
// append new root node, get back result node
pDocument->appendChild(pElem, &pNode);
::SysFreeString(sNodeName);
pElem->Release();

// new node named "firstNode"
sNodeName = ::SysAllocString("firstNode");
pDocument->createElement(sNodeName,&pElem);
pNode->appendChild(pElem, &pNode);
::SysFreeString(sNodeName);
pElem->Release();

BSTR sText = ::SysAllocString("New Text Node");
pDocument->createTextNode(sText, &pText);
pNode->appendChild(pText, &pNode);
::SysFreeString(sText);
pText->Release();
```

This code creates a new root node for the document, named "rootNode." It then creates an Element named firstNode, which it appends to the root node. Finally, it creates a new Text node with the text "New Text Node," which is appended as the first child of the node firstNode. The resulting document structure looks like this:

```
<rootNode>
    <firstNode>New Text Node</firstNode>
</rootNode>
```

Iterating Through a Document's Nodes

This example uses the MSXML DOM methods to iterate over the document's nodes, starting with the document itself. The function `IterateNodes()` takes a pointer to a node and recursively calls itself for each of the node's child nodes.

```
IXMLDOMDocument *pDocument;

void IterateNodes(IXMLDOMNode *pNode)
{
    IXMLDOMNode *pChildNode, *pNextNode;

    ProcessNode(pNode); // do your node processing in here

    pNode->get_firstChild(&pChildNode);
    while (pChildNode)
    {
        IterateNodes(pChildNode);
        pChildNode->get_nextSibling(&pNextNode);
        pChildNode = pNextNode;
    }
}

// assume we retrieved a document pointer somewhere
IterateNodes(pDocument);
```

Parsing Files and Memory Buffers

The MSXML parser provides two Microsoft-specific APIs for parsing XML files and memory buffers. The `load()` method loads an XML file from persistent disk storage, and the `loadXML()` method parses a string buffer and builds a document. In each case, you must first create an empty DOMDocument before calling these methods.

The `load()` method will load an XML file from a file path, URL, another DOMDocument, or any other object that supports the COM interfaces IStream, IPersistStream, or ISequentialStream. For example, to load an XML file from a file path, you could write this code:

```
IXMLDOMDocument *pDocument;
BSTR filePath;

// assume we retrieve a pointer to a document
```

```
pDocument->put_async(VARIANT_FALSE); // no asynchronous loading
VARIANT vPath;
VARIANT_BOOL bSuccess;
// initialize the first argument to be the file path
VariantInit(&vPath);
vPath.vt = VT_BSTR;
V_BSTR(filePath);
// call the load() method
pDocument->load(vPath, &bSuccess);
```

Loading an XML document from a string buffer is even easier: you just pass the method the BSTR that contains the document string. This example shows how to do this:

```
IXMLDOMDocument *pDocument;

// assume we somehow retrieve a pointer to a document
CString myDoc("<book><chapter>Chapter1</chapter></book>");
BSTR bDocStr = myDoc.SysAllocString();
VARIANT_BOOL bSuccess;
HRESULT hr = pDocument->loadXML(bDocStr, &bSuccess)
ASSERT(hr == S_OK);
```

Serializing a Document

Serializing a document using the MXSML parser is very straightforward: the parser provides a custom property named `xml` that represents the XML string of the entire document. An MSXML application only needs to call the `get_xml` method on the DOM document to retrieve the XML string for the contents. The following code shows how to retrieve the XML string for a given DOM document:

```
HRESULT hr = S_OK;
BSTR bstr = NULL;
CString XMLText;
hr = pDocument->get_xml(&bstr);
XMLText = bstr;

if( bstr )
     SysFreeString(bstr);
```

Once your application has the XML string, it can do whatever it wants with it— save it to a file, place it in a text field, and so on.

MSXML also supports the `save()` method, which can be used to save an IXMLDOMDocument to an output location. The syntax for the `save()` method is

```
HRESULT save(VARIANT destination);
```

The destination parameter can be a URL, file path, or another object that supports persistent streaming.

Useful Utilities

The MSXML parser provides several useful utility methods that are not a part of the core W3C DOM specification, but they can make certain node and other programming tasks less cumbersome.

The `selectNodes()` and `selectSingleNode()` methods available on the IXMLDOMNode interface can be used to select a single node or create a NodeList of nodes using an XPath expression. For example, the following code snippet selects all of the data nodes in a document:

```
BSTR bstr = NULL;
IXMLDOMNodeList *pList = NULL;
IXMLDOMDocument *pDocument;

// assume we have a pDocument pointer
bstr = ::SysAllocString("//data");
HRESULT hr = pDocument->selectNodes(bstr,&pList);
::SysFreeString(bstr);
```

The MSXML documentation contains a complete XPath reference that describes how to use XPath notation in your DOM applications.

The IXMLDOMDocument's `createNode()` method can be used to create arbitrary node types. Its syntax is

```
RESULT createNode(VARIANT Type,BSTR name,BSTR namespaceURI,
    IXMLDOMNode **node);
```

This example creates nodes based upon a parameter passed to the function `CreateNewNode`:

```
IXMLDOMNode *CreateNewNode(IXMLDOMDocument* pDoc, BSTR nodeName,
    int nodeType)
{
    VARIANT vtype;
    IXMLDOMNode * newNode;
```

```
    vtype.vt = VT_I4;
    V_I4(&vtype) = (int)nodeType;

    pDoc->createNode(vtype, nodeName, NULL, &newNode);
    return newNode;
}
```

Where to Get More Information About MSXML

The MSDN website (http://msdn.microsoft.com/xml/) is a good source of information for Microsoft's XML implementation. In addition, several websites, such as XML.com (www.xml.com) and Perfect XML (www.perfectxml.com) have recently run articles on using MSXML.

Macromedia Dreamweaver

Macromedia's Dreamweaver application is a popular HTML authoring tool that exposes a DOM interface to its documents. Developers can create extensions to Dreamweaver using the familiar HTML and JavaScript languages, and these extensions have full access to the documents open in the application as well as in persistent storage. In this section, we'll examine Dreamweaver's support for the DOM and take a look at how Dreamweaver differs in its support from browsers such as Netscape Navigator and Internet Explorer.

Where to Get Dreamweaver

Dreamweaver is available directly from Macromedia as well as third-party software resellers. A trial version is also downloadable from the Macromedia website (macromedia.com/software/dreamweaver/), which will last for 30 days. This version is fully functional, and you can try out the examples in this chapter in the trial version.

The DOM in Dreamweaver

Dreamweaver supports a limited subset of DOM Level 1, along with the Internet Explorer attributes `innerHTML` and `outerHTML`. Table 6-2 lists the DOM methods and properties supported by Dreamweaver.

DOM Method or Property	Notes
nodeType	Supported by all document objects
parentNode	Supported by all document objects
childNodes	Supported by all document objects
documentElement	Supported by the Document object
body	Supported by the Document object
URL	Supported by the Document object
tagName	Supported by all HTML tag elements
innerHTML	Supported by all HTML tag elements
outerHTML	Supported by all HTML tag elements
data	Supported by Text and Comment nodes
getElementsByTagName()	Supported by the Document object and all HTML tag elements
hasChildNodes()	Supported by all document objects
getAttribute()	Supported by all HTML tag elements
setAttribute()	Supported by all HTML tag elements
removeAttribute()	Supported by all HTML tag elements

Table 6-2   *Supported DOM Methods and Properties in Dreamweaver*

Getting to Know the API

The Dreamweaver application supports a very rich and robust API for creating all kinds of extensions with different capabilities and intended uses. For the purposes of this section, we will focus on one kind of Dreamweaver extension that allows developers the most power and flexibility when working with documents: the Dreamweaver Command extension.

Command extensions are written as HTML files with embedded JavaScript and/or JavaScript contained within external .js files. The HTML file can contain an optional HTML <FORM> tag, which, if present, signals the application that the extension has a user interface. When the user invokes the command, the extension's form (if it has one) is displayed in a modal dialog box, where the user is allowed to enter values for whatever form elements the extension developer has made available. The extension can then use this input to perform its work. Commands are not required to have such a form, however, and if they do not, then whatever JavaScript code is contained within the onLoad event handler of the HTML file's <BODY> tag is executed when the user invokes the command.

Command extensions are stored inside the Commands folder, which is located inside the Configuration folder, which is located in the same folder as the Dreamweaver application itself. When a command is placed inside this folder, it shows up in Dreamweaver's Commands menu, as shown in Figure 6-3. Each command is listed in the menu according to the contents of its <TITLE> tag.

The following code illustrates a sample Dreamweaver command extension that displays an alert when invoked from the Commands menu:

```
<HTML>
<HEAD>
<TITLE>Sample Extension</TITLE>
</HEAD>

<BODY onLoad="alert('hello world!')">
</BODY>
</HTML>
```

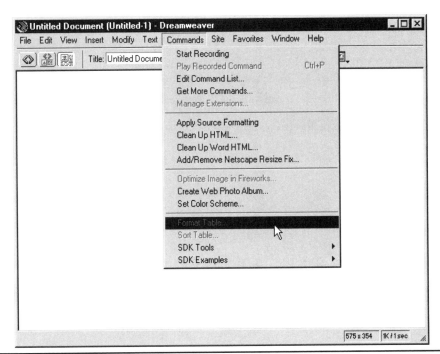

Figure 6-3   *The Dreamweaver Commands menu*

There is a global object in Dreamweaver's JavaScript namespace that represents the application object, called dreamweaver (or dw for short). Many of the application's properties and methods are accessed using the dreamweaver object, as you'll see in the following section.

Using the Dreamweaver DOM

Using the Dreamweaver DOM API is strikingly similar to using the DOM in a regular browser, with some notable exceptions. Because Dreamweaver is an editing application, not just a viewing application, there are methods and properties available to do things such as manipulate the current selection in the document, create new documents, and load and save documents from disk.

In this section, we'll examine how some common DOM operations are accomplished using the Dreamweaver API. To create the command extensions that will be needed to run the code, we will use this document as a template:

```
<HTML>
<HEAD>
<TITLE>Sample Extension</TITLE>
<SCRIPT>
function doIt()
{
   // scripts will go here
}
</SCRIPT>
</HEAD>

<BODY onLoad="doIt()">
</BODY>
</HTML>
```

For each example, the corresponding script code will be inserted into the `doIt()` function and the file will be saved into the Commands folder.

Creating Documents and Getting Document References

Creating a document in Dreamweaver is very straightforward. The method to do this is called `createDocument()`, and it is called from the global dreamweaver application object:

```
var oDOM = dreamweaver.createDocument();
```

NOTE

To see this or any other Dreamweaver script in action, enter this code into the `doIt()` *function in the extension template listed in the preceding section, give the file a name, and save it in the Dreamweaver Commands folder.*

The `createDocument()` method returns a reference to the DOM for the newly created document. To obtain a DOM reference for the currently active document in Dreamweaver, your extension calls the `getDocumentDOM()` method on the dreamweaver object:

```
var currentDOM = dreamweaver.getDocumentDOM();
```

In addition, the `getDocumentDOM()` method can be used to retrieve the DOM of a file stored on disk by passing the "file://" URL of the file to the method. Note that this does not actually open the document in a Dreamweaver window, it just returns the DOM for that file. For example, this code returns the DOM of a file myfile.html on the C drive:

```
dreamweaver.getDocumentDOM("file://C|/myfile.html");
```

Most of the document-related methods in Dreamweaver are methods of the document object. For this reason, it is almost impossible to write a useful Dreamweaver extension without using the `getDocumentDOM()` method.

Creating and Manipulating Document Content

The Dreamweaver DOM API does not support the W3C methods `appendChild()`, `insertBefore()`, and so on. So, how do you get new content into a document? There are several ways; one is to use the `innerHTML` and `outerHTML` element properties, along with certain Dreamweaver-specific methods used to insert text in a document.

Recall that the `innerHTML` and `outerHTML` properties are defined by Microsoft Internet Explorer (see Chapter 5). In Dreamweaver, these properties can be used to simulate the various DOM methods that are missing. For example, the `appendChild()` method appends a node to the end of the node list of an existing node. This is functionally equivalent to

```
oParentNode.innerHTML = oParentNode.innerHTML + HTML_for_new_node;
```

where `HTML_for_new_node` is a string of HTML code that represents the HTML tag to be appended. Similarly, the `insertBefore` function can be simulated by

```
oParentNode.innerHTML = HTML_for_new_node + oParentNode.innerHTML;
```

Using these properties, you can create nodes as strings of text and then insert them into the document. For example, the following code will insert an `IMG` tag at the end of the document's `BODY` section:

```
var oDOM = dreamweaver.getDocumentDOM();
var oBody = oDOM.getElementsByTagName("BODY")[0];
oBody.innerHTML = oBody.innerHTML + "<IMG name='myImage.gif'>";
```

There are also methods provided to insert text directly into the document, such as `insertText()` and `insertHTML()`. The `insertText()` method inserts text content into the document at the current insertion point. For example, the following code inserts `&lt;b&gt;Dreamweaver&lt;/b&gt;` into the document:

```
var DOM = dreamweaver.getDocumentDOM();
DOM.insertText("<b>Dreamweaver</b>");
```

The `insertHTML()` method also inserts content into the document but inserts it as HTML source code, not as text in the document. To see the difference, if the `insertHTML()` method were called with the same argument as in the preceding example, a bold "Dreamweaver" string would be inserted into the document instead of the escaped version of the HTML just shown.

Retrieving and Setting the Document Selection

As an editing application, Dreamweaver must keep track of what the user has selected in the current document so it knows which element to apply edits to. Extensions can retrieve the current selection and change it to be any arbitrary object or range of text within the document by using Dreamweaver's built-in selection methods. There are methods for both retrieving and setting the selection as a range of text or as a document node, as listed in Table 6-3.

Selection Method	Description
getSelection	Returns the current selection as an array of two integers
getSelectedNode	Returns the currently selected document node
setSelection	Sets the current selection range in the document
setSelectedNode	Sets the given node as the current selection in the document

Table 6-3 *Dreamweaver's Selection Manipulation Methods*

All of these methods are called from a document object, which is usually obtained from a call to `dreamweaver.getDocumentDOM()`. For example, the following code illustrates the process of retrieving the selected node, surrounding it with a bold tag (`<B></B>`) and adding an ID attribute of `"somenode"`.

```
var oSelectedObj;

oSelectedObj = dw.getDocumentDOM().getSelectedNode();
oSelectedObj.setAttribute("ID","somenode");
oSelectedObj.outerHTML = "<B>" + oSelectedObj.outerHTML + "</B>";
```

Examining Document Content

In addition to modifying document nodes directly using the `innerHTML` and `outerHTML` methods, Dreamweaver provides support for the W3C standard `getElementsByTagName()` method. Thus, you can write code that works just like it does in the browser, with very minimal changes. Recall from Chapter 5 our function for finding images in a browser page that did not have an `ALT` attribute defined:

```
function checkAltTags()
{
    var oImgList = document.getElementsByTagName("img");
    var i=0;

    if (oImgList.length > 0)
    {
        for (i=0; i<oImgList.length; i++)
        {
            var altText = oImgList.item(i).getAttribute("alt");
            if (altText == "")
                alert("Image: " + oImgList.item(i).src +
                    " has no ALT attribute!");
        }
    }
}
```

To turn this code into a Dreamweaver extension that looks for images with no `ALT` attributes is very straightforward. First, to operate on the currently active document, you need to call the `getDocumentDOM()` method. This means you need to change the line that reads

```
var oImgList = document.getElementsByTagName("img");
```

to read

```
var oImgList = dreamweaver.getDocumentDOM().getElementsByTagName("img");
```

This will return a list of all of the IMG tags in the document. Now, you need to find images that have no ALT attribute. It turns out that Dreamweaver's implementation of the getAttribute() method returns null in the case that an attribute is not specified instead of an empty string, so you need to change the line that reads

```
if (altText == "")
```

to read

```
if (altText == null)
```

Now, you need to package the whole thing up as a Command extension and save it in the Commands folder. The following code shows the finished command:

```
<HTML>
<HEAD>
<TITLE>Check Missing ALT attributes</TITLE>
<SCRIPT>
function checkAltAttrs()
{
    var oImgList = dw.getDocumentDOM().getElementsByTagName("img");
    var i=0;

    if (oImgList.length > 0)
    {
        for (i=0; i<oImgList.length; i++)
        {
            var altText = oImgList.item(i).getAttribute("alt");
            if (altText == null)
                alert("Image: " + oImgList.item(i).src +
                    " has no ALT attribute!");
        }
    }
}
</SCRIPT>
</HEAD>
<BODY onLoad="checkAltAttrs()">
</BODY>
</HTML>
```

When this command is saved in the Commands folder, it appears in Dreamweaver's Commands menu. When invoked by the user, it examines the current Dreamweaver document for images with missing `ALT` attributes and displays an alert if it finds any.

Serializing Documents

To save a document to disk, an extension can call the `saveDocument()` method from the dreamweaver object. The function takes two arguments: the first argument is the DOM of the document to save, and the second argument is the file URL to save the document to. The following code, for example, saves the current document to the root of the C drive on the user's computer:

```
dreamweaver.saveDocument(dreamweaver.getDocumentDOM(),
    "file://C|/myfile.html");
```

Where to Get More Information About the Dreamweaver DOM

These examples just barely scratch the surface of what can be accomplished with Dreamweaver extensions. To learn more about writing Dreamweaver extensions, the Macromedia Exchange website is a good place to get information about extending Dreamweaver (macromedia.com/exchange/dreamweaver). There is an SDK available for download, and most of the extensions available on the site are free and can be downloaded and examined in depth (after all, most are just HTML and JavaScript files).

Dreamweaver also ships with online documentation detailing the workings of the Dreamweaver extensibility mechanism; it can be found under the Help menu by choosing Extending Dreamweaver.

There are also several books available that deal with extending Dreamweaver, such as *Dreamweaver 4: The Complete Reference* by Jennifer Kettell (McGraw-Hill/Osborne, 2001) and *Building Dreamweaver 4 and UltraDev 4 Extensions* (McGraw-Hill/Osborne, 2001) by Tom Muck and Ray West. Both are very good sources of information for building Dreamweaver extensions.

Conclusion

In this chapter, we examined the DOM support available in various nonbrowser applications, from standalone DOM implementations to commercially available software packages that expose a DOM structure. Two of these implementations, Xerces from the Apache Software Foundation and MSXML from Microsoft, are standalone implementations that can be used by applications that need to work with XML documents. The third, Macromedia Dreamweaver, is a commercial HTML editing application that can be extended via HTML and JavaScript to create and manipulate HTML and XML documents.

In the next chapter, we will take a look at some debugging strategies and utility code that may be useful when developing DOM applications. In particular, we'll look at different strategies and code for debugging browser-based applications, as well as other DOM implementations.

Debugging DOM Applications

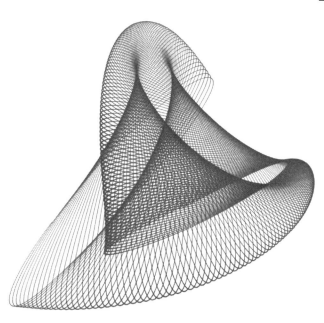

S o far in Part II, we've examined some DOM algorithms that you can use to perform operations that are common among document processing applications, and we've taken a look at the extent of DOM support available in today's browsers and other applications. In this section, we'll examine some debugging strategies and useful code that you can use in your own DOM programs to help make them as robust and stable as possible.

Importance of Good Debugging Skills

It probably comes as no surprise that at some point during the development of your killer DOM application, you're going to have to debug your code. It's just a fact of programming life: even the best programmers among us run into trouble from time to time when writing applications and need tools to help iron out the kinks. Indeed, sometimes debugging a problematic program can take as long as (or even longer than) writing the code itself. The art of debugging is perhaps one of the most important yet most neglected skills that programmers need to develop. The reason for this is really quite simple: getting rid of bugs as quickly as possible translates directly into earlier shipping dates.

Unfortunately, if you're a JavaScript developer, you've got it tough when it comes to debugging. Most browsers and other applications that use JavaScript today don't have good a debugger built in, and even those that do sometimes can't catch certain types of problems or have debuggers that are painfully slow. This is compounded by the fact that JavaScript is a "loosely typed" language and does not force developers to explicitly declare what types of data their variables will contain.

NOTE

Things will get a little better for JavaScript developers with the release of Mozilla 1.0, the open-source browser from mozilla.org, that will include tools such as a DOM Inspector for examining DOM structures and Venkman, a full-featured JavaScript debugger. For more information, visit www.mozilla.org. In addition, Microsoft is shipping a new version of its script debugger in Internet Explorer 6.

Java and C++ developers have it much better—their development environments usually come with superb debuggers—but there's still more that can be done to help the DOM application writer debug code and catch problems before they come up in production.

In this chapter, we're going to take a look at some useful utilities and strategies that you can take advantage of in your own DOM applications. The examples in this chapter will emphasize browser-based debugging, though you should find the information useful regardless of what language or platform you're developing for.

Be Assertive: Use ASSERT()

One of the best ways to rid your applications of bugs is to expose them as early as possible during the development and testing process. The faster you can force bugs to the surface, the faster you can exterminate them from your program. One simple yet effective debugging tool that most C++ programmers have been using for quite some time is the humble ASSERT() function (technically, a macro in the C++ language). This function evaluates a Boolean condition and "asserts" that the outcome is true. If everything is OK, the program continues on its merry way. If the Boolean condition is not met, it displays an error message. The typical syntax for calling ASSERT() is simple:

```
ASSERT(someBooleanCondition);
```

When an ASSERT() condition fails the test, there is usually some kind of feedback presented to the application user, such as the dialog in Figure 7-1.

Let's take a closer look at how the ASSERT() function is actually defined.

Defining ASSERT()

The ASSERT() function is defined a little differently for different platforms. In JavaScript, the ASSERT() function can be defined like this:

```
function ASSERT(bCondition, strMsg)
{
   if (!bCondition)
      alert("ASSERTION FAILURE " + strMsg);
}
```

Here, we've defined ASSERT() to take an optional second argument, the message to display in the event that the condition evaluates to false. In addition, because JavaScript doesn't support the concept of macros, you have to define ASSERT() as an actual function. In practice, this function would probably be defined in an external .js file and then included in the source file where it is used by a <SCRIPT> tag. In

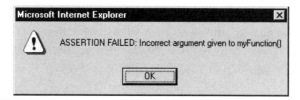

Figure 7-1 *Error message showing an assertion failure*

this case, there is a simple if statement that evaluates the condition and shows an alert if the condition evaluates to false.

In C++, ASSERT() is usually defined as a macro that expands during the precompile phase, like this:

```
#define ASSERT(bCondition)
    if (f) {} \
    else { \
        /* Platform-specific error display code here */ \
        /* just print the error to whatever stderr is */ \
        fflush(NULL); /* flush open buffer before calling abort() */ \
        fprintf(stderr, "Assertion failed! File: %s, Line: %d", \
                _ _FILE_ _, _ _LINE_ _); \
        fflush(stderr); \
        abort();\
    }
```

NOTE

ASSERT() is usually defined to be a debug-only macro or function, and release-quality code has the ASSERT() macro defined to be an empty function. This is so that, in practice, the release version of the code runs a little faster (because the code to do all the condition checking is absent), and the user doesn't see frightening ASSERT() failure messages when things go wrong or when the programmer uses ASSERT() incorrectly.

In this case, the ASSERT() macro also evaluates the condition and displays an error to the stderr output stream. Most common development environments today define the _ _FILE_ _ and _ _LINE_ _ macros to be the current file and line of the source code where ASSERT was called. In case you're wondering, that empty if() section at the start of the macro is not a mistake: it has to be there to prevent dangling if-else situations. For example, guess what will happen if you define ASSERT() as

```
#define ASSERT(bCondition)
   if (!f) { \
      fflush(NULL); \
      fprintf(stderr, "Assertion failed! File: %s, Line: %d", \
              _ _FILE_ _, _ _LINE_ _); \
      fflush(stderr); \
      abort();\
   }
```

and you try to use it in the following code snippet:

```
if (someExpression)
   ASSERT(someCondition);
else
   everythingIsOK();
```

The `else` clause will never execute in the way it was intended. Why? Because it is being paired up with the `if` clause defined in the `ASSERT()` macro. Remember, the `ASSERT()` macro gets expanded in place in the code, which can have unforeseen consequences. Using the if-else form in the macro definition prevents this problem from happening.

Using ASSERT() Effectively

In general, the `ASSERT()` function should be used to catch conditions in the code that are illegal and should never happen during the normal course of the program's execution. For example, consider the following JavaScript function:

```
function getTextNodeData(objNode)
{
   return objNode.data;
}
```

This function seems innocent enough: it simply returns the `data` property of a Text node (recall from Chapter 2 that Text nodes inherit from the CharacterData interface, which provides the `data` property). There's just one not-so-small problem with this code: it may not have been passed a Text node in the first place. Of course, you could just add some error-checking code, like this:

```
function getTextNodeValue(objNode)
{
   if (objNode.nodeType == 3) // 3 means text node
```

```
        return objNode.data;
    else
        return "";
}
```

However, then you're just masking the problem, which is that somewhere in your code you may be asking for the value of a Text node that isn't a Text node. This code does nothing to help you find this problem; in fact, it only hides it from you even further because it isn't clear why an empty string was returned. Did the function return an empty string because the text node had no content? Was it because there was an error somewhere in the function? This becomes even more of a problem when someone who's unfamiliar with the code tries to use this nifty getTextNodeData() function that you've written, only to get back an empty string. There's no quick way to tell exactly what's happening without tracking down your function and determining how it works, which, in turn, slows down development.

Use ASSERT() to Catch Errors

Fortunately, there is a better way. Using the ASSERT() function we have defined, you could instead write the getTextNodeData() function like this:

```
function getTextNodeData(objNode)
{
    ASSERT(objNode != null && objNode.nodeType == 3,
            "Not a text node!");
    return objNode.data;
}
```

In this example, the code first checks to see if the objNode argument is not null and that its nodeType is indeed that of a text node. If these conditions are both met, the function is allowed to continue and return the data property. Otherwise, an error alert is displayed. In this case, it would be obvious to another user of your function that their code is providing input to getTextNodeData() that isn't valid. Programming this way forces developers to always do the right thing in their code because problems will surface pretty quickly if the constraints of the code aren't followed.

Here's another example of how using an ASSERT() statement can save you a little money on aspirin costs. Consider this simple JavaScript routine:

```
function add(i, j)
{
```

```
    return (i + j);
}
```

What does this function do? If you said "it returns the sum of two numbers," you're right. Well, almost: you'd be right *as long as the two supplied arguments were both numbers*. What if the caller didn't give you numbers, but strings instead? The result would indeed be very different! If you needed this routine to be absolutely sure that it was given two numbers to add, you could do so by making a simple modification:

```
function add(i, j)
{
    ASSERT(typeof(i) == "number" && typeof(j) == "number");
    return (i + j);
}
```

Anyone trying to pass this function anything other than two numbers would be quickly made aware of the error of their ways.

Finally, a good example of using ASSERT() arises when checking the values of if and case statements to make sure that legal values are passed in and processed correctly. For example, a common programming construct such as switch-case usually handles multiple possible values and takes action depending on each, such as in this code listing:

```
switch (someValue)
{
case 1:
  // do the first case
  break;
case 2:
  // do the second case
  break;
// . . . and so on for the rest of the cases
}
```

In many instances where switch() statements are used, the values of each of the case handlers are the only ones that are valid, and any other values are illegal. For example, if you were to write a function that returned a text string description of a given node type, you might write it using a switch() statement, where each case handler examines the node's nodeType property and returns an appropriate string. There are only 12 node types, so any values outside of 1 and 12 would be invalid. A good way to catch illegal values in this case would be to use the default handler for the `switch()` statement and have it `ASSERT()` if the code ever reaches that point, like this:

```
// . . . code from the previous 11 cases
case 12:
  // do case 12 stuff;
  break;
default:
  ASSERT(FALSE); // should never get here normally
  break;
```

Now, should this `switch` statement ever try to execute the default case, an `ASSERT` would automatically be raised because the only way the code can reach this point is if an illegal value had been given earlier.

When Not to Use ASSERT()

In general, the `ASSERT()` function should be used *to catch illegal conditions in your code.* In other words, use `ASSERT()` to make sure that things are the way you expect them to be, such as legal values for a function's arguments. Don't use `ASSERT()` to try and trap conditions that are honest-to-goodness error conditions that can arise in your program under perfectly normal circumstances and that must be handled by your application.

A good example of when not to use an `ASSERT()` statement looks like this:

```
function f()
{
   var age;
   ASSERT((age = getAgeFromUser()) >= 21);
}
```

There are two problems with this code. First, it uses an `ASSERT()` to make sure that the user entered a value greater than or equal to 21. However, it's entirely possible and even likely that the user may enter an age that's less than 21. This isn't a bug in the code; it's a situation that your application needs to anticipate and handle correctly. For example, the age may not be mandatory, and hence can be ignored. On the other hand, if it is mandatory, the user should be prompted to enter it before continuing. The second problem is that the code that detects this condition tries to be clever and save some space by wrapping the `ASSERT()` statement and the code that retrieves the input into one line. The problem here is that if the `ASSERT()` function is disabled for some reason, such as building a release version of the application, the line won't get executed because it will evaluate to an empty statement.

The basic rules to follow here are simple: first, don't put code that must always execute into `ASSERT()` calls; and second, use `ASSERT()` to catch bugs, not garden-variety errors that are going to happen in the normal course of the program.

Getting Fancy with ASSERT()

Once you get used to the idea of how `ASSERT()` works and where to effectively use it, you can define a whole bunch of useful, special-purpose `ASSERT()` functions that perform very specific tasks. For example, you can write an `ASSERT()` that checks to see if a given node is indeed a "valid" node—that is, that the `nodeType` property actually exists (in the JavaScript case) and it is between 1 (for Element nodes) and 12 (for Notation nodes). The `ASSERT()` function for this in JavaScript looks like this:

```
function ASSERT_VALID_NODE(objNode)
{
    if (objNode == null)
    {
        alert("Invalid node -- node is null");
        return;
    }
    if (typeof(objNode.nodeType) == "undefined")
    {
        alert("Invalid node -- no nodeType property!");
        return;
    }
    if (objNode.nodeType < 1 || objNode.nodeType > 12)
    {
        alert("Invalid node -- nodeType is invalid!");
        return;
    }
}
```

This version of `ASSERT()`, named `ASSERT_VALID_NODE`, accepts a single argument and determines whether the node argument is, in fact, a valid node. The first test is whether an object was even specified. If the argument is `null`, you definitely don't have a valid node. The next test makes sure that the `nodeType` property of the object is actually present (note that this test is specifically for JavaScript—Java and C++ wouldn't need to do this). If the supplied object has no `nodeType` property, the node can't be valid. Finally, you check to make sure that the `nodeType` property is inside the range of acceptable node types.

This example is pretty basic; it only determines whether the basic structure of a DOM node is present or not. You could get a lot more fancy by adding individual checks for each node type. For example, this improved version makes sure that the `tagName` property is present for Element nodes:

```
function ASSERT_VALID_NODE(objNode)
{
   if (objNode == null)
   {
      alert("Invalid node -- node is null");
      return;
   }
   if (typeof(objNode.nodeType) == "undefined")
   {
      alert("Invalid node -- no nodeType property!");
      return;
   }
   if (objNode.nodeType < 1 || objNode.nodeType > 12)
   {
      alert("Invalid node -- nodeType is invalid!");
      return;
   }
   if (objNode.nodeType == 1)
   {
      if (typeof(objNode.tagName) == "undefined")
      {
         alert("Invalid Element -- no tagName property!");
         return;
      }
   }
}
```

Another example of using `ASSERT()` is to make sure that your own application logic is running correctly. For example, suppose there is a point in your DOM application that requires you to act on the document element node. You can make sure of this by using a specialized `ASSERT()` function such as `ASSERT_IS_DOC_ELEMENT`:

```
function ASSERT_IS_DOC_ELEMENT(objNode)
{
   if (objNode != document.documentElement)
```

```
        alert("ASSERT Failure: this is not the document element!");
}
```

You get the idea. When properly used, simple tools like ASSERT() can really increase the effectiveness of your debugging efforts by forcing bugs to appear sooner in the testing process. Using them throughout your code is definitely a good programming habit to develop.

If you're using a development environment such as Microsoft's Visual Studio, you've already got ASSERT() at your disposal. If not, it's easy to define your own version for your particular environment.

Tracing Your Steps with TraceConsole

Although using the ASSERT() function will help find errors in programming logic by exposing illegal conditions in the code, sometimes bugs take on more insidious forms that cannot be detected or caught by an ASSERT() statement. To find these bugs, you need a slightly more advanced debugging tool.

The TraceConsole is a utility for browser-based JavaScript DOM developers that displays a program's variables and other interesting objects as they change while the application is running. It essentially provides a record of program execution that can be examined after the program has run to help pinpoint logic errors in the code. Figure 7-2 shows a sample screenshot of the TraceConsole.

Almost every JavaScript developer has used the alert() function at some point in their debugging process; it's almost a rite of passage as a web developer. The basic premise is that at some point in your application, you need to verify that a certain variable contains a certain value, or that an array contains the right data. The main problem with alert() is that it isn't very flexible. First, you have to deal with a pop-up window every time the alert() function is called, which can make using alert() inside loops very unpractical. Second, the amount of data that can be reasonably displayed inside an alert() window is pretty small. Once you start getting more than a half dozen or so lines of output, the readability of the information rapidly diminishes. Third, the information displayed by alert() is fleeting. Once you dismiss the dialog box, that information is gone (unless you've manually written it down, which can become a huge pain).

Enter the TraceConsole. Think of TraceConsole as alert() on steroids: instead of constantly bugging you with pop-up windows that must be manually dismissed before the execution of the code can continue in the browser, the data that would normally be displayed by the alert() function is routed to a separate window

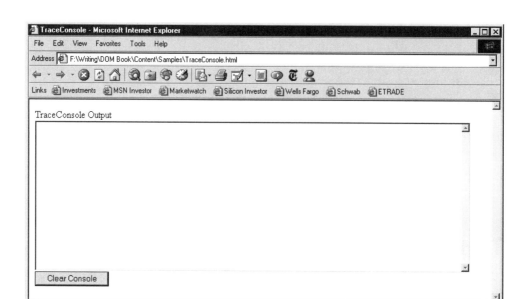

Figure 7-2 *The TraceConsole window*

instead. This output can then be copied and pasted into a text editor or saved as a log file for future reference. This eliminates the modal alert dialog, the amount of data, and the persistence problems presented by the `alert()` method.

Listing 7-1 contains the code for the TraceConsole.html file.

Listing 7-1 *The TraceConsole HTML Source*

```
<HTML>
<HEAD>
<TITLE>TraceConsole</TITLE>
</HEAD>
<BODY>
<FORM NAME="form1" METHOD="post" ACTION="">
  TraceConsole Output<BR>
  <TEXTAREA NAME="consoletext" ROWS="15" COLS="90"></TEXTAREA>
  <BR>
  <INPUT TYPE="BUTTON" NAME="btnClear" VALUE="Clear Console"
      onClick="document.forms[0].consoletext.value=''">
</FORM>
```

```
</BODY>
</HTML>
```

The TraceConsole window essentially consists of a <FORM> with a text field, where the trace output will be sent, and a button that can be used to clear its contents.

Using the TraceConsole

To use the TraceConsole, your script needs to include the TraceConsole.js file, like this:

```
<SCRIPT SRC="TraceConsole.js"></SCRIPT>
```

You also need to make sure that the file TraceConsole.html is available to the script. The code begins by declaring some global variables:

```
var g_sIndentStr = '   '; // string to use to indent trace output
var gTraceWin=null;  // holds a reference to the trace window
var g_TimeStart = 0; // stores the time when the timer was started
```

The function openTraceWindow() calls the window.open() method to create an instance of the console:

```
function openTraceWindow()
{
     gTraceWin = window.open("TraceConsole.html");
}
```

You can modify the URL path to the TraceConsole file in this function if you want to store it in a global place. When called, a global reference to the trace window is created and stored in the gTraceWin variable.

Once you've included the JavaScript source file for the console, you need to create an instance of the console window before you can trace output to it. The openTraceWindow() does this for you. Once you've called openTraceWindow(), you can start calling the other tracing functions. If at any point your script needs to clear the console window, it can call the clearTrace() function:

```
function clearTrace()
{
     gTraceWin.document.forms[0].consoletext.value ='';
}
```

This will delete all the existing content in the console.

The TraceConsole Functions

The TraceConsole provides a set of useful functions for recording several different kinds of variables and objects. In addition, the TraceConsole API provides functions that can be used to perform basic performance timing of sections of code, which can help you identify areas to focus on in order to improve performance.

Basic Output

The most basic function available in the TraceConsole is `traceString()`. It takes a single string as an argument and writes it out to the console window. JavaScript allows you to build strings rather easily using the + operator, so it's simple to write out a string that shows the content of a variable:

```
var myName = "Joe";
traceString("myName is currently set to " + myName);
```

Using `traceString()` is the closest available comparison to using the `alert()` function because both take string arguments. The `traceString()` function is written as

```
function traceString(str)
{
   if (gTraceWin)
      gTraceWin.document.forms[0].consoletext.value += str;
}
```

Sometimes it is useful to trace a whole bunch of variables to the output at once. The `traceValues()` function does this in the TraceConsole. It accepts a variable number of arguments and traces them to the output window:

```
var a=1;
var b=3;
var c=9;
traceString("first batch:\n");
traceValues(a,b,c);
a++;
b = c + a;
traceValues(a,b);
traceString("second batch:\n");
```

The result of the previous code snippet in the trace window is shown in Figure 7-3. The source for the `traceValues()` function is listed as follows:

```
function traceValues( /*, [param 1], [param 2], ... */)
{
    var cArgs = arguments.length;
    var i=0;
    var sStr='';

    for (i=0; i<cArgs; i++)
    {
        sStr += '[' + arguments[i];
        sStr += '] \n';
    }

    traceString("traceValues: Tracing " + arguments.length +
        " arguments:\n");
    traceString(sStr + "\n");
}
```

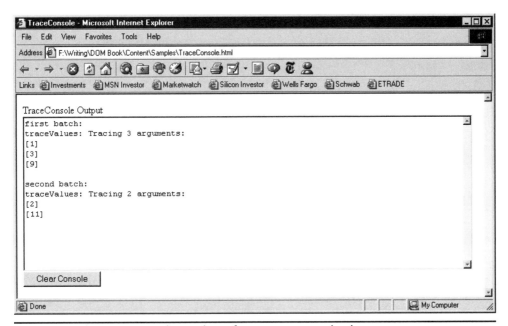

Figure 7-3   *The TraceConsole window after tracing several values*

Tracing Complex Objects

The TraceConsole can also be used to trace complex objects to the console window, such as arrays, Document nodes, and generic objects. Each object type has a corresponding trace function in the API, such as `traceArray()`, `traceNode()`, and `traceObject()`.

Listing 7-2 shows the code for the `traceArray()` function.

Listing 7-2   *The* `traceArray()` *Function*

```
function traceArray(aTheArray, bIncludeLength, bIncludeElemTypes,
    bRecursiveTrace)
{
   var thestr='';
   var i=0;

   if (bIncludeLength)
      traceString("-- Tracing Array with length: " +
              aTheArray.length + \n");
   else
      traceString("-- Tracing Array object: \n");

   for (i=0; i < aTheArray.length; i++)
   {
      thestr = g_sIndentStr + "element "+i;

      if (bIncludeElemTypes)
         thestr += (" (type: " + typeof(aTheArray[i]) + ") value: ");
      else
         thestr += "value: ";

      thestr += aTheArray[i];

      traceString(thestr);

      if (bRecursiveTrace && typeof(aTheArray[i]) == "object")
      {
      // if the object has a length property, then it is an array.
      // Otherwise, just pass the object to the traceObject routine
         if (typeof(aTheArray[i].length) == "undefined")
            traceObject(aTheArray[i], bIncludeElemTypes, true,
                  bRecursiveTrace);
```

```
      else
         traceArray(aTheArray[i], bIncludeLength,
                  bIncludeElemTypes, bRecursiveTrace);
      }
   }
}
```

The `traceArray()` function takes four arguments. The first argument is the array to be traced. The remaining three arguments are Boolean values that specify whether to include the array length in the output, whether to show the type of each element, and whether the array should be traced recursively (that is, when an array element is itself another array, whether that array should be traced as well).

The `traceNode()` method traces the contents of a DOM node to the console window. The source for the function is shown in Listing 7-3.

Listing 7-3   *The `traceNode()` Function*

```
function traceNode(oTheNode, bShowType, bShowContent, bShowParent,
     bShowChildCount)
{
   var sOutputString='';
   var sID = '';

   if (typeof(oTheNode.nodeType) != "undefined")
   {
      if (oTheNode.nodeType == 1)
         sID = oTheNode.getAttribute("id");

      sOutputString = 'Node: ' + sID + '\n';

      if (bShowType)
      {
         sOutputString += '   Type: ' + getNodeDescription(oTheNode)
                        + "\n";
      }

      if (bShowParent)
      {
         sOutputString += '   Parent: ' + getNodeDescription(
                        oTheNode.parentNode ) + "\n";
```

```
      }
      traceString(sOutputString);

      traceString("   Child Nodes: ");
      if (oTheNode.hasChildNodes())
      {
         traceString(oTheNode.childNodes.length + " child nodes.\n")
      }
      else
         traceString("None.\n");

      if (bShowContent)
      {
         sOutputString = "Content: ";

         switch (oTheNode.nodeType)
         {
         case 1:
            sOutputString += oTheNode.innerHTML + "\n";
            break;
         case 3:
            sOutputString += oTheNode.data + "\n";
            break;
         case 8:
            sOutputString += oTheNode.data + "\n";
            break;
         case 9:
            sOutputString += "[Body Content not shown for
                     document nodes]" + "\n";
            sOutputString += "   URL: " + oTheNode.URL + "\n";
            break;
         }
         traceString(sOutputString);
      }
   }
   else
      traceString("traceNode(): Invalid node type specified.
                     'nodeType' property undefined.");
}
```

The traceNode() function takes five arguments. The first is the node to be traced. The four remaining Boolean arguments specify whether to show the node type, its text content, its parent node, and the number of child nodes it has. To output the node's content, the `traceNode()` method uses the `innerHTML` property that is not part of the DOM standard but is supported by both Internet Explorer 6 and Netscape 6.

This version of the `traceNode()` function has been abbreviated to handle only the common types of document nodes (Element, Text, Comment, and Document), although adding support for the other types would be trivial. The `getNodeDescription()` function used by `traceNode()` is basically a big `switch` statement that returns a text description of each node type, as shown in Listing 7-4.

Listing 7-4   *The* `getNodeDescription()` *Method*

```
function getNodeDescription(oTheNode)
{
     if (oTheNode == null)
          return "null";

     switch (oTheNode.nodeType)
     {
     case 1:
          return "Element Node (Tag: " + oTheNode.tagName + ")";
     case 2:
          return "Attribute Node";
     case 3:
          return "Text Node";
     case 4:
          return "CDATA Node";
     case 5:
          return "Entity Reference Node";
     case 6:
          return "Entity Node";
     case 7:
          return "Processing Instruction Node";
     case 8:
          return "Comment Node";
     case 9:
          return "Document Node";
     case 10:
          return "Document Type Node";
     case 11:
```

```
            return "Document Fragment Node";
    case 12:
            return "Notation Node";
    default:
            return "Unknown Node Type";
    }
}
```

The output of the `traceNode()` function provides a concise description of
the properties of a given node. For example, consider a node represented by an
unordered list:

```
<UL ID="oList">
    <LI>item 1</LI>
    <LI>item 2</LI>
    <LI>item 3</LI>
    <LI>item 4</LI>
</UL>
```

Figure 7-4 shows the trace output when `traceNode()` is called for the
unordered list.

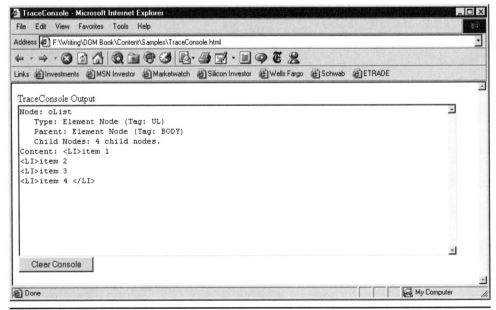

Figure 7-4   *Tracing a node*

The `traceObject()` function performs almost the same function as `traceNode()`, but with generic JavaScript objects. The source for the function is shown in Listing 7-5.

Listing 7-5   *The* `traceObject()` *Function*

```
function traceObject(oTheObj, bIncludeElemTypes, bIncludeStaticProps,
     bRecursiveTrace /* , cIndentLevel */)
{
   var x;
   var theStr='';
   var sIndentStr = '';
   var typeStr='';
   var i, cIndentLevel;

   // if the object defines a length property, trace it as array
   if (typeof(oTheObj.length) != "undefined")
      traceArray(oTheObj, true, true, bIncludeElemTypes,
                 bRecursiveTrace);

   // get the indent level if it was specified
   if (arguments.length == 5)
      cIndentLevel = arguments[4];
   else
      cIndentLevel = 1;

   // indent each string
   for (i=0; i<cIndentLevel; i++)
      sIndentStr += g_sIndentStr;

   // First list the static properties and methods
   if (bIncludeStaticProps)
   {
      traceString(sIndentStr + "-- Static Methods and
                  Properties:\n");

      for (x in oTheObj.constructor)
      {
         theStr = sIndentStr + "static property: " + x;
         typeStr = typeof(oTheObj.constructor[x]);
         if (bIncludeElemTypes)
```

```
            theStr += " (type: " + typeStr + ")";
        if (typeStr != "function")
            theStr += " value: " + oTheObj.constructor[x];
        traceString(theStr);
    }
    traceString("\n");
}


// now list the object's properties and methods
traceString(sIndentStr + "-- Object Methods and Properties:\n");
for (x in oTheObj)
{
    theStr = sIndentStr + "property: " + x;
    typeStr = typeof(oTheObj[x]);
    if (bIncludeElemTypes)
        theStr += " (type: " + typeStr + ")";
    if (typeStr != "function")
        theStr += " value: " + oTheObj[x];
    traceString(theStr);

    if (typeof(oTheObj[x]) == "object" && bRecursiveTrace)
        traceObject(oTheObj[x], bIncludeElemTypes,
                         bIncludeStaticProps, bRecursiveTrace,
                         cIndentLevel+1);
    }
    traceString("\n");
    traceString(sIndentStr + "----- End of Object -----\n");
}
```

The traceObject() function takes four arguments: the object to trace, the Boolean values indicating whether to show property types, whether to show static (class) properties, and whether to trace recursively. The traceObject() function can also recursively trace subobjects, as traceArray() does with elements that are arrays. For example, if an object defines a property that is itself an object, traceObject() can trace its properties as well. The fifth argument is the current indent level; this is provided so that traceObject() can indent its output in the trace window for each subobject it encounters.

Using the Timer Functions

When trying to find parts of your code that could use a little speed improvement, it helps to have something like a stopwatch to time how long it takes to perform certain operations. The TraceConsole provides a simple timer that can be used to gauge approximately how long a part of your code takes to complete. You just need to bracket the code in question with the trace function to start the timer and the trace function to stop it: the console handles the rest. The code for the two timer functions, startTimer() and stopTimer(), are listed here:

```
function startTimer()
{
     var timeStart = new Date();
     g_TimeStart = timeStart.getMilliseconds();
     traceString("+-+-+ Timer Started: " + g_TimeStart + "\n");
}

function stopTimer()
{
     var timeStop = new Date();
     var endTime = g_TimeStart + timeStop.getMilliseconds();
     traceString("+-+-+ Timer Stopped: " + endTime + "\n");
     traceString("+-+-+ Time Difference: " + (endTime-g_TimeStart)
                    + "\n");
}
```

NOTE

JavaScript is an interpreted language, so a script's execution speed will depend largely on the power of the machine on which it is running and what other processes are running concurrently. Because of this, the timer functions should only be used to determine an approximation of relative performance; these routines do not provide any type of specific accuracy in their measurements.

For example, the following code can be used to measure how long an array operation takes:

```
function timerTest()
{
     startTimer();

     var arr = new Array(10);
     var i=0;
     for (i=0; i<10; i++)
          arr[i] = i * i;

     stopTimer();
}
```

Figure 7-5 shows the console window output when this script is run.

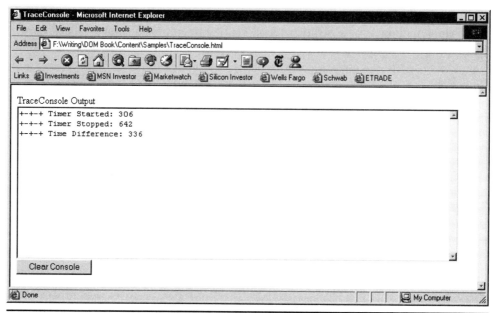

Figure 7-5 *Trace output from timer functions*

The TraceConsole is certainly more complicated and sophisticated than using plain `alert()` functions; but once you start using it and become familiar with the functions, you will find it a welcome replacement for plain vanilla alerts.

NOTE

If you're developing in C++ or Java, your platform likely already has built-in support for some form of trace, such as `System.out.println()` *for Java and the* `TRACE` *macro in VisualC++. Check the documentation for your development environment for more information.*

The DOMDumper

Sometimes it's not practical to sift through the output of a program's execution, or maybe you don't need that level of detail. What you need is a way of seeing the big picture: a snapshot of your application's DOM document structure in real time. This is the kind of situation that the DOMDumper tool is ideally suited for.

Essentially, the DOMDumper tool takes a picture of the current state of a DOM structure in a web page starting from a given node in the document tree and dumps it into a separate browser window for examination. Each line in the output corresponds to a particular node in the tree, and the interesting parts of each node are included in the output. This type of tool is really useful when you want to make sure that your application is correctly manipulating a document tree because you can visually inspect the structure of the document at any given point in time.

First, we'll examine some of the sample output generated by the DOMDumper, and then we'll walk through the code to see how it works.

DOMDumper Output

Listing 7-6 shows a simple HTML document with an ordered list containing three list items.

Listing 7-6   *Sample Document with an Ordered List*

```
<!DOCTYPE HTML PUBLIC "-//W3C//DTD HTML 4.0 Transitional//EN">
<HTML>
<HEAD>
<TITLE>Untitled Document</TITLE>
<SCRIPT src="DOMDumper.js"></SCRIPT>
</HEAD>
<BODY BGCOLOR="#FFFFFF" onLoad="DumpDOM(document,'    ')">
<OL ID="list1">
     <LI>item 1</LI>
     <LI>item 2</LI>
     <LI>item 3</LI>
</OL>
</BODY>
</HTML>
```

The document's BODY tag has an onLoad handler that calls the DOMDumper functions to create the output shown in Figures 7-6 and 7-7. Figure 7-6 shows the output of the DOMDumper for this sample document viewed in Netscape 6. Figure 7-7 shows the same output from Internet Explorer 6.

Each figure shows the structure of the document from the point of view of the Document node. Right away, it's obvious that Netscape and IE view different types of nodes very differently. The output from Netscape 6 more closely resembles the W3C structure than IE does in a number of ways. First, IE treats the DOCTYPE declaration as a comment, whereas Netscape 6 correctly identifies it as a DocumentType

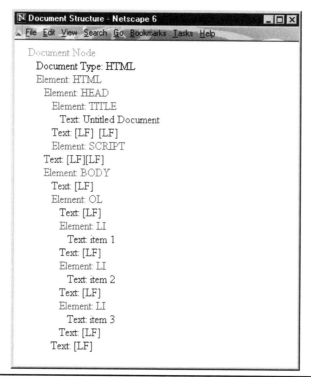

Figure 7-6 *DOMDumper output in Netscape 6*

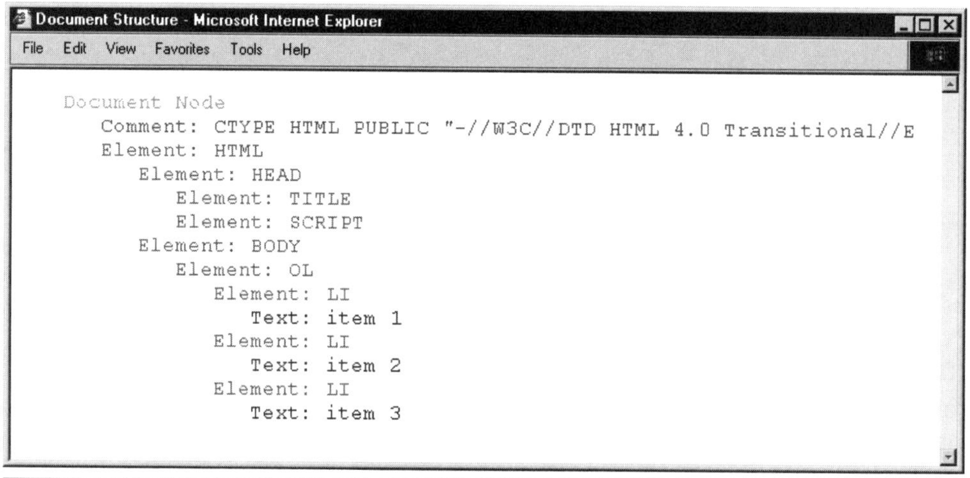

Figure 7-7 *DOMDumper output in Internet Explorer 6*

node. Second, Netscape 6 identifies the text of the <TITLE> tag as a text node, whereas IE skips it. Finally, Netscape 6 identifies the carriage returns in the source code as empty text nodes; IE skips over those as well.

Let's examine the code that produced this output.

DOMDumper Code

The code for DOMDumper, contained in the file DOMDumper.js, is broken up among three routines, the second of which does the core of the work. The first and third routines basically create the output window and clean up after the output has been generated, respectively. Listing 7-7 shows the code for the function that creates the window that the document structure will be dumped into.

Listing 7-7   *Code for Creating the Dump Window*

```
var gDumpWindow;
// change this to as many spaces as you want nodes indented
var gIndentStr = "    ";
var g_I = 1;
var gbShowCRLF = true; // show \n and \r in text output

var gElemColor = "red";
var gAttrColor = "black";
var gTextColor = "blue";
var gCDATAColor = "yellow";
var gEntityRefColor = "black";
var gEntityColor = "black";
var gPIColor = "black";
var gCommentColor = "green";
var gDocElemColor = "orange";
var gDocTypeColor = "black";
var gDocFragColor = "black";
var gNotationColor = "black";

function DumpDOM(startNode, indentStr)
{
     gDumpWindow = window.open(
          '','DumpDOM'+g_I,'width=600,scrollbars=yes,resizable=yes,
          menubar=yes');
     gDumpWindow.document.write(
          '<HTML>\n<HEAD>\n<TITLE>Document Structure ' + g_I++ +
```

```
                    '</TITLE>\n' +
                    '<STYLE TYPE="text/css">\nPRE {font-family:sans serif;' +
                    'font-size:12pt}\n</style>\n</head>\n\n' +
                    '<BODY BGCOLOR="#FFFFFF">\n\n<pre>');
          Dump(startNode, indentStr);
          CloseDumpDocument();
}
```

The code begins by defining some global variables that will be used throughout the rest of the code. The gDumpWindow variable will be used to hold a reference to the dump window that is created to hold the output. The gIndentStr variable holds the string that is used to indent each line of the output. The gbShowCRLF controls whether \n and \r characters in the source are displayed as [LF] and [CR]. The remaining variables control the colors used in the output to make the various parts of document structure easier to identify.

The DumpDOM() function performs only a few functions. First, it calls the window.open() method to create a new window to hold the output. Next, it uses the document.write() method to write the HTML infrastructure to the output document. The entire body content of the document is wrapped in a <PRE> element so that the indentation of each string will be displayed properly by the browser. After the document has been created and initialized, the Dump() function is called to write the contents of the DOM to the window's document. Finally, the CloseDumpDocument() function is called to clean up and write the closing HTML code to the dump window.

The workhorse of the DOMDumper tool is the function that generates the output. Listing 7-8 contain the code for the Dump() function.

Listing 7-8   *The* Dump() *Function*

```
function Dump(oNode,indentString)
{
      var sNodeContent = '';
      var sNodeStr = '';
      var arrChildren = oNode.childNodes;

      // check the node type
      switch (oNode.nodeType)
      {
      case 1: // Element Node
            sNodeContent = "<span style='color:" + gElemColor + "'>";
            sNodeContent += "Element: " + oNode.tagName;
```

```
        if (oNode.getAttribute("id") != "")
            sNodeContent += ", ID=" + oNode.getAttribute("id");
        break;
case 2: // Attribute Node
        sNodeContent = "<span style='color:" + gAttrColor + "'>";
        sNodeContent += "Attr: " + oNode.name + "=" + oNode.value;
        break;
case 3: // Text Node
        sNodeContent = "<span style='color:" + gTextColor + "'>";
        var theNodeData = oNode.data;
        if (gbShowCRLF)
        {
            theNodeData = theNodeData.replace(/\n/g,"[LF]");
            theNodeData = theNodeData.replace(/\r/g,"[CR]");
        }
        sNodeContent += "Text: " + theNodeData;
        break;
case 4: // CDATA Node
        sNodeContent = "<span style='color:" + gCDATAColor + "'>";
        sNodeContent += "CDATA Section: " + oNode.data;
        break;
case 5: // Entity Reference Node
        sNodeContent = "<span style='color:" + gEntityRefColor + "'>";
        sNodeContent += "Entity Reference";
        break;
case 6: // Entity Node
        sNodeContent = "<span style='color:" + gEntityColor + "'>";
        sNodeContent += "Entity: publicId=" + oNode.publicId +
                        " systemId=" + oNode.systemId + " notationName="
                        + oNode.notationName;
        break;
case 7: // Processing Instruction Node
        sNodeContent = "<span style='color:" + gPIColor + "'>";
        sNodeContent += "Processing Instruction target=" +
        oNode.target + " data=" + oNode.data;
        break;
case 8: // Comment Node
        sNodeContent = "<span style='color:" + gCommentColor + "'>";
        sNodeContent += "Comment: " + oNode.data;
        break;
case 9: // Document Node
        sNodeContent = "<span style='color:" + gDocElemColor + "'>";
        sNodeContent += "Document Node";
        break;
case 10: // Document Type Node
        sNodeContent = "<span style='color:" + gDocTypeColor + "'>";
        sNodeContent += "Document Type: " + oNode.name;
        break;
case 11: // Document Fragment Node
```

```
                        sNodeContent = "<span style='color:" + gDocFragColor + "'>";
                        sNodeContent += "Document Fragment";
                        break;
            case 12: // Notation Node
                        sNodeContent = "<span style='color:" + gNotationColor + "'>";
                        sNodeContent += "Notation publicId=" + oNode.publicId +
                                            " systemId=" + oNode.systemId;
                        break;
            };
            sNodeContent += "</span>";

            sNodeStr = indentString + sNodeContent + "\n";

            gDumpWindow.document.write(sNodeStr);

            for (var i=0; i < arrChildren.length; i++)
            {
                    Dump(arrChildren[i], indentString + gIndentStr);
            }
    }
```

There's no real magic behind the `Dump()` function: it's essentially a giant `switch()` statement that writes out certain properties of a node depending upon the node type. For example, for Element nodes, the `Dump()` function writes out the `tagName` property and ID attribute, if one exists for the node. After it writes out the node string, the `Dump()` function recursively calls itself for each of the node's child nodes.

Listing 7-9 shows the code that finishes up writing the output to the dump window.

Listing 7-9   *The Closing HTML for the Dump Window*

```
function CloseDumpDocument()
{
        gDumpWindow.document.write('</pre></body></html>');
}
```

The `CloseDumpDocument()` function writes the closing HTML code to the output window.

Using the DOMDumper

To use the DOMDumper tool, your application needs to include the JavaScript source file DOMDumper.js. Then, when you need to view the document structure, you call the dump functions to create the output window.

Listing 7-10 shows Listing 7-5 modified to use the DOMDumper when triggered by a button click event. The source for the dump functions is included via a `<SCRIPT>` tag, and a button has been added to trigger the dump routines. In addition, a button has been added to delete list items from the document.

Listing 7-10   *Using the DOMDumper*

```
<!DOCTYPE HTML PUBLIC "-//W3C//DTD HTML 4.0 Transitional//EN">
<HTML>
<HEAD>
<TITLE>Untitled Document</TITLE>
<SCRIPT src="DOMDumper.js"></SCRIPT>
<SCRIPT>
function deleteItem(listNode)
{
      listNode.removeChild(listNode.lastChild);
}
</SCRIPT>
</HEAD>
<BODY BGCOLOR="#FFFFFF">
<OL ID="list1">
      <LI>item 1</LI>
      <LI>item 2</LI>
      <LI>item 3</LI>
</OL>
<INPUT type="button" value="Delete Node"
    onClick="deleteItem(document.getElementById('list1'))" name="delBtn">
<INPUT type="button" value="Dump Structure" onClick="DumpDOM(
    document.getElementById('list1'), ' ' )" name="dumpBtn">
</BODY>
</HTML>
```

When the document is in its initial state, its structure looks like Figure 7-8.

If you close the dump window and click the Delete Node button twice, the two last list items will be removed. When the Dump Structure button is clicked again, the structure looks like Figure 7-9.

Clearly, using DOMDumper makes it a lot easier to quickly verify that a DOM application is in fact manipulating a document correctly. Listing 7-8 doesn't even begin to write out all of the possible information that could be helpful when viewing the structure; modifications are left to the reader as an exercise.

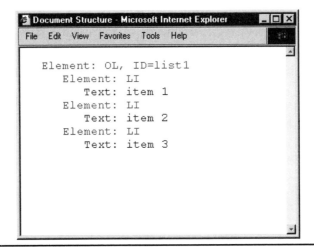

Figure 7-8 *Initial document structure*

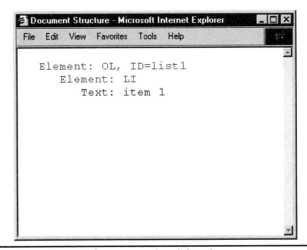

Figure 7-9 *Document structure after two nodes deleted*

Conclusion

In this chapter, you saw how some simple debugging tools and strategies can make finding and eradicating bugs in DOM applications much easier. First, we examined the humble ASSERT() function, and you saw how it can be used to force bugs to appear sooner in the testing process by making sure that illegal conditions in the code are checked for and caught quickly. We also looked at some ways to make the ASSERT() function more specialized for DOM applications by having it check for DOM-specific error conditions such as invalid node types and specific nodes in the document.

Then we looked at a debugging tool called the TraceConsole, which can be used to trace program output as it happens in an application. Using the methods available in the TraceConsole API, a DOM application can record the logical progression of an application over the course of the program's execution, similar to the way that a web server saves statistical information to a log file. After the program has been put through a few tests, the trace output can be examined to help pinpoint hard-to-find logic bugs.

Finally, we looked at DOMDumper, a tool that can display a real-time picture of the DOM substructure of any node in the document. Using the Dump() function, the DOM Dumper creates an HTML document that displays a document's DOM structure beginning at a given node and encompassing all of that node's children. The DOMDumper can be used to investigate the structure of a document at a particular point in time, helping to verify that an application is modifying a document in the intended way.

This chapter brings us to the end of Part II, where we've examined how the DOM is supported in some real-world implementations. In Part III, we'll use the foundations and theory learned in Part I along with our real-world experience gained in Part II to examine some practical examples of how the DOM can be used to provide effective user interfaces and perform useful document processing in your DOM applications. We'll also take a look at where the DOM is headed in the future.

Practical Uses of the DOM

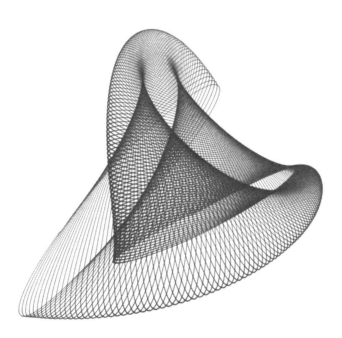

Providing Automatic Document Navigation

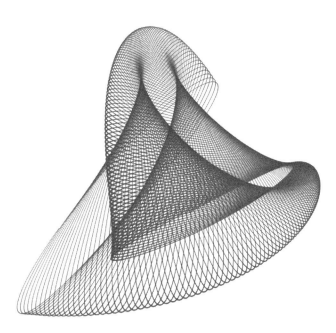

Part I introduced the concepts of the DOM and discussed the basic interfaces of the DOM API. In Part II, we focused mostly on DOM theory and contrived examples to illustrate concepts. In Part III, starting here with Chapter 8, we're going to concentrate on examples of practical uses of the DOM that you can put to work in your applications to make them more usable, dynamically engaging to the user, and processor efficient. We'll conclude by taking a look at future directions of the DOM and what you can expect to see as the DOM matures and evolves.

In this chapter, we will look at practical ways to use the DOM to make your documents and the information that they present more usable and easier to navigate. In particular, we'll examine different ways of using the DOM to improve the presentation and navigability of the document's structure and information. We'll begin by looking at how you can quickly provide a user with a list of interesting places in the document that they can link to immediately. Next, we'll look at how your documents can automatically build tables of contents for the user that correspond to the document's sections. Finally, we'll build an example that allows users to mark their current place in the document so they can read another section and easily find their previous place in the page.

NOTE

This chapter is not intended to serve as an official information design reference or tutorial for creating usable websites in accordance with W3C or other accepted standards. There are plenty of good resources available on the Web you can refer to for this information. The purpose here is to illustrate how the DOM can be used to achieve certain practical design objectives. For more information on creating accessible web pages, refer to the W3C's Web Accessibility Initiative at www.w3.org/WAI/.

Using the DOM to Provide Better Document Navigation

Documents presented on the Web in a modern, DOM-capable browser have the distinct advantage of being live—that is, they are more than just static words printed on a piece of paper, as in this book. Because the content and structure of the information in a web page can be discovered by a DOM application on-the-fly, the developer can take advantage of some unique abilities of the browser to improve the way this information is displayed and consumed by the viewer.

For example, long documents (such as the W3C DOM specification itself) can often be difficult to read or comprehend because there is too much information presented right up front. Navigating documents of this size becomes a challenge in itself because users often scroll through documents and read information in a nonlinear, random-access fashion. Using the DOM, your documents can automatically adapt to their content by making themselves easier to navigate. This is accomplished by reading the structure of the content and modifying the page in the browser to provide user-interface elements that allow users to quickly jump to certain points in the document.

Another good example is enabling the user to keep track of where they are in a document by placing a temporary "marker" at a certain point in the document; they can then use this marker to find the same location later. For instance, if a user is reading a rather lengthy page and wants to refer to some particular information earlier or later in the document, they can just click the paragraph they are reading to mark it with a visual indicator. They can later scroll through the document and easily return to that section by looking for the marker.

Let's begin by taking a look at how the DOM can be used to improve the way a user jumps to specific information in a document.

Example: On-the-Fly Bookmarks

One example of using the DOM to make a document easier to navigate is by providing a list of bookmarks that is generated on-the-fly for a particular page. This is especially useful if the page contains locations that you want to expose as bookmark destinations that don't necessarily correspond exactly to tag locations in the document (such as <H1> tags, images, and so on). In this example, the DOM is used to dynamically create a list of virtual bookmarks or places of interest that the user can select from a standard <SELECT> list and automatically jump to. Figure 8-1 shows the bookmark list in the page as seen in Internet Explorer 6.

Each bookmark entry is created from a specially marked <SPAN> tag that has a bookmark attribute on it. The content of the bookmark attribute becomes the text displayed in the <SELECT> list. For example, a bookmark named Hotels in the list would be indicated in the document source as

```
<SPAN bookmark="Hotels">Hotels Section</SPAN>
```

Listing 8-1 shows the code that is used to generate the bookmark list. This code is stored in a separate file named Bookmarks.js and is included in the target web page using a <SCRIPT> tag with a SRC attribute, like this:

```
<SCRIPT SRC="Bookmarks.js"></SCRIPT>
```

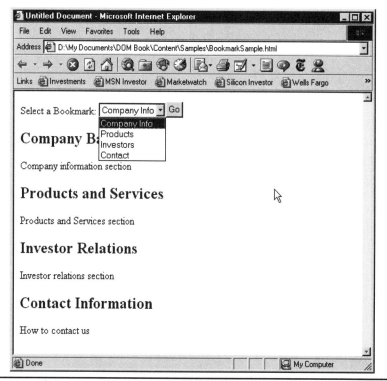

Figure 8-1 *List of dynamically generated bookmarks*

Listing 8-1 *buildBookmarks()* **Source**

```
var g_anchorCount;
var g_docLoc;

function buildBookmarks()
{
    var i;
    g_anchorCount = 0;
    // save off the original URL
    g_docLoc = new String(document.location);

    // build the FORM to hold the controls
    var oForm = document.createElement("FORM");
    // create the SELECT element for the bookmarks
    var oSelect = document.createElement("SELECT");
```

```
   oSelect.setAttribute("id","bookmarks");

   // label for the SELECT list
   var oText = document.createTextNode("Select a Bookmark: ");
   oForm.appendChild(oText);
   oForm.appendChild(oSelect);

   // build the "Go" button
   var oBtn = document.createElement("INPUT");
   oBtn.setAttribute("type","button");
   oBtn.setAttribute("value","Go");
   oBtn.setAttribute("onClick","jumpToBookMark()");
   oForm.appendChild(oBtn);

   // get all the SPAN elements
   var aMarkElements = document.getElementsByTagName("SPAN");
   // for each span, see if it has a bookmark attribute
   for (i=0; i<aMarkElements.length;i++) {
      if (aMarkElements[i].getAttribute("bookmark") != "") {
         // build named anchor for the location
         var oAnchor = buildNamedAnchor();
         aMarkElements[i].innerHTML = oAnchor +
            aMarkElements[i].innerHTML;

         // build an OPTION tag for the SELECT list
         var sName = aMarkElements[i].getAttribute("bookmark");
         var oOption = buildBookmarkRef(sName);
         // add the OPTION tag to the SELECT
         oSelect.appendChild(oOption);

         g_anchorCount++; // increment the anchor count
      }
   }
   insertBookmarkList(oForm);
}

function buildBookmarkRef(sName)
{
   var oOptionTag = document.createElement("OPTION");

   // set the value
   oOptionTag.setAttribute("value","bookmark"+g_anchorCount);
   // create the display name
```

```
    var oOptionText = document.createTextNode(sName);
    oOptionTag.appendChild(oOptionText);

    return oOptionTag;
}

function buildNamedAnchor()
{
    // use innerHTML to get around IE "name" attr bug:
    // IE won't let you set the "name" attr of A tags
    return "<A NAME=bookmark" + g_anchorCount + "></A>";
}

function insertBookmarkList(oBookMarkNode)
{
    // get the BODY tag
    var oBody = document.getElementsByTagName("BODY")[0];

    // insert the bookmark list as the first child
    oBody.insertBefore(oBookMarkNode,oBody.firstChild);

    // IE BUG: IE won't trigger form elements with attached
    // event handlers that have been inserted via the DOM
    // unless you force it to reparse the document by setting
    // the innerHTML property of the BODY tag. Netscape doesn't
    // mind this, so we just do it for both browsers.
    oBody.innerHTML = oBody.innerHTML;
}

function jumpToBookMark()
{
    var oSelect = document.getElementById("bookmarks");
    var selOption = oSelect.selectedIndex;
    var newURL = g_docLoc + "#" + oSelect.options[selOption].value;
    document.location = newURL;
}
```

Let's examine the code in Listing 8-1 by each function to see how it all works.

Setting Up

The buildBookmarks() function is the one that is called to create the bookmarks from the document's <SPAN> tags. The function starts by setting up some global variables that will be used to build the bookmarks: `g_anchorAcount` is used to create named anchor tags to serve as bookmark destinations, and the `g_docLoc` string holds the initial URL of the document. The script stores this value aside in a variable because it needs to work with the original document's URL each time the user chooses a bookmark. Note also that the value of `g_docLoc` is set by creating a new String object and initializing it with the value of the document's location property. Just writing the following code wouldn't work.

```
g_docLoc = document.location
```

Why? Because the `g_docLoc` variable would just point to the same underlying string object as the document.location property, and when it changed, you would lose the original value of the document URL.

Creating the User Interface Elements

The `buildBookmarks()` function next creates the user interface controls that will be needed to display the bookmarks. First, the enclosing `<FORM>` tag is created, then the `<SELECT>` list that will hold the bookmarks is created:

```
// build the FORM to hold the controls
var oForm = document.createElement("FORM");
// create the SELECT element for the bookmarks
var oSelect = document.createElement("SELECT");
oSelect.setAttribute("id","bookmarks");
```

The `<SELECT>`list is also given the ID of "bookmarks" so it can be referred to later. After the select list is created, a text node is created to serve as a label for the list:

```
var oText = document.createTextNode("Select a Bookmark: ");
```

Then the text label and `<SELECT>`list are added to the form element:

```
oForm.appendChild(oText);
oForm.appendChild(oSelect);
```

Finally, the Go button is created and added to the form:

```
var oBtn = document.createElement("INPUT");
oBtn.setAttribute("type","button");
oBtn.setAttribute("value","Go");
oBtn.setAttribute("onClick","jumpToBookMark()");
oForm.appendChild(oBtn);
```

The script sets the value of the `onClick` attribute to be the `jumpToBookMark()` function, which is part of the script that is included in the page (discussed shortly).

Building the Bookmark List

Once the user interface controls have been created, the script scans the document for all <SPAN> tags and builds the list of bookmarks. The line

```
var aMarkElements = document.getElementsByTagName("SPAN");
```

retrieves all of the <SPAN> elements in the page. However, the page may already be teeming with existing <SPAN> tags, and you are only interested in the ones that have been marked as representing a bookmark. The <SPAN> tags have special "bookmark" attributes, so you need to filter these tags out and use them to build the bookmark list. This is done by iterating over the list of <SPAN> elements and looking for those with bookmark attributes:

```
for (i=0; i<aMarkElements.length;i++) {
     if (aMarkElements[i].getAttribute("bookmark") != "") {
```

If the `getAttribute()` call indicates the presence of a bookmark attribute, a bookmark entry is constructed. This is done in two steps: first, the named anchor tag that will serve as the destination for the bookmark link is created.

```
var oAnchor = buildNamedAnchor();
aMarkElements[i].innerHTML = oAnchor +
     aMarkElements[i].innerHTML;
```

You have to be a little tricky here because IE has a bug in it that prevents the setting of the NAME attribute on <A> tags. The workaround is to build the string of HTML to represent the <A> tag and then use the `innerHTML` property to add it to the document. The `buildNamedAnchor()` function takes care of creating the HTML string for the <A> tag:

```
function buildNamedAnchor()
{
     . . .
     return "<A NAME=bookmark" + g_anchorCount + "></A>";
}
```

The string returned is then inserted into the `innerHTML` of the <SPAN> tag that represents the bookmark.

After the named anchor has been created, the second step is that each of the <OPTION> tags for the <SELECT> list needs to be created. This is accomplished by the buildBookmarkRef() function:

```
var sName = aMarkElements[i].getAttribute("bookmark");
var oOption = buildBookmarkRef(sName);
```

The buildBookmarkRef() function takes the value of the bookmark attribute and creates an <OPTION> tag for it:

```
function buildBookmarkRef(sName)
{
    var oOptionTag = document.createElement("OPTION");

    // set the value
    oOptionTag.setAttribute("value","bookmark"+g_anchorCount);
    // create the display name
    var oOptionText = document.createTextNode(sName);
    oOptionTag.appendChild(oOptionText);

    return oOptionTag;
}
```

The <OPTION> tag is created by a call to createElement, and the value attribute is set to the string bookmarkX, where X is the value of the g_anchorCount global counter. The display name for the <OPTION> tag is created as a text node and appended to the <OPTION> element, which is then returned and added to the <SELECT> node. Then the g_anchorCount counter is incremented, and the process repeats for each of the remaining <SPAN> tags:

```
oSelect.appendChild(oOption);

g_anchorCount++; // increment the anchor count
```

Inserting the Bookmark List into the Document

After the main loop in the buildBookmarks() function completes, the user interface controls are inserted into the top of the document by the insertBookmarkList() function with the <FORM> node as the argument:

```
insertBookmarkList(oForm);
```

The function finds the <BODY> tag of the document by calling getElementsByTagName().

```
// get the BODY tag
var oBody = document.getElementsByTagName("BODY")[0];
```

Then the form node, passed as the oBookMarkNode argument, is inserted into the document's body as the first child node:

```
oBody.insertBefore(oBookMarkNode,oBody.firstChild);
```

At this point, you once again have to resort to some trickery in Internet Explorer. It seems that IE will not call any JavaScript methods or event handlers if the document's DOM has been modified directly unless the document is forcibly reparsed. This can be accomplished by setting the <BODY> tag's innerHTML property to itself:

```
oBody.innerHTML = oBody.innerHTML;
```

Netscape doesn't require this trick; however, because this has no adverse effect in Netscape, you simply have it happen in both browsers without enclosing it inside a browser-specific function.

Responding to the User's Bookmark Selection

Now all that is left is to handle the user's clicking the Go button. When the Go button is clicked, the jumpToBookMark() function is called:

```
function jumpToBookMark()
{
     var oSelect = document.getElementById("bookmarks");
     var selOption = oSelect.selectedIndex;
     var newURL = g_docLoc + "#" + oSelect.options[selOption].value;
     document.location = newURL;
}
```

The function finds the <SELECT> list by calling getElementById() with the ID that you previously assigned to it ("bookmarks"). It then extracts the value of the currently selected option, which will be the name of a named anchor tag in the document. It then sets the document's location property to the original URL plus the name of the anchor tag, which causes the browser to jump to that location in the document.

Now, to use this script, the developer needs to identify the places in a given document that will be accessible as bookmarks, place the special bookmark <SPAN> tags at those locations, include the Bookmarks.js file in the page, and trigger the `buildBookmarks()` function from the `<BODY>` tag's `onLoad` handler to automatically build the list of bookmarks for that page.

Example: Automatic Table of Contents

Although the on-the-fly bookmark generator works well, its main drawback is that it isn't fully automatic. The author has to manually go through the document and mark each place where a bookmark should appear, which can be time consuming if you have a large number of documents or documents with a lot of content in them. A better solution would be totally automatic and would allow the user to control the visibility of the user-interface elements.

The automatic table of contents generator accomplishes these requirements. It builds a table of contents for a given page by reading the content of the document when it is loaded and creating a list of links to the `<H1>` and `<H2>` tags contained within the page. When finished, the list can be displayed at the top of the page in the form of an ordered or unordered list, as shown in Figure 8-2.

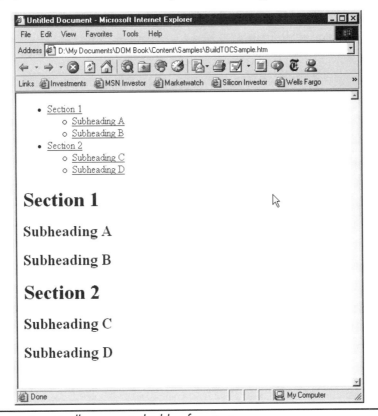

Figure 8-2   *Automatically generated table of contents*

Listing 8-2 lists the code for generating a table of contents automatically. This code is stored in a separate file named buildTOC.js and is included in the target web page using a <SCRIPT> tag with a SRC attribute, like this:

```
<SCRIPT SRC="buildTOC.js"></SCRIPT>
```

To create the list of bookmarks, your page should call the buildTOC() function from the web page's onLoad event handler.

Listing 8-2   *Automatic Table of Contents Generator*

```
var gNodeCounter = 1; // keeps track of the current indent level
var gbDoH1=true, gbDoH2=true; // flags for H1 and H2
var oCurNode = null;
var sLastNodeAdded="";
var gTOCNode = null;

function buildTOC()
{
   // create the root of the TOC as an unordered list
   gTOCNode = document.createElement("UL");
   oCurNode = gTOCNode; // initialize the current node
   oBodyNode = document.getElementsByTagName("BODY")[0];

   nodeScanner(oBodyNode); // build the table of contents

   // insert the TOC at the top of the BODY
   oBodyNode.insertBefore(gTOCNode, oBodyNode.firstChild);
}

// scans all of the nodes in the document in document order
function nodeScanner(oNode)
{
   processNode(oNode);
   var chld;

   chld = oNode.firstChild;
   while (chld) {
      nodeScanner(chld);
      chld = chld.nextSibling;
   }
```

```
}

function processNode(oNode)
{
    var oLINode = null;
    if (oNode.nodeType == 1) {
        // we have an element node -- see if it is a HEADING element
        if ((oNode.nodeName == "H1" && gbDoH1) ||
            (oNode.nodeName == "H2" && gbDoH2))
        {
            // make a new List Item for TOC
            oLINode = document.createElement("LI");

            // create A tag for the list item to link to the heading
            var oAnchor = document.createElement("A");
            oAnchor.setAttribute("href","#"+gNodeCounter);
            oLINode.appendChild(oAnchor);

            // text content for the A tag is innerHTML of the H1 or H2
            var textContent = oNode.innerHTML;
            var oTextNode = document.createTextNode(textContent);
            oAnchor.appendChild(oTextNode);

            // IE BUG: For some reason, IE doesn't allow you to create
            // named anchors by setting the "name" attribute on an
            // "a" tag, so we have to workaround it by setting the
            // innerHTML property of the target heading node
            oNode.innerHTML = "<a name=\""+
                    gNodeCounter++ + "\"></A>" + oNode.innerHTML;
        }
        if (oLINode)
            addTOCNode(oLINode,oNode);
    }
}

function addTOCNode(oNewNode, oRefNode)
{
    if (oCurNode == gTOCNode) {
        gTOCNode.appendChild(oNewNode);
        oCurNode = oNewNode;
        sLastNodeAdded = "H1";
    }
    else {
```

```
        if (oRefNode.nodeName == "H1") {
            // h1 nodes are always children of the root UL
            gTOCNode.appendChild(oNewNode);
            oCurNode = oNewNode;
            sLastNodeAdded = "H1";
        }
        else if (oRefNode.nodeName == "H2") {
            // if current node is H1, add it as a child of the H1.
            if (sLastNodeAdded == "H1") {
                var oUL = document.createElement("UL");
                oCurNode = oCurNode.appendChild(oUL);
                oCurNode.appendChild(oNewNode);
            }

            // if current node is H2, add the new node as a sibling.
            if (sLastNodeAdded == "H2")
                oCurNode.parentNode.appendChild(oNewNode);

            oCurNode = oNewNode;
            sLastNodeAdded = "H2";
        }
    }
}
```

Let's examine the code piece by piece to see how the TOC is created.

Setting Up

The script begins by initializing some global variables that will be used throughout the code. Specifically, the `gbDoH1` and `gbDoH2` variables can be set to create TOC entries for <H1> and <H2> tags, respectively.

The `buildTOC()` function is the only method that users of the script need to call directly, usually from the `onLoad` handler of the web page that the TOC will be created for. Using the `onLoad` handler creates the TOC automatically once the page has been loaded. To create the TOC manually, a control such as a button or hyperlink can be added to the page to call the `buildTOC()` method when triggered.

The `buildTOC()` method creates an unordered list (UL) that will serve as the table of contents list and assigns it to the global `gTOCNode`. It then retrieves the <BODY> tag for the document:

```
gTOCNode = document.createElement("UL");
oCurNode = gTOCNode; // initialize the current node
oBodyNode = document.getElementsByTagName("BODY")[0];
```

Next, `buildTOC()` calls the function `nodeScanner()` with the BODY tag as its argument:

```
nodeScanner(oBodyNode); // build the table of contents
```

The `nodeScanner()` method recursively visits all of the nodes in the document and builds the TOC as it goes along. After it is finished, the TOC is inserted into the document at the top of the body section:

```
oBodyNode.insertBefore(gTOCNode, oBodyNode.firstChild);
```

Scanning the Document's Nodes

The `nodeScanner()` method is the same as the depth-first traversal algorithm you first saw in Chapter 4. It walks through all of the document nodes in document order and calls the `processNode()` method for each node that it finds.

It is important that the nodes be scanned in document order because the TOC must reflect the nodes in the same order they appear in the document.

Building a TOC Destination

The `processNode()` method is where most of the work is done. The function declares a local variable named oLINode to hold the list item node that will become the TOC entry.

```
var oLINode = null;
```

Next, the function checks to see if the node being processed is an element node. If it is, it then checks to see if it is an <H1> or <H2> and whether that particular heading tag type is desired for inclusion in the TOC:

```
if (oNode.nodeType == 1) {
    // we have an element node -- see if it is a HEADING element
    if ((oNode.nodeName == "H1" && gbDoH1) ||
        (oNode.nodeName == "H2" && gbDoH2))
    {
```

If these conditions are met, a new TOC entry is created for the heading tag. First, a new list item element is created:

```
// make a new List Item for TOC
oLINode = document.createElement("LI");
```

Next, an anchor tag is created that will link the list item in the TOC to the location of the heading tag in the text. The text for the anchor tag that will appear in the TOC is the same as the text content of the heading node:

```
// create A tag for the list item to link to the heading
var oAnchor = document.createElement("A");
oAnchor.setAttribute("href","#"+gNodeCounter);
oLINode.appendChild(oAnchor);
// text content for the A tag is innerHTML of the H1 or H2
var textContent = oNode.innerHTML;
var oTextNode = document.createTextNode(textContent);
oAnchor.appendChild(oTextNode);
```

Now you just need to insert a named anchor in the heading tag that will serve as the link destination for the TOC entry. Internet Explorer has issues with setting the name of an <A> tag directly via the DOM, so you should do it using the innerHTML property of the heading node. This also works in Netscape, so you don't need to enclose it in browser-specific checking code.

```
oNode.innerHTML = "<a name=\""+
     gNodeCounter++ + "\"></A>" + oNode.innerHTML;
```

Finally, the list item is added to the TOC by calling addTOCNode():

```
if (oLINode)
     addTOCNode(oLINode,oNode);
```

Adding the TOC Entry

The addTOCNode() takes the list item that will be the TOC entry and adds it to the global gTOCNode object. You want the entries for <H2> tags to be properly indented underneath the <H1> entries, so the script has to keep track of what kind of heading tag the most recently added TOC entry was for.

The addTOCNode() method first checks the special case where the very first TOC entry is being added.

```
if (oCurNode == gTOCNode) {
     gTOCNode.appendChild(oNewNode);
     oCurNode = oNewNode;
     sLastNodeAdded = "H1";
}
```

If this is not the first TOC entry, the code checks to see what kind of heading tag the TOC entry corresponds to. If it is an <H1> tag, the TOC entry is added at the top level of the TOC list:

```
if (oRefNode.nodeName == "H1") {
    // h1 nodes are always children of the root UL
    gTOCNode.appendChild(oNewNode);
    oCurNode = oNewNode;
    sLastNodeAdded = "H1";
}
```

Otherwise, if the TOC entry is for an <H2> tag, the script checks to see what the most recently added TOC entry was for. If it was for an <H1>, the TOC list needs to first indent the new entry under the most recent one:

```
else if (oRefNode.nodeName == "H2") {
    // if current node is H1, add it as a child of the H1.
    if (sLastNodeAdded == "H1") {
        var oUL = document.createElement("UL");
        oCurNode = oCurNode.appendChild(oUL);
        oCurNode.appendChild(oNewNode);
    }
```

If the most recently added TOC entry was for an H2 tag, the code simply adds the new TOC entry as a sibling of the previous one:

```
    // if current node is H2, add the new node as a sibling.
    if (sLastNodeAdded == "H2")
        oCurNode.parentNode.appendChild(oNewNode);

    oCurNode = oNewNode;
    sLastNodeAdded = "H2";
}
```

When the code is finished, the TOC represents all of the H1 and H2 tags in the document, and the user simply clicks one to be taken to that section of the document.

Example: Document Placeholders

Both of the previous examples allow the user to navigate a document by quickly jumping to various locations within the page. In this example, we'll provide the user with a simple mechanism for marking their current place in the page so they can easily find it again if they scroll away from it. I came up with this idea while reading the W3C specification because I found myself reading one section and needing to quickly refer to another section in a different part of the page. Finding my previous location was a bit of pain because the document has a lot of sections that look very similar to each other.

The general idea is to temporarily modify the appearance of the part of the page the user is viewing by performing a simple task, such as clicking the paragraph of text they are reading to highlight it. When the user clicks, the paragraph's background color changes slightly so it can easily be spotted again later. Figure 8-3 shows two paragraphs, one highlighted and one normal.

Listing 8-3 lists the code for highlighting the selected paragraph in the browser when the user clicks it. This code is stored in a separate file named buildPlaceholders.js and is included in the target web page using a <SCRIPT> tag with a SRC attribute, like this:

```
<SCRIPT SRC="buildPlaceholders.js"></SCRIPT>
```

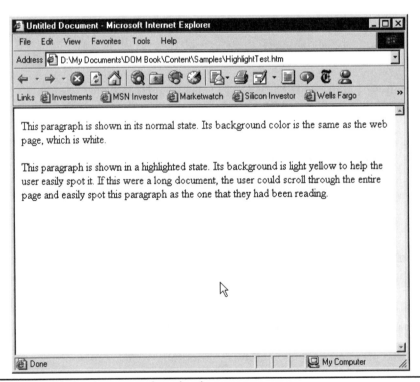

Figure 8-3   *Highlighted paragraph in the document*

Listing 8-3   *Highlighting Paragraph Tags in the Page*

```
var currentNode;
var curBackColor;

function initPlaceholders()
{
      var oBody = document.getElementsByTagName("BODY")[0];

      if (window.event)
            oBody.attachEvent("onclick",handleClick);
      else
            oBody.addEventListener("click",handleClick,true);

      currentNode = null;
}

function handleClick(evt)
{
      var targetNode;

      if (window.event)
            targetNode = window.event.srcElement;
      else
            targetNode = evt.target;

      // if text node, set to parent
      if (targetNode.nodeType == 3)
            targetNode = targetNode.parentNode;

      if (currentNode)
            currentNode.style.backgroundColor = curBackColor;

      if (targetNode.nodeType == 1) {
            var pNode;

      if(targetNode.nodeName != "P")
            pNode = getContainingParaNode(targetNode);
      else
            pNode = targetNode;

      if (pNode) {
            curBackColor = pNode.style.backgroundColor;
```

```
                    pNode.style.backgroundColor="#ffff99";
                    currentNode = pNode;
            }
            else
                    currentNode = null;
            }
    }

function getContainingParaNode(oNode)
{
        var testNode;

        testNode = oNode.parentNode;
        while (testNode)
        {
                if (testNode.nodeName == "P")
                        return testNode;
                testNode = testNode.parentNode;
        }
        return null;
}
```

Using the code is simple—in the onLoad handler of the document in which you want to use placeholders, you simply call the initPlaceholders() function. This function attaches event handlers to the <BODY> tag of the document, and all subsequent clicks are examined to see if the clicked element is within a <P> tag and needs to be highlighted.

Let's examine the code to see how each piece works.

Setting Up

The initPlaceholders function is where the placeholder code is set up:

```
function initPlaceholders()
{
        var oBody = document.getElementsByTagName("BODY")[0];

        if (window.event)
                oBody.attachEvent("onclick",handleClick);
        else
                oBody.addEventListener("click",handleClick,true);

        currentNode = null;
}
```

The code begins by retrieving the <BODY> tag for the document because this is the page element that the event listener will be installed on. To install the event handler, the code first needs to see if the script is running in Internet Explorer or Netscape; IE's event model is slightly different than the DOM Events module that Netscape implements. More information on IE's event model can be found at msdn.microsoft.com/library/default.asp.

Internet Explorer doesn't pass an event object to the handler for an event as Netscape does and as the DOM Level 2Events module specifies. Instead, IE uses a global event object accessed from the window object. Thus, if the window object has a property named event, you know that the script is running inside IE; if it doesn't, it is in Netscape.

Attaching events to objects in IE is almost the same as in Netscape. Instead of calling the function addEventListener, IE uses the function attachEvent. The event names are also slightly different in that they keep their "on" prefix; for example, a click event is named onclick.

Handling Click Events

Once the browser has been determined, the <BODY> tag has an event handler attached to it named handleClick(). This handler will determine the clicked element and will highlight it if it is a paragraph tag:

```
function handleClick(evt)
{
    var targetNode;

    if (window.event)
        targetNode = window.event.srcElement;
    else
        targetNode = evt.target;

    if (currentNode)
        currentNode.style.backgroundColor = curBackColor;

    var pNode;

    if (targetNode.nodeName != "P")
        pNode = getContainingParaNode(targetNode);
    else
        pNode = targetNode;

    if (pNode) {
```

```
                curBackColor = pNode.style.backgroundColor;
                pNode.style.backgroundColor="#ffff99";
                currentNode = pNode;
        }
        else
                currentNode = null;
}
```

When a click in the document is detected, the handleClick() function is called. The function (again) determines whether the script is in IE or Netscape because the target element is accessed slightly differently in each case. In the Netscape case, the target element is contained in the target property of the event argument passed to the function. In IE, the target element is stored in the srcElement property of the window.event object.

If there is already a selected node in the document, it is first unhighlighted by setting the backgroundColor property of the node's style attribute to a previously saved value. Next, you check to see if the clicked node is a <P> node or is contained within a <P> node by calling the getContainingParaNode() function. If so, the current background color of the node is saved and is changed to be a light yellow color. This node is then set to be the currently selected node.

Finding a Containing Paragraph Node

The getContainingParaNode() method determines if the given node is contained within a paragraph node:

```
function getContainingParaNode(oNode)
{
        var testNode;

        testNode = oNode.parentNode;
        while (testNode)
        {
                if (testNode.nodeName == "P")
                        return testNode;
                testNode = testNode.parentNode;
        }
        return null;
}
```

The function walks up the document hierarchy starting from the given node until it finds a paragraph tag or traverses above the document root. It returns the <P>

node if it finds one, or it returns `null` if the given node is not contained within a `<P>` tag.

This particular example may or may not be useful in all cases. It is primarily intended to provide a working example of one way of giving users a method of marking their current place in the document. Possible customizations of this code include changing the highlight color based upon the clicked element type, using different CSS style rules other than background color, and changing the color of the text itself. Alternative methods might involve outlining the selected paragraph or moving a layer containing a special symbol next to the paragraph tag. You should choose the method most appropriate for your web pages according to your desired design specifications.

Conclusion

In this chapter, you saw several ways of using the DOM to make web pages more usable and approachable by dynamically adapting to the content contained within the page. First, you saw how a document can build a list of bookmarks on-the-fly by searching the content for specially marked tags that indicate where bookmark destinations should be. Next, you saw how to automatically generate a table of contents for a web page by scanning the page for `<H1>` and `<H2>` tags and building a list of links to the tags in the document. Finally, you saw how to help users save their place in a web page by highlighting a portion of the page, making it easy to spot if the user decides to temporarily read another section of the page and then return.

In the next chapter, we'll examine ways of using the DOM to provide more dynamic user interfaces for your web pages that minimize browser-specific coding, such as creating a color picker, implementing in-place list editing, and pop-up menus.

Dynamic User Interfaces

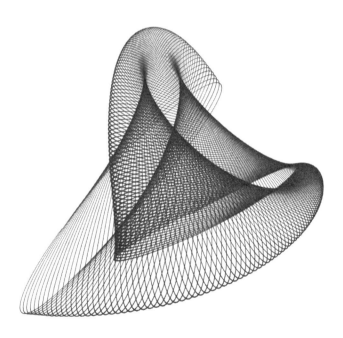

I n Chapter 8, you saw some examples of how to build web pages that can use the DOM to provide automatic navigational aids to users by adapting to a document's content on-the-fly. This is accomplished by reading the structure and content of the page and dynamically configuring some common user interface controls to allow the user to easily move around within the document. These navigation controls, such as tables of contents, bookmarks, and so on, can then be reused across multiple pages.

In this chapter, we'll take a look at how to build web pages with dynamic, interactive, cross-browser user interfaces using the DOM API. We'll start with an example that illustrates how to create a dynamically generated color picker that allows users to interactively select a color. Then we'll look at how to create lists of items that can be edited in-place. Finally, we'll examine how to create pop-up menus using the DOM methods.

Building Dynamic User Interfaces with the DOM

Prior to the DOM, building dynamic, engaging user interfaces for web pages usually meant dealing with Dynamic HTML (DHTML). This, in turn, usually meant dealing with incredible headaches because there was no official standardization between the major browser vendors with respect to their proprietary object models and scripting APIs. As a result, browser-specific code often needed to be created to accomplish the same user interface results in different browsers from different vendors, and sometimes even between different versions of the same browser from one vendor.

Though it still isn't quite seamless to build highly interactive user interfaces using completely browser-independent code today, the situation has improved significantly with the introduction of the latest DOM-capable browsers such as Netscape 6.2 and Internet Explorer 6. In fact, most of the actual document manipulation itself can be accomplished with browser-independent code; it's the interactivity part that's still not quite standardized, such as event processing and style handling. Whereas Netscape 6.2.x faithfully supports the DOM Level 2 Events module, Internet Explorer implements its own event handling system. Even so, processing events across different browsers isn't as hard as it used to be because Internet Explorer at least follows the same general principles as the DOM specification in its event handling APIs, such as event capture and event bubbling.

One of the key benefits of using the DOM instead of DHTML to create web-based user interfaces is that every aspect of the page can be modified by the application, not just the parts of the page that the older DHTML browsers specifically make available for manipulation (such as layers and images). In addition, because the

DOM makes it possible to create entirely new page elements, your applications can achieve user interactions that weren't possible before: elements can come and go, text can change colors and styles, and even forms and form elements can be created and processed dynamically.

Let's begin by taking a look at how to create a color picker user interface.

Creating a Color Picker

One of the more complex user-interface gadgets I've always admired is the color picker. Color pickers usually have several characteristics in common: they display a range of colors from which the user can choose, they display the currently selected color, and they display the color that the mouse is currently over. Using the DOM, you can create a color picker that performs all of these tasks.

Figure 9-1 shows a page that contains a dynamically generated color picker that allows a user to select a color and then displays that color in a box. In addition, as

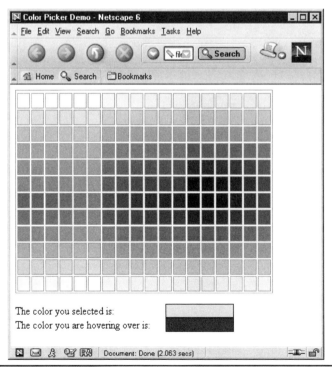

Figure 9-1 *Selecting a color with the color picker*

the mouse is being moved over the picker, the color that the mouse is currently hovering over is also displayed.

Creating the color picker involves three major steps. First, the code generates a table whose cells represent the various background colors. Next, each table cell has the appropriate event handlers registered to detect mouse click and mouse-over events. Finally, the event handlers are written to respond to the events and allow the user to select a color.

Listing 9-1 lists the code for the color picker HTML page.

Listing 9-1   *Color Picker HTML Page*

```
<HTML>
<HEAD>
<TITLE>Color Picker Demo</TITLE>
<SCRIPT SRC="CreateColorPicker.js"></SCRIPT>
</HEAD>

<BODY BGCOLOR="#FFFFFF">
<SCRIPT>
var oBody = document.getElementsByTagName('BODY').item(0);
oBody.insertBefore(createColorTable(),oBody.firstChild);
</SCRIPT>
<P>
<TABLE CELLSPACING="0" CELLPADDING="0" WIDTH="339">
    <TR>
        <TD WIDTH="232">The color you selected is:</TD>
        <TD STYLE="BORDER:1px solid #000000" ID="colorCell"
                WIDTH="105"> </TD>
    </TR>
    <TR>
        <TD WIDTH="232">The color you are hovering over is:</TD>
        <TD STYLE="BORDER:1px solid #000000" ID="hoverCell"
                WIDTH="105"> </TD>
    </TR>
</TABLE>
</BODY>
</HTML>
```

The page includes an external JavaScript file called ColorPicker.js, which contains the code that controls the picker. The body section contains a script that creates the color picker user interface and inserts it as the first child of the body section, along with a static table that displays the selected color and the color that the mouse is hovering over.

Listing 9-2 shows the code that controls the color picker.

Listing 9-2   *CreateColorPicker.js*

```
function createColorTable()
{
    var tableNode = document.createElement("TABLE");
    var oTableHead = document.createElement("THEAD");
    var oTableBody = document.createElement("TBODY");
    var colorArray = new Array("00","33","66","99","CC","FF");
    var i,j;
    var oTR, oTD;
    var colorStr = "";
    var color1,color2,color3;

    tableNode.appendChild(oTableHead);
    tableNode.appendChild(oTableBody);

    tableNode.setAttribute("border","1");
    tableNode.setAttribute("width","400");
    tableNode.setAttribute("id","colorTable");
    for (i=0; i < 6; i++)
    {
        color2 = colorArray[(6-i)-1];
        oTR = document.createElement("TR");
        for (j=0; j < 6; j++)
        {
            color1 = colorArray[5];
            color3 = colorArray[j];
            colorStr = "#"+color1+color2+color3;
            oTR.appendChild(createColorCell(colorStr));
        }
        for (j=0; j < 6; j++)
        {
            color1 = colorArray[3];
            color3 = colorArray[(6-j)-1];
            colorStr = "#"+color1+color2+color3;
            oTR.appendChild(createColorCell(colorStr));
```

```
            }
            for (j=0; j < 6; j++)
            {
                    color1 = colorArray[1];
                    color3 = colorArray[j];
                    colorStr = "#"+color1+color2+color3;
                    oTR.appendChild(createColorCell(colorStr));
            }
            oTableBody.appendChild(oTR);
        }

    for (i=0; i < 6; i++)
    {
            color2 = colorArray[i];
            oTR = document.createElement("TR");
            for (j=0; j < 6; j++)
            {
                    color1 = colorArray[4];
                    color3 = colorArray[j];
                    colorStr = "#"+color1+color2+color3;
                    oTR.appendChild(createColorCell(colorStr));
            }
            for (j=0; j < 6; j++)
            {
                    color1 = colorArray[2];
                    color3 = colorArray[(6-j)-1];
                    colorStr = "#"+color1+color2+color3;
                    oTR.appendChild(createColorCell(colorStr));
            }
            for (j=0; j < 6; j++)
            {
                    color1 = colorArray[0];
                    color3 = colorArray[j];
                    colorStr = "#"+color1+color2+color3;
                    oTR.appendChild(createColorCell(colorStr));
            }
            oTableBody.appendChild(oTR);
        }
    return tableNode;
}

function createColorCell(colorStr)
{
```

```
        oTD = document.createElement("TD");
        oTD.style.backgroundColor=colorStr;
        addClickHandler(oTD,selectColor);
        addMouseOverHandler(oTD,hoverColor);
        oTD.innerHTML = " ";

        return oTD;
}

function addClickHandler(oNode, oFunction)
{
        if (typeof(window.event) != "undefined")
                oNode.attachEvent("onclick",oFunction);
        else
                oNode.addEventListener("click",oFunction,true);
}

function addMouseOverHandler(oNode, oFunction)
{
        if (typeof(window.event) != "undefined")
                oNode.attachEvent("onmouseover",oFunction);
        else
                oNode.addEventListener("mouseover",oFunction,true);
}

function selectColor(evt)
{
        var oTarget;
        if (typeof(window.event) != "undefined")
                oTarget = window.event.srcElement;
        else
                oTarget = evt.currentTarget;

        document.getElementById("colorCell").style.backgroundColor =
                        oTarget.style.backgroundColor;
}

function hoverColor(evt)
{
        var oTarget;
        if (typeof(window.event) != "undefined")
                oTarget = window.event.srcElement;
        else
```

```
            oTarget = evt.currentTarget;

    document.getElementById("hoverCell").style.backgroundColor =
                oTarget.style.backgroundColor;
}
```

The `createColorTable()` function creates a `<TABLE>` node and populates it with 12 rows of 18 cells, each representing a web-safe color. Each table row is generated in 3 groups of 6 cells at a time. As each cell is created, a new color value is computed and assigned to the cell. When it is finished, the table contains 216 colors.

Let's examine the code to see how it works.

Set up the Color Picker User Interface

The `createColorTable()` function begins by creating the TABLE, THEAD, and TBODY nodes that will hold the table structure:

```
var tableNode = document.createElement("TABLE");
var oTableHead = document.createElement("THEAD");
var oTableBody = document.createElement("TBODY");
```

Next, some local variables are declared, including an array of 6 base hexadecimal numbers that will be used to create the RGB colors:

```
var colorArray = new Array("00","33","66","99","CC","FF");
```

The THEAD and TBODY are appended to the TABLE element, and some common table settings are initialized and set as attributes on the table:

```
tableNode.appendChild(oTableHead);
tableNode.appendChild(oTableBody);

tableNode.setAttribute("border","1");
tableNode.setAttribute("width","400");
tableNode.setAttribute("id","colorTable");
```

Now the color cells are generated. In order to achieve a certain continuous tone and look to the table, the cells are generated in a particular pattern. There are 12 rows of colors divided into two groups, consisting of 6 rows each. Within the row groups, there are three groups of cells, each consisting of 6 cells.

For each row group, a TR node is created first, followed by the TDs for the TR. When each TD is created, it is assigned a color by the function createColorCell(). The function takes a single argument, the RGB background color for the cell, and returns a newly created TD node whose background color matches the argument:

```
function createColorCell(colorStr)
{
oTD = document.createElement("TD");
oTD.style.backgroundColor=colorStr;
addClickHandler(oTD,selectColor);
addMouseOverHandler(oTD,hoverColor);
oTD.innerHTML = " ";

return oTD;
}
```

The   entity is required in Netscape 6 so that the table cell will render properly. In addition to setting the background color of the cell, the createColorCell() function assigns click and mouse-over handlers to the TD node. These event handlers allow the user to select a color and display the color that the mouse is hovering over.

Respond to User Events

The selectColor() method is called in response to a mouse click. It extracts the background color from the cell's style and sets the color of the TD with ID "colorCell" in the color selection table to match the selected color:

```
function selectColor(evt)
{
var oTarget;
if (typeof(window.event) != "undefined")
      oTarget = window.event.srcElement;
else
      oTarget = evt.currentTarget;

document.getElementById("colorCell").style.backgroundColor =
          oTarget.style.backgroundColor;
}
```

The `hoverColor()` method performs a similar function, except that it displays the color that the mouse is currently hovering over in the TD with ID "hoverCell" in the color selection table:

```
function hoverColor(evt)
{
var oTarget;
if (typeof(window.event) != "undefined")
     oTarget = window.event.srcElement;
else
     oTarget = evt.currentTarget;

document.getElementById("hoverCell").style.backgroundColor =
          oTarget.style.backgroundColor;
}
```

The end result is a dynamically generated color picker that can be used to allow the user to select a color. This example doesn't make use of the color that the user selects, but doing so would simply require changing the `selectColor()` method to perform whatever function was desired for the newly selected color.

In-Place List Editing

Lists are common in web pages—common enough that the HTML language provides several different list types, such as definition lists, ordered (numbered) lists, and unordered (bulleted) lists. Lists are great for displaying information in a columnar form, especially information that lends itself to list format, such as sorted information. Unfortunately, HTML contains no built-in way for a user to dynamically edit the content of a list. For example, a to-do list application needs to let the user add and delete list items, as well as edit the text description of each item. In addition, the application might allow the user to specify the priority of each to-do item and its required completion date.

You can achieve most of these requirements using standard form controls in DHTML, such as a standard <SELECT> list, along with buttons to add and delete items and an edit field to change the item's content. These types of lists, however, don't have very many formatting options, and they certainly can't display more than one column of information. In addition, indenting subitems is not automatic the way it is with HTML lists, and it requires a bit of a hack to work correctly (each item in the select list needs to be prepended with some spaces to "indent" them in the list).

Building the same interface using the DOM, however, provides a much higher level of interactivity and a richer user experience. Your application can use regular HTML lists and at the same time provide in-place editing of the contents of each list item. Figure 9-2 shows an HTML list with editing controls for changing and deleting the list item, as well as canceling the edit operation.

Let's examine the code involved in creating and controlling the document shown in Figure 9-2. Listing 9-3 shows the code for the document in Figure 9-2.

Listing 9-3   *List Editing Sample Document*

```
<HTML>
<HEAD>
      <TITLE>Untitled Document</TITLE>
      <SCRIPT SRC="ListEditing.js"></SCRIPT>
</HEAD>
<BODY BGCOLOR="#FFFFFF" onLoad='initListEditor("theList")'>
      <H2>List Editing Example</H2>
      Click on a list item to edit or delete it.
      <FORM NAME="form1" METHOD="post" ACTION="">
            <UL id="theList">
                  <LI>New Item</LI>
            </UL>
            <INPUT TYPE="BUTTON" NAME="Button" VALUE="Add New Item"
                                    onClick="addNewItem()">
      </FORM>
</BODY>
</HTML>
```

This HTML page is pretty simple: it contains a form with a basic unordered list and a button for adding new items. The list has an ID attribute named `theList` to make it easier to refer to the node in the script. The page includes an external JavaScript file named ListEditing.js, which contains all of the script code to handle in-place list editing.

There are only two functions that the page needs to call to get the in-place list editing functionality: `initListEditor()` and `addNewItem()`. Everything else is handled directly by the ListEditing script. In this example, the document's `<BODY>` tag has an `onLoad` event handler, which is used to initialize the script code for editing the list. The script calls the `initListEditor()` function, which takes the ID of the script that will support in-place editing. When the user wants to

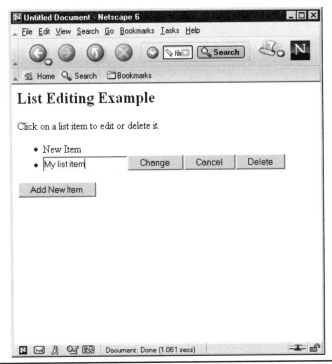

Figure 9-2   *In-place editing of a list item*

add a new item to the list, they click the Add New Item button, which in turn calls the `addNewItem()` function. Listing 9-4 contains the code for ListEditing.js.

Listing 9-4   *ListEditing.js—A Script for In-place List Editing*

```
var gTheList;
var gOldContent="";

function initListEditor(whichList)
{
      // get the list element
      gTheList = document.getElementById(whichList);

      // add the click handler to handle item clicks
      if (typeof(window.event) != "undefined")
          gTheList.attachEvent("onclick", itemClick);
```

```
        else
              gTheList.addEventListener("click", itemClick, true);
}

function itemClick(evt)
{
        var oTarget;
        // get the event target
        if (typeof(window.event) != "undefined")
              oTarget = window.event.srcElement;
        else
              oTarget = evt.target;


        // if the event target was a text node, get its parent LI tag
        if (oTarget.nodeType == 3)
              oTarget = getParentLITag(oTarget);


        if (oTarget && oTarget.nodeName == "LI") {
              // are we already editing another item? If so,
              // remove the current controls and move them to the new
              // item.
              var curEditItem = document.getElementById("itemText");
              if (curEditItem) {
                    var oLItag = getParentLITag(curEditItem);
                    oLItag.innerHTML = gOldContent;
              }
              gOldContent = oTarget.firstChild.data; // save old value
              editListItem(oTarget);
        }
}

// get the parent LI tag for the given node, if it has one.
function getParentLITag(oNode)
{
        var oParent = oNode.parentNode;

        while (oParent)
        {
              if (oParent.nodeName == "LI")
                    return oParent;
              oParent = oParent.parentNode;
        }
        return null;
```

```
}

// adds click handlers to the list item editing buttons
function addClickHandler(oNode, oFunc)
{
    if (typeof(window.event) != "undefined")
        oNode.attachEvent("onclick", oFunc);
    else
        oNode.addEventListener("click", oFunc, true);
}

function addNewItem()
{
    // add a new list item to the list
    var oLINode = document.createElement("LI");
    var oLIText = document.createTextNode("New Item");
    oLINode.appendChild(oLIText);
    gTheList.appendChild(oLINode);
}

function editListItem(oLIItem)
{
    var sTextContent = oLIItem.firstChild.data;

    // create the text field for editing the content
    var oTextField = document.createElement("INPUT");
    oTextField.setAttribute("type","text");
    oTextField.setAttribute("value",sTextContent);
    oTextField.setAttribute("id","itemText");

    // replace the text content of the LI with the textfield
    oLIItem.replaceChild(oTextField,oLIItem.firstChild);

    // add the Change, Cancel, and Delete Buttons
    var oBtnOK = document.createElement("INPUT");
    oBtnOK.setAttribute("type","button");
    oBtnOK.setAttribute("value","  Change  ");
    addClickHandler(oBtnOK, commitEdit);

    var oBtnCancel = document.createElement("INPUT");
    oBtnCancel.setAttribute("type","button");
    oBtnCancel.setAttribute("value","  Cancel  ");
    addClickHandler(oBtnCancel, cancelEdit);
```

```
        var oBtnDEL = document.createElement("INPUT");
        oBtnDEL.setAttribute("type","button");
        oBtnDEL.setAttribute("value","  Delete  ");
        addClickHandler(oBtnDEL, deleteItem);

        // add the buttons to the list
        oLIItem.appendChild(oBtnOK);
        oLIItem.appendChild(oBtnCancel);
        oLIItem.appendChild(oBtnDEL);
}

function commitEdit(evt)
{
        // get the value from the text field
        var oTextField = document.getElementById("itemText");
        // we have to actually refer to the value property here;
        // doing a getAttribute() has no effect in Netscape 6.2
        var sTextContent = oTextField.value;

        // set the innerHTML of the LI to the text.
        // this has the dual purpose of removing the controls.
        oTextField.parentNode.innerHTML = sTextContent;
}

function deleteItem(evt)
{
        // delete the selected list item
        var oTextField = document.getElementById("itemText");
        gTheList.removeChild(oTextField.parentNode);
}

function cancelEdit(evt)
{
        // cancel the current list item being edited
        var oTextField = document.getElementById("itemText");
        oTextField.parentNode.innerHTML = gOldContent;
}
```

The script code for ListEditing.js is broken up into nine separate functions. Each function is responsible for handling one piece of the list editing functionality: initialization, event handling, cleanup, and so on.

The `initListEditor()` function takes one argument, the ID of the list to edit, and calls `getElementById()` to retrieve the node for that list. The script stores that node in a global variable named `gTheList`. It then adds an event handler for click events to the list. IE and Netscape handle events slightly differently, so the script needs to detect which browser is running and call the appropriate API. Because only IE 6 has a window property named `event`, the script tests for the existence of the `window.event` property and calls the `attachEvent()` method if it is present. If not, the script calls the DOM Level 2 Events method `addEventListener()` because that is what Netscape 6 uses. This event handler, named `itemClick()`, will be the one that processes mouse clicks on all of the list items.

When the user clicks a list item, the `itemClick()` event handler method is called. If the function is running under Netscape 6, the function will be called with a single argument, an Event data structure. Under IE, the function is called with no arguments; the global property `window.event` contains all of the event information. The function retrieves the target of the mouse click and stores it in a local variable, `oTarget`. The next line checks to see if the mouse clicked a text element, which would be the text child node of an `<LI>` tag. If so, the `getParentLITag()` function is called to retrieve the corresponding `<LI>` tag of the text node.

Once the `<LI>` tag that was clicked has been determined, the script is ready to create the controls to handle the in-place editing. However, if the controls are already editing another item, they must first be moved to the new item. The script calls `getElementById()` with the `itemText` argument, which is the ID for the edit field. If this returns a non-`null` value, the script calls `getParentLITag()` to retrieve the parent list item for the edit field and resets its `innerHTML` to the contents of the global variable `gOldContent`. The first time the list is clicked, there will be no current list item being edited, so this code will not execute, and thus the `gOldContent` variable does not need to be initialized. Instead, the next line of the script, which sets the content of the `gOldContent` variable to the text content of the `<LI>` tag, will be executed. This variable is used to store away the original contents of the `<LI>` tag in case the user decides to cancel editing the item or clicks another item. Finally, the script calls `editListItem()` with one argument, the LI node that is about to be edited.

The `editListItem()` function begins by retrieving the text content of its child Text node, which will be used to initialize the value of the edit field. Next, the script uses the `createElement()` DOM method to create an `<INPUT>` element for the edit field. The `setAttribute()` method is used to set the `type`, `value`, and `id` attributes for the edit control. The script then calls the `replaceChild()` method on the `<LI>` node to replace the child Text node with the edit field.

Once the edit control has been added, the script creates the Change, Cancel, and Delete buttons by calling the `createElement()` and `setAttribute()` methods. Each button is assigned a click event handler by calling the `addClickHandler()` function, which is a simple utility function that takes a node and assigns a click event handler to it, depending on which browser the script is running under. The Change button is assigned the `commitChange()` handler, the Cancel button is assigned the `cancelEdit()` handler, and the Delete button is assigned the `deleteItem()` handler. Once each button has been created, it is added as a child of the LI node by calling `appendChild()`.

When the `editListItem()` function completes, the controls have all been created and placed in position. Now, the script just needs to handle the button clicks for the item being edited.

The `commitChange()` event handler, which is called when the user clicks the Change button, retrieves the node for the edit control and extracts the value that the user has entered into the control. The script then sets the `innerHTML` attribute of the `<LI>` tag to the text string. This has two purposes: first, it stores the value that the user entered into the control as the new text for the `<LI>` tag. Second, it has the side effect of deleting the controls because the document will be reflowed by the browser when the `innerHTML` property is set.

NOTE

Even though the `innerHTML` property is not part of the official W3C DOM specification, it is supported by both IE 6 and Netscape 6, which makes it safe to use for scripts where you know the code will be used in one of those browsers. In addition, it is often more convenient and practical to use this property than it is to manually set each child node of a given parent.

If the user decides to cancel editing the item by clicking the Cancel button, the `cancelEdit()` function resets the `innerHTML` property of the LI node to the text that was stored in the `gOldContent` variable when the item was first clicked. As in the case of the `commitChange()` function, this sets the text value of the LI tag, as well as deleting the controls.

Deleting an item by clicking the Delete button calls the `deleteItem()` function. The function retrieves the node for the edit control, then gets the parent `<LI>` tag using the `parentNode` property. The script then calls the `removeChild()` DOM method on the global gTheList variable, using the `<LI>` tag as the argument. This effectively removes the list item along with the editing controls.

Adding new items to the list is accomplished with the `addNewItem()` method. This function uses the `createElement()` and `createTextNode()` DOM methods to make a new `<LI>` tag, which is appended to the list being edited via the `appendChild()` method.

A few notes about the ListEditing.js script: first, the script does not do any error checking. If this script were to be used in a real production environment, it would need to be significantly improved with error checking and handling code, such as `ASSERT` statements (see Chapter 7). Also, the script makes several assumptions about the list being edited, such as that the first child item of each `<LI>` tag is a text node. This may not always be the case, and again, this should be checked for in a production setting.

DOM-Based Pop-up Menus

Implementing pop-up menus has always been one of the more complex user interface tasks that web developers have been faced with, usually because making it work across multiple browsers was difficult. Using the DOM together with Cascading Style Sheets (CSS), the task becomes somewhat simpler.

Figure 9-3 shows a web page with a pop-up menu displayed over a hyperlink.

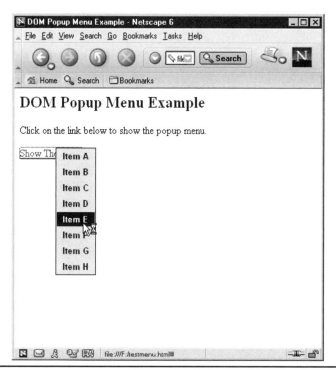

Figure 9-3   *Pop-up menu*

The menu itself is a standard `DIV` element. It starts out invisible in the page and is positioned over the link and made visible when the user clicks the link. When the user moves the mouse off the `DIV`, the menu becomes invisible again.

Each menu item is a separate anchor tag inside the `DIV`. The anchors have an associated CSS style sheet that changes their appearance when the mouse is moved over them. Clicking the item causes the browser to jump to the new URL represented by the link, which may also be a `javascript:` URL that causes a particular action to occur.

Let's examine the code that controls the pop-up menu. Listing 9-5 shows the code for the document in Figure 9-3.

Listing 9-5　*Document with Pop-up Menu*

```
<HTML>
<HEAD>
<TITLE>DOM Popup Menu Example</TITLE>
<SCRIPT SRC="PopupMenu.js"></SCRIPT>
<STYLE TYPE="text/css">
a.menuItemStyle {
  color: #000000;
  border: 0px solid #000000;
  display: block;
  font-family: sans-serif;
  font-size: 10pt;
  font-weight: bold;
  padding: 4px 10px 4px 10px;
  text-decoration: none;
}
a.menuItemStyle:hover {
  background-color: #000000;
  border: 1px solid #ffffff;
  padding: 3px 9px 3px 9px;
  color: #ffffff;
}

.menuStyle {
  background-color: #dddddd;
  border: 1px solid #000000;
  position: absolute;
  left: 0px;
  top: 0px;
```

```
    visibility: hidden;
}
</STYLE>
</HEAD>
<BODY>
<DIV ID="menu1" class="menuStyle">
  <A HREF="#" class="menuItemStyle">Item A</A>
  <A HREF="#" class="menuItemStyle">Item B</A>
  <A HREF="#" class="menuItemStyle">Item C</A>
  <A HREF="#" class="menuItemStyle">Item D</A>
  <A HREF="#" class="menuItemStyle">Item E</A>
  <A HREF="#" class="menuItemStyle">Item F</A>
  <A HREF="#" class="menuItemStyle">Item G</A>
  <A HREF="#" class="menuItemStyle">Item H</A>
</DIV>
<H2>DOM Popup Menu Example</H2>
Click on the link below to show the popup menu.
<P>
  <A HREF="#" onMouseOver="doMenu(event, 'menu1');return false;">
      Show The Menu</A>
</P>
</BODY>
</HTML>
```

The HTML page defines some styles that are used for the menu items and includes a JavaScript file named Pop-upMenu.js, which contains the code that controls the menu behavior. The page defines three CSS styles that govern the appearance of the menus. The first two, menuItemStyle and menuItemStyle:hover, are defined as class selectors of the <A> tag, so you can assign these styles to the anchor tags inside the DIV that defines the menu. In addition, by defining the menuItemStyle:hover style as a :hover pseudostyle for the <A> tag, you get automatic mouse-over functionality. When the mouse moves over the <A> tag, the menuItemStyleOver style will be automatically applied and automatically removed when the mouse moves off it. The third CSS style, menuStyle, defines the basic appearance for the DIV. Its visibility property is initially set to hidden so that the menu will not be visible when the page is first loaded. To make the menu visible, the code toggles this setting.

TIP

The border property of the menuItemStyle's hover pseudoclass is one pixel shorter on each side than the regular menuItemStyle. This is because the hover style includes a 1-pixel white border as the highlight color. The hover border is made smaller to account for this and to avoid an unpleasant redraw effect when the mouse is moved over each item.

The body of the page contains the definition for the `DIV` element that implements the menu. It, in turn, contains eight `<A>` tags, each of which represents a menu item. In this example, the `href` attribute of each `<A>` tag is set to "#" so that the mouse-over functionality will work, but in actual use each menu item's `href` would be set to the URL of the destination page.

The Show The Menu link has an `onClick` handler that displays the menu when clicked. The `return false` part of the handler is needed to keep the browser from trying to follow the link specified by the href attribute. The call to the `doMenu()` function displays the menu. It is contained in the PopupMenu.js code, which is shown in Listing 9-6.

Listing 9-6   *PopupMenu.js*

```
var gMenuOffsetX = 3;
var gMenuOffsetY = 3;

// IE has a native function for this, but Netscape doesn't,
// so we'll use our own version.
function containsNode(containerNode, testNode)
{
  while (testNode.parentNode)
  {
    testNode = testNode.parentNode;
    if (testNode == containerNode)
      return true;
  }
  return false;
}

function doMenu(event, id)
{
  var theNode;
  var menuX, menuY;
```

```
  // get the node that represents the menu
  theNode = document.getElementById(id);

  // in IE, position the menu relative to where the user
  // clicked. Have to take into account the scroll amount
  // of the document's body because that's how IE
  // calculates mouse offsets. On Netscape, just need to
  // include the amount that the window is scrolled.
  if (typeof(window.event)!= "undefined") {
    menuX = window.event.clientX +
                document.documentElement.scrollLeft +
                document.body.scrollLeft;
    menuY = window.event.clientY +
                document.documentElement.scrollTop +
                document.body.scrollTop;
  }
  else {
    menuX = event.clientX + window.scrollX;
    menuY = event.clientY + window.scrollY;
  }
  // start the menu underneath the mouse a little bit.
  menuX -= gMenuOffsetX;
  menuY -= gMenuOffsetY;

  // position the menu by setting the style's left and top
  // CSS selectors. Append the "px" designation.
  theNode.style.top = menuY + "px";
  theNode.style.left = menuX + "px";

  // make the menu visible!
  theNode.style.visibility = "visible";

  // set up an onmouseout handler so the menu will go away
  // when the mouse leaves the DIV.
  theNode.onmouseout = doMouseOut;
}

function doMouseOut(evt)
{
  var curNode;
  var newNode;

  // on IE, retrieve the event information from the "this"
```

```
    // reference to the element and the global window.event
    // property. On Netscape, use the evt argument provided
    // by the browser.
    if (typeof(window.event) != "undefined")
    {
      curNode = this;
      newNode = window.event.toElement;
    }
    else
    {
      curNode = evt.currentTarget;
      newNode = evt.relatedTarget;
    }


    // if the mouseout event occurred in one of the child anchor
    // tags, then we don't want the menu to go away. We only want
    // the menu to disappear when the mouseout event is happening
    // on the DIV element. Here, we check to see if the new element
    // is different from the current event target and make sure
    // that the new element is not contained by the DIV tag.
    if (curNode != newNode && !containsNode(curNode, newNode))
      curNode.style.visibility = "hidden";
}
```

When the doMenu() function is called, the script retrieves the DIV element that represents the menu by calling getElementById() with the ID of the menu:

```
theNode = document.getElementById(id);
```

Next, the script calculates the point at which the upper-left corner of the menu should be displayed. This is done slightly differently for IE and Netscape because IE 6 uses the <BODY> tag as its base reference for calculating mouse offsets when rendering page elements in compatibility mode. When running in standards mode, however, it uses the document element as its base. Fortunately, IE sets the values of the body's scrollOffset fields to zero when using the document element and vice versa, so that the correct measurement is produced, regardless of which mode IE is running in. The offset for the DIV is thus arrived at by adding the coordinates of the mouse click to the scroll offsets of the body and documentElement. In Netscape 6's case, the window property contains the global scroll offsets, so those are added to the mouse click location to arrive at the point where the menu should be displayed. Finally, the menu's location is offset by a few pixels to ensure that it is placed under the mouse pointer:

```
if (typeof(window.event)!= "undefined") {
  menuX = window.event.clientX +
                document.documentElement.scrollLeft +
                document.body.scrollLeft;
  menuY = window.event.clientY +
                document.documentElement.scrollTop +
                document.body.scrollTop;
}
else {
  menuX = event.clientX + window.scrollX;
  menuY = event.clientY + window.scrollY;
}
// start the menu underneath the mouse a little bit.
menuX -= gMenuOffsetX;
menuY -= gMenuOffsetY;
```

Once the position for the menu has been calculated, the menu is moved to its location by setting the top and left properties of the DIV's style:

```
theNode.style.top = menuY + "px";
theNode.style.left = menuX + "px";
```

Next, the menu is made visible by setting the visibility property of the style:

```
theNode.style.visibility = "visible";
```

Finally, the script sets an onMouseOut handler for the DIV so that it will be notified when the mouse leaves the menu. This is done so the menu can be hidden:

```
theNode.style.visibility = "visible";
```

At this point, the menu is visible on the screen, and the user can interact with it using the mouse. As each item is moved over by the mouse, it highlights and unhighlights. When the mouse is moved off the DIV, the doMouseOut() method is called, which hides the menu. First, the menu determines the current target of the event and the new target where the mouse is moving to:

```
if (typeof(window.event) != "undefined")
{
  curNode = this;
```

```
    newNode = window.event.toElement;
}
else
{
  curNode = evt.currentTarget;
  newNode = evt.relatedTarget;
}
```

Next, things get a little tricky. Because the `mouseout` event will be generated for the `DIV`'s child `<A>` tags, it is necessary to make sure that the new element that the mouse is moving to is not the `DIV` itself or one of the `<A>` tags that constitute the menu items. Otherwise, the menu would disappear as soon as you moved the mouse, even if you kept it within the confines of the `DIV` tag!

The solution is to make sure that new target and current targets are different *and* that the new target is not one of the child elements of the `DIV` element. If these conditions are met, the menu is hidden again by setting the visibility property of the style to `hidden`:

```
if (curNode != newNode && !containsNode(curNode, newNode))
  curNode.style.visibility = "hidden";
```

The `containsNode()` method is a utility function that determines whether a node contains another node. Internet Explorer provides a native implementation of this function, but unfortunately Netscape does not, so the script uses its own version. Given the test node and the node that might be the container, the code successively examines each parent of the test node to see if it is the container node:

```
while (testNode.parentNode)
{
  testNode = testNode.parentNode;
  if (testNode == containerNode)
    return true;
}
return false;
```

If the container node is found as one of the ancestors of the test node, the function returns `true`. Otherwise, the top of the document is eventually reached, and the function returns `false`.

Conclusion

In this chapter, you saw how to accomplish some common user interface techniques using the DOM that used to require browser-specific DHTML programming (and in some cases, couldn't even be accomplished with DHTML). First, you saw how to create a web page-based color picker that allows users to select colors from a palette of web-safe color values. This example used mouse-move and click events to update the color selection fields. Next, you examined a new way to provide list editing functionality that allows a user to edit items in a list directly in-place by dynamically creating form controls when the user clicks a list item. Finally, you took a crack at a DOM-oriented solution to a familiar problem: cross-browser pop-up menus, written entirely using the DOM and CSS.

In the next chapter, we'll focus on how to use the DOM to perform client-side data-driven document processing. These techniques can make web pages even more powerful and useful to users because the information contained within them can be processed and manipulated without having to wait for round trips to the server each time. This results in saved bandwidth, improved responsiveness, and a lighter processing load on the server.

Client Processing of
Data-Driven Documents

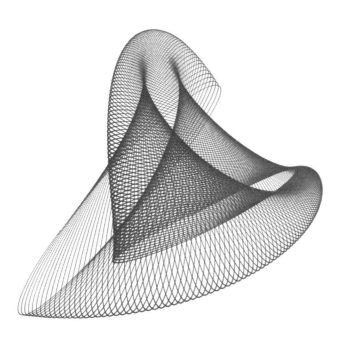

I n Chapters 8 and 9, you saw how to use the DOM to improve the usability of web pages and create more engaging user interfaces than were possible with earlier, DHTML-based scripts. Creating these types of interfaces is made possible mainly because the DOM provides two important capabilities: the ability to access and modify any part of the document, and the ability to create entirely new elements in the document.

In this chapter, we'll examine how to use these DOM capabilities, along with some browser JavaScript code to provide rich, client-side data processing functionality to users of your applications. We'll start by looking at a simple example of sorting a list of items and continue with a more advanced demonstration of sorting any table in a web page. Next, you'll see how to use the DOM to perform what's commonly known as "screen-scraping," in which a browser script post-processes the contents of a server-generated document to provide additional data presentation to the end user. For example, some pages are generated by server-side ASP or JSP scripts, and even though their exact contents cannot be known at design time, your scripts can discover the data contained within the page and perform additional processing on it. Finally, we'll look at how to embed XML data in a web page and use the DOM to create an advanced data-presentation application.

Processing Data-Driven Documents on the Client

By using the DOM to process data directly in the client, your applications can help relieve the workload on the server and provide the user with a much more responsive application. The client will not need to hit the server each time the user wants to manipulate the information in the page, so the round-trip time from the server is eliminated, and data manipulation that would normally be done on the server can be performed locally.

For example, using the DOM, it is entirely possible to provide advanced features such as client-side data sorting, dynamic HTML generation, and advanced data analysis in your web pages. Along with some JavaScript code, your DOM applications can sort tables and lists, perform complex calculations, and even derive new data, all completely on the client. These capabilities become even more powerful when you combine client-side data processing with embedded XML data in your web pages, a capability supported either directly or indirectly by both Netscape Navigator 6.x and Internet Explorer 5 and later. Both Internet Explorer and Netscape allow you to embed XML data fragments, called "data islands," inside web pages. This enables applications to provide advanced data presentation to users by employing standard DOM, CSS, and JavaScript technologies.

Let's begin by taking a look at a common use of client-side data manipulation: data sorting in tables and lists.

Client-Side Sorting

One of the more obvious applications of client-side data processing is the sorting of information. There are all kinds of instances where a user might want to sort the information displayed to them in a web page: listing their credit card transactions by date or amount, sorting lists of data alphabetically, displaying college courses grouped by prerequisite classes and grade level, and so on.

Usually, this kind of data sorting would be performed on the server. Typically, the user clicks a link in the first row of a table column whose URL links to a server-side ASP or JSP script. The server script then sorts the data, regenerates the table (along with the rest of the page), produces the finished document, and retransmits it to the client for display.

That whole round-trip process can take a fairly long time, depending on the amount of processing load on the server at any given moment. In modern DOM-capable browsers, however, implementing the same sorting functionality using the DOM API along with some standard JavaScript is pretty straightforward. Let's look at a simple example of sorting the contents of a list.

Sorting a List

Figure 10-1 shows a sample document containing an ordered list of items representing a grocery shopping list.

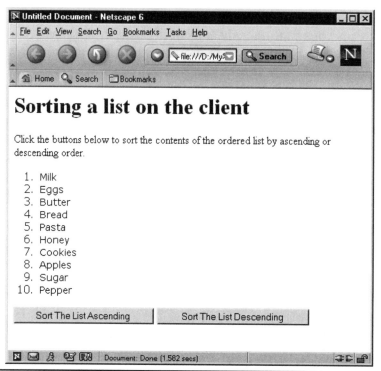

Figure 10-1   *Sample document to be sorted*

The source code for this document is shown in Listing 10-1.

Listing 10-1   *HTML Code for Shopping List Document*

```
<html>
<head>
<title>Untitled Document</title>
<meta http-equiv="Content-Type" content="text/html; charset=iso-8859-1">
<style type="text/css">
<!--
li {        font-family: Verdana, Arial, Helvetica, sans-serif;
            font-size: 14px;
            color: #000000
}
-->
</style>
<script src="SortList.js"></script>
```

```
</head>
<body bgcolor="#FFFFFF" text="#000000">
<h1>Sorting a list on the client</h1>
Click the buttons below to sort the contents of the ordered list
by ascending or descending order.
<ol id="theList">
  <li>Milk</li>
  <li>Eggs</li>
  <li>Butter</li>
  <li>Bread</li>
  <li>Pasta</li>
  <li>Honey</li>
  <li>Cookies</li>
  <li>Apples</li>
  <li>Sugar</li>
  <li>Pepper</li>
</ol>
<input type="button" name="sortBtnAsc" value="Sort The List Ascending"
      onClick="gbAscending = true; sortList('theList')">
<input type="button" name="sortBtnDesc" value="Sort The List Descending"
      onClick="gbAscending = false; sortList('theList')">
</body>
</html>
```

The grocery list page allows the user to sort the list in one of two directions by providing two buttons: one to sort the list in an ascending order, and one for descending order. When the ascending button is clicked, the list sorts the items alphabetically, as shown in Figure 10-2.

When they are clicked, each of the two buttons in the document performs two JavaScript actions. First, each sets a global variable, gbAscending, to indicate whether the list is being sorted in an ascending or descending order. Then, each calls the sortList() function with the ID of the list node to be sorted. The code to perform the sorting is contained in the SortList.js JavaScript file, shown in Listing 10-2.

Listing 10-2   *SortList.js—Sorting a List*

```
var gbAscending = true;
function sortList(sListID)
{
   var oListToSort = document.getElementById(sListID);

   // retrieve the LI tags in the list
   var listItems = oListToSort.getElementsByTagName("LI");
```

```
// store a count of the number of LI tags
var numItems = listItems.length;
// create an array the same size as the number of tags.
// this will hold the sorted results.
var aStrings = new Array(numItems);

// build the array of strings to sort
for (var i=0; i < numItems; i++) {
   aStrings[i] = new String(listItems.item(i).firstChild.data);
}
// sort the list using JavaScript's built-in sorting function.
// Pass our custom callback function as the argument to do the
// actual sorting of the data.
aStrings.sort(sortCallBack);

// once the list has been sorted, replace the list items
// with the sorted ones by replacing the text of each
// list item with the contents of the sorted array.
for (var i=0; i < numItems; i++) {
   var newLIText = document.createTextNode(aStrings[i]);
   listItems.item(i).replaceChild(
      newLIText,listItems.item(i).firstChild);
}
}

function sortCallBack(a,b)
{
   if (a < b)
      return gbAscending ? -1 : 1;
   else if (a > b)
      return gbAscending ? 1 : -1;
   else return 0;
}
```

Prepare the Data for Sorting

The `sortList()` function begins by calling document.`getElementById()` to
retrieve the node for the list to be sorted:

```
var oListToSort = document.getElementById(sListID);
```

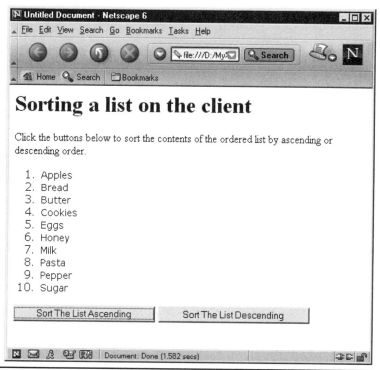

Figure 10-2   *List sorted in ascending order*

Once the list has been located in the page, the script uses the
`getElementsByTagName()` method to get the list of `<LI>` tags for the list
node and stores the number of tags in a local variable to use as a loop control.

```
var listItems = oListToSort.getElementsByTagName("LI");
var numItems = listItems.length;
```

To make the sorting easier, you're going to take advantage of JavaScript's built-in
array sorting functionality. There are two reasons for doing it this way, rather than
sorting the data manually. The first is that the JavaScript Array class provides built-in
sorting functionality via the `sort()` method. The second is to prevent screen flicker
during the sorting process. If you just sorted the list in-place by rearranging the table
row nodes, the user would see the list as it was being rearranged, which, in the case
of large list, would be noticeable. To prevent this from happening, you can store the
data in a temporary array, sort it there, and then replace the list contents all at once.

Of course, there's no reason you can't use a custom sorting algorithm to accomplish the same thing—this way just keeps the example simple and takes advantage of the increased performance of JavaScript engine's platform-native sorting code.

To do this, the code needs to store the contents of each list item in a temporary array and then call the Array class's `sort()` method. The script first creates an array the same size as the number of `<LI>` tags:

```
var aStrings = new Array(numItems);
```

Next, the script needs to store the contents of each `<LI>` tag's child text node in the array so they can be sorted. To do this, the script extracts the contents of the `<LI>` tag's child text node, creates a JavaScript String object for it, and inserts it into the array:

```
for (var i=0; i < numItems; i++) {
    aStrings[i] = new String(listItems.item(i).firstChild.data);
}
```

Performing the Sort

Once the array has been filled with the text data, it just needs to be sorted. The JavaScript Array class has a built-in method, `sort()`, that sorts the contents of the array. It accepts one argument, which is the name of a callback function that will be used to compare the items in the array and tell the JavaScript engine which one is "larger" than the other. JavaScript then uses this information to sort the items in the array. If the function returns a number greater than 0, the first argument will sort before the second argument. If the function returns a value less than 0, the second argument will sort before the first one. If the function returns 0, the two items are equal.

The script invokes the array's sorting method by calling the `sort()` function:

```
aStrings.sort(sortCallBack);
```

The callback function is named `sortCallBack()`, and it accepts two arguments. When called by the JavaScript engine, each of the two arguments will represent a string in the array. The function uses the global variable `gbAscending` to determine whether the user has selected ascending or descending sorting, and it compares each string to determine its sort order:

```
if (a < b)
    return gbAscending ? -1 : 1;
else if (a > b)
```

```
        return gbAscending ? 1 : -1;
else return 0;
```

Here, the comparison function uses the standard greater-than (<) and less-than (>) operators to compare the strings, which compares them using ASCII values. The benefit of this is that you don't have to write separate code to compare strings and numbers.

Replacing the Original Data with the Sorted Data

After the `sort()` method has compared all of the items, the contents of the array will be rearranged to reflect the new sorting. All that is left to do is replace the contents of the list's `<LI>` tags with the newly sorted array contents. The script iterates over each item in the array, creates a new text node for the string in each item, and calls `replaceChild()` on each `<LI>` tag in the list to replace the `<LI>` tag's existing text node (which is the `firstChild`) with the new one:

```
for (var i=0; i < numItems; i++) {
    var newLIText = document.createTextNode(aStrings[i]);
    listItems.item(i).replaceChild(newLIText,listItems.item(i).firstChild);
}
```

Sorting a Table

A slightly more complex example involves sorting a table. In this case, you want to provide the user with the ability to sort each table column in ascending and descending order by clicking a link in the top row of each column, just as they would in a web page that used server-side sorting.

To illustrate, let's take the same document as in the list sorting example, modified by adding prices to each of the items on the shopping list and displaying it as a table, as shown in Figure 10-3.

Here, the user has the option to sort either column in ascending or descending order by clicking one of the links in the table header. The source HTML for this document is shown in Listing 10-3:

Listing 10-3   *HTML Source for Table-Based Shopping List Document*

```
<html>
<head>
<title>Untitled Document</title>
<style type="text/css">
<!--
```

```
th,td {          font-family: Verdana, Arial, Helvetica, sans-serif;
            font-size: 18px;
            color: #000000
}
-->
</style>
<script src="SortTable.js"></script>
</head>
<body bgcolor="#FFFFFF" text="#000000">
<h1>Sorting a table on the client</h1>
<table border="1" cellpadding="2" id="theList">
  <thead>
      <tr>
      <th>
            Item (<a href="#"
              onClick="javascript:sortTable('theList',0,true);return false;"
               >Asc</a>)
            (<a href="#"
              onClick="javascript:sortTable('theList',0,false);return false;"
             >Desc</a>)
      </th>
      <th>
            Price (<a href="#"
              onClick="javascript:sortTable('theList',1,true);return false;"
              >Asc</a>)
            (<a href="#"
              onClick="javascript:sortTable('theList',1,false);return false;"
              >Desc</a>)
      </th>
      </tr>
  </thead>
  <tbody>
  <tr>
      <td>Milk</td>
      <td>1.99</td>
  </tr>
  <tr>
      <td>Eggs</td>
      <td>2.29</td>
  </tr>
  <tr>
      <td>Butter</td>
      <td>3.49</td>
  </tr>
  <tr>
      <td>Bread</td>
      <td>0.99</td>
```

```
   </tr>
   <tr>
      <td>Pasta</td>
      <td>1.19</td>
   </tr>
   <tr>
      <td>Honey</td>
      <td>4.39</td>
   </tr>
   <tr>
      <td>Cookies</td>
      <td>2.99</td>
   </tr>
   <tr>
      <td>Apples</td>
      <td>0.59</td>
   </tr>
   <tr>
      <td>Sugar</td>
      <td>1.78</td>
   </tr>
   <tr>
      <td>Pepper</td>
      <td>1.56</td>
   </tr>
   </tbody>
</table>
</body>
</html>
```

The table contains both a <THEAD> and <TBODY> section, which will make it easier to sort (because you're only interested in the contents of the TBODY node). Note that both IE and Netscape assume the presence of the TBODY node, regardless of whether the actual HTML source contains one, so you should include one in your tables to reduce any confusion that may arise over which table child node you are working with.

The <THEAD> contains two columns, each containing a label ("Item" and "Price") and two links. Each link allows the user to sort the corresponding column in an ascending or descending fashion. The links each have an HREF attribute that contains JavaScript code to call the sortTable() function. The sortTable() function is called with a different set of parameters depending upon the link that is clicked: the ID of the table, the index of the column to sort, and whether to sort

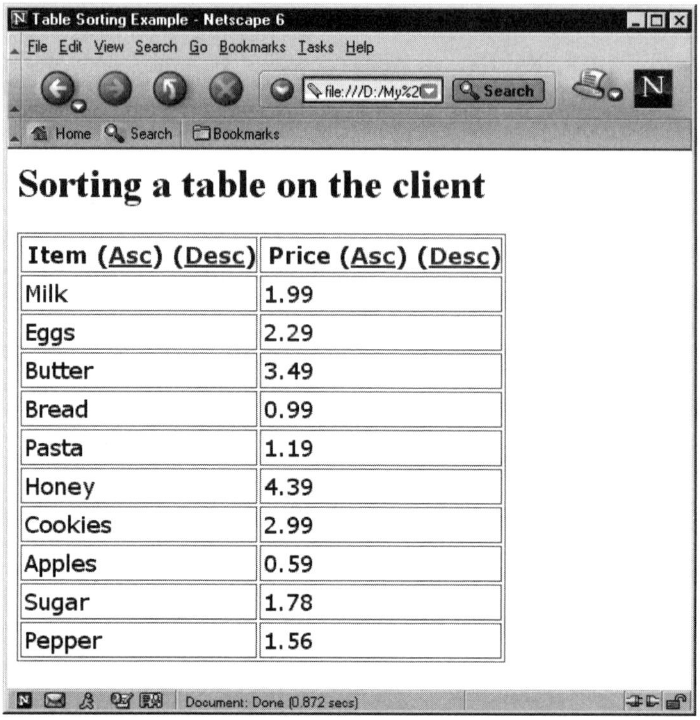

Figure 10-3 *The shopping list document presented as a table with items and prices*

ascending (`true`) or descending (`false`). The code to sort the table is shown in Listing 10-4.

Listing 10-4   *SortTable.js*

```
var gbAscending = true;
var gbCol = 0;
function sortCallBack(a,b)
{
    // each of the arguments passed to this function is a TR node
    // with one or more child TD nodes.
    // get the child node of each TR element that corresponds
    // to the column to be sorted.
    var col1 = a.getElementsByTagName("TD")[gbCol];
    var col2 = b.getElementsByTagName("TD")[gbCol];
```

```
        // now get the text node for each col
        var text1 = col1.firstChild.data;
        var text2 = col2.firstChild.data;

        // now that we have the text nodes, do the sorting
        if (text1 < text2)
                return gbAscending ? -1 : 1;
        else if (text1 > text2)
                return gbAscending ? 1 : -1;
        else return 0;
}


function sortTable(whichTable, whichCol, sortDir)
{
        // Find the table to be sorted
        var oTable = document.getElementById(whichTable);
        // begin by getting the node for the TBODY because that
        // node contains all the rows to be sorted
        var oTBody = oTable.getElementsByTagName('TBODY')[0];
        // get all of the TR tags within the tbody
        var aTRows = oTBody.getElementsByTagName('TR');
        // store the length of the TR array
        var numRows = aTRows.length;

        gbAscending = sortDir;
        gbCol = whichCol;

        // make an array to hold each TR tag in the body.
        var theSortedRows = new Array(numRows);

        // copy each TR tag into the array. Do a "deep clone" on
        // each TR so that all of the child TD tags come along
        // with it.
        var i;
        for (i=0; i < numRows; i++) {
                theSortedRows[i] = aTRows[i].cloneNode(true);
        }

        // now -- sort the array!
        theSortedRows.sort(sortCallBack);

        // now that the array has been sorted, we put back all of the
        // table rows that we had copied out earlier.
```

```
        // First, get rid of the current TBODY.
        oTable.removeChild(oTBody);
        // make a new one in its place
        oTBody = document.createElement("TBODY");
        oTable.appendChild(oTBody);
        // now copy in all of the sorted TR tags
        for (i=0; i< numRows; i++) {
                oTBody.appendChild(theSortedRows[i]);
        }
}
```

The `sortTable()` function works similarly to the `sortList()` function in the previous example, with some notable exceptions. First, when sorting a table, it is necessary to rearrange all of the rows for each of the columns in the table, not just for the column being sorted. In the list example, all the code had to keep track of was the contents of each `<LI>` tag. Here it's a little more complex because the code needs to keep track of the entire row contents. Second, when sorting the list, it was okay to process all of the list's child nodes because they were all `<LI>` tags. In the case of the table, there are some child nodes of the table tag that need to be left alone, such as the header section. This job is made somewhat easier because the two sections of the table are divided into `<THEAD>` and `<TBODY>` sections.

Prepare the Data for Sorting

Just as in the list sorting example, the `sortTable()` function begins by gathering some necessary information about the table to be sorted. The first argument, `whichTable`, is the ID of the table to be sorted. The function calls `getElementById()` to find the table node with the given ID:

```
var oTable = document.getElementById(whichTable);
```

Next, the function retrieves the TBODY node for the table because that section contains the nodes for the rows that need to be sorted. Once the TBODY has been found, its child `<TR>` tags are retrieved, and the number of rows is stored in a local variable:

```
var oTBody = oTable.getElementsByTagName('TBODY')[0];
var aTRows = oTBody.getElementsByTagName('TR');
var numRows = aTRows.length;
```

The `sortTable()` code then sets the `gbAscending` global variable just as in the list sorting example, but in this case also remembers which column is being sorted by storing the index of the column in `gbCol`:

```
gbAscending = sortDir;
gbCol = whichCol;
```

Now an array is created to hold all of the TR nodes. This is the array that will be sorted:

```
var theSortedRows = new Array(numRows);
```

After the array has been created, each <TR> tag is copied into it using the `clone()` method of the DOM's Node interface. The clone is performed as a deep copy, so that all of the TR node's child nodes, such as the TD and Text nodes, are copied as well. This will minimize the amount of code needed to replace the original data with the sorted data later:

```
var i;
for (i=0; i < numRows; i++) {
      theSortedRows[i] = aTRows[i].cloneNode(true);
}
```

After the array has been filled with the TR nodes, the `sort()` method is called for the array. As in the list sorting example, the only argument is the name of the callback function to perform the actual sorting:

```
theSortedRows.sort(sortCallBack);
```

Performing the Sort

The Array class's `sort()` method will repeatedly call the `sortCallBack()` function that it was given as an argument to compare two items together. In the list sorting example, this was easy because each item in the array was just a JavaScript string that could be compared to another string. In the case of the table sorting, however, each item will be a document fragment consisting of a TR node with a number of TD and Text child nodes.

To compare each item, the `sortCallBack()` function retrieves the <TD> tag representing the column that is being sorted from each of the TR nodes. It does this by using the `gbCol` global variable to index the TD array for each TR:

```
var col1 = a.getElementsByTagName("TD")[gbCol];
var col2 = b.getElementsByTagName("TD")[gbCol];
```

After extracting the <TD> tag, the function retrieves the text from the Text node child of the column:

```
var text1 = col1.firstChild.data;
var text2 = col2.firstChild.data;
```

Now, the function can perform the comparison function, just as in the list sorting example. If the function returns > 0, the first argument will sort before the second argument. If the function returns < 0, the second argument will sort before the first one. If the function returns 0, the two items are equal:

```
if (text1 < text2)
       return gbAscending ? -1 : 1;
else if (text1 > text2)
       return gbAscending ? 1 : -1;
else return 0;
```

After all of the items have been compared, the array of TR nodes will have been rearranged into the proper order for the selected column.

Replace the Original Data with the Sorted Data

Once the <TR> tags have all been sorted, the only remaining task is to copy them back into the table structure. This is a little trickier than the list example because you're replacing an entire structure of nodes and not just a text string. To make things a little easier, the code removes any existing <TBODY> tag and replaces it with a new, empty one:

```
oTable.removeChild(oTBody);
oTBody = document.createElement("TBODY");
oTable.appendChild(oTBody);
```

Once the <TBODY> has been replaced, the function iterates over the array of sorted <TR> tags and appends each one, child tags and all, to the new <TBODY>:

```
for (i=0; i< numRows; i++) {
       oTBody.appendChild(theSortedRows[i]);
}
```

That's it! The new table rows are in place, and the screen is updated to show the newly sorted table.

Post-Processing Server-Generated Documents

So far, the examples you've seen have all dealt with static HTML pages whose contents were known at the time the processing script was written. However, there will be times when your application will need to perform post-processing of documents that were created by a script on the server. For example, you might segment your application to split the responsibilities for the data presentation between the server, which will extract data from a database and generate the basic HTML, and the client, which will perform data transformation and display locally. This type of technique is often referred to as "screen-scraping," which means post-processing data that has already been generated for presentation by another source.

Let's use the document in Listing 10-5 as an example of the kinds of post-processing you can do within the client. This listing contains a table that represents the closing prices of the stock ticker for an imaginary company, JOEM, for seven days. Assume that this document was created by a server-side script that reads the prices from a database and generates the raw HTML output for display in the browser.

Listing 10-5   *Server-Generated HTML Page*

```
<html>
<head>
<title>Screen Scraping Example</title>
<script src="CalcStockData.js"></script>
</head>
<body bgcolor="#FFFFFF" onLoad="calcStockData('stockData')">
<table id="stockData" border="1" width="193">
     <thead>
     <tr>
          <th colspan="2">JOEM Historical Prices</th>
     </tr>
     <tr>
          <th>Date</th>
          <th>Price</th>
     </tr>
     </thead>
     <tbody>
     <tr>
          <td>4-1-02</td>
          <td>25.35</td>
     </tr>
     <tr>
          <td>4-2-02</td>
```

```
                <td>28.02</td>
        </tr>
        <tr>
                <td>4-3-02</td>
                <td>31.45</td>
        </tr>
        <tr>
                <td>4-4-02</td>
                <td>29.34</td>
        </tr>
        <tr>
                <td>4-5-02</td>
                <td>27.10</td>
        </tr>
        <tr>
                <td>4-6-02</td>
                <td>24.00</td>
        </tr>
        <tr>
                <td>4-7-02</td>
                <td>25.35</td>
        </tr>
        </tbody>
</table>
<p>Share Price Calculations:</p>
<form>
        <table border="0" width="337">
                <tr>
                        <td>The highest closing price was:</td>
                        <td>
                                <input type="text" name="txtHigh" id="txtHighField">
                        </td>
                </tr>
                <tr>
                        <td>The lowest closing price was: </td>
                        <td>
                                <input type="text" name="txtLow" id="txtLowField">
                        </td>
                </tr>
                <tr>
                        <td>The average 7-day price was:</td>
                        <td>
                                <input type="text" name="txtAvg" id="txtAvgField">
                        </td>
                </tr>
        </table>
```

```
</form>
</body>
</html>
```

Suppose further that you wanted to perform some post-processing on the document, such as calculating the high and low closing prices for the week, along with the average stock price over the seven-day time frame. The results would then be displayed in a results table below the stock table, as shown in Figure 10-4.

To accomplish this, you would need to extract the data from the raw HTML and perform the calculations on the client side. The JavaScript code in Listing 10-6 calculates the low and high prices and the seven-day average and inserts the results into the text form fields in the results table.

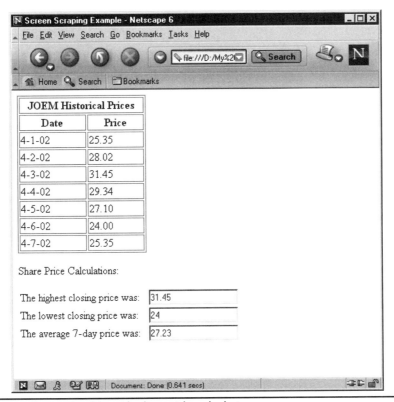

Figure 10-4   *The stock table with client-side calculations*

Listing 10-6 *CalcStockData.js*

```
function calcStockData(idTable)
{
  var highPrice=0.0, lowPrice=100000.0, avgPrice=0.0;
  var oTable = document.getElementById(idTable);
  var i=0;

  // get the rows from the table body
  var oBODY = oTable.getElementsByTagName('TBODY')[0];
  var aTRs = oBODY.getElementsByTagName('TR');
  for (i=0; i < aTRs.length; i++)
  {
    // for each row, get the price for the day
    var thePrice =

parseFloat(aTRs[i].getElementsByTagName('TD')[1].firstChild.data);
    if (thePrice < lowPrice)
      lowPrice = thePrice;
    if (thePrice > highPrice)
      highPrice = thePrice;
    avgPrice += thePrice;
  }
  // store the results in the table
  document.getElementById("txtHighField").value=highPrice;
  document.getElementById("txtLowField").value=lowPrice;
  avgPrice = avgPrice/7.0;
  avgPrice = Math.round(avgPrice*100.0)/100.0;
  document.getElementById("txtAvgField").value=avgPrice;
}
```

The `calcStockData()` function is called by the `<BODY>` tag's `onLoad` handler, which passes the ID of the table to extract the data from. In this case, the data is not very complex—it's just a series of dates and floating-point numbers, but it's not hard to imagine more complex examples where the required data is buried within a long string of text, such as a phone number, a postal code, or an employee number. In such cases, it is not uncommon to have to use regular expression (RegExp) syntax to extract the required data from the text.

Here, the `calcStockData()` function extracts the stock price from the table using the native JavaScript function `parseFloat()`, which takes a string argument and returns a floating-point number represented by the string. You know that the only contents of the cell will be a floating-point number, so extracting it is easy. If the text were prepended with a $ sign or some other text, the code would need to strip off the extraneous information to get the price datum (again, probably using a regular expression). The function uses this value to record the highest and lowest prices it finds, and calculates a seven-day average price using the `Math.round()` function to round the number to two decimal places.

Once the necessary data has been calculated, the function uses the `getElementById()` method to retrieve the text field objects and set their contents to the calculated high, low, and average price values.

Working with Embedded XML Data in Web Pages

The potential power of client-side data processing becomes even more evident when combined with embedded XML. Both Internet Explorer and Netscape Navigator allow XML code fragments to be embedded directly in a web page or referenced from an external XML file. DOM applications can use these XML data "islands" to provide true data-driven web pages entirely on the client browser.

NOTE

There is currently no accepted W3C standard for working with embedded XML in HTML web pages, although Microsoft is working with the W3C to define one. There is no word yet on if or when this will be adopted as an official W3C recommendation, but stay tuned.

A data island is a section of XML code that is either directly embedded within the web page (called "inline" XML) or referenced via a separate XML file (called "external" XML). For example, the following code fragment illustrates an inline XML data island embedded in the body section of an HTML file:

```
<body>
<xml id="myDataIsland">
   <people>
      <person>
         <name>John</name>
      </person>
   <person>
      <name>Paul</name>
   </person>
   <person>
      <name>George</name>
```

```
    </person>
    <person>
        <name>Ringo</name>
    </people>
</xml>
</body>
```

Once XML data has been embedded in a web page, it can be used to generate HTML to present that data. For example, the XML data island listed previously might appear in a web page as an HTML table or as the contents of a select list, as shown in Figure 10-5.

In this section, you'll examine how to embed XML data in web pages that will work across multiple browsers, and you'll see how to write DOM code to manipulate the XML information and build HTML to display the data.

Let's begin by taking a look at the XML support currently provided by Internet Explorer 6, which provides robust built-in support for data islands.

Data Islands in Internet Explorer

Internet Explorer provides native support for XML data islands, along with several methods for working with them. For example, IE allows certain types of HTML elements to be "bound" to XML data islands for automatic data-driven HTML code generation. When the page is viewed in the browser, Internet Explorer automatically populates the HTML element with the data from the associated XML data island. In addition, IE supports using XSLT to transform the XML data island into HTML.

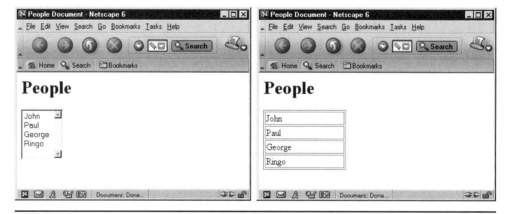

Figure 10-5   *XML as an HTML select list (left) and as an HTML table (right)*

Data islands can be defined in Internet Explorer as either inline or external. Inline data islands embed their XML code directly within the page. External data islands reference an external XML source, just as an < IMG > tag points to its image source file.

Inline Data Islands

To define an inline XML data island in Internet Explorer, your application needs to enclose the XML code within an <XML> tag. This XML tag is then assigned a unique ID that can be used to refer to the element throughout the document and bind the island to an HTML element that supports data binding. Listing 10-7 shows a sample HTML page with an embedded XML data island, along with an HTML table that uses the data island to populate the table cells.

Listing 10-7   *HTML Document with an XML Data Island*

```
<html>
<head>
      <title>Inline XML Sample Document</title>
</head>
<body bgcolor="#FFFFFF">
<xml id="myDataIsland">
<people>
      <person>
            <name>John</name>
      </person>
      <person>
            <name>Paul</name>
      </person>
      <person>
            <name>George</name>
      </person>
      <person>
            <name>Ringo</name>
      </person>
</people>
</xml>
</body>
</html>
```

The XML tag identifies an individual section of XML within the HTML document and uses the ID myDataIsland to assign the island a unique ID within the page. This ID attribute can be used to bind the XML data island to a data-driven HTML tag in IE 5 and later versions (discussed shortly).

The XML element is parsed and stored within the DOM document tree just as any other element is, so you can use the DOM to interact with the contents of the data island. For example, to count the number of `<person>` tags within the data island, you can use code like the following, which will produce an alert displaying the number 4:

```
var xmlDoc = document.getElementById('myDataIsland');
var tagList = xmlDoc.getElementsByTagName('person');
alert (tagList.length);
```

External Data Islands

In addition to specifying an XML data island inline, the XML tag can refer to an external XML document using the SRC attribute. The syntax for this is

```
<XML ID="myDataIsland" SRC="http://localhost/docs/myxmldoc.xml"></XML>
```

The URL for the SRC attribute can be either a local file, as in the previous example, or it can be a path to an XML file on a remote computer. Using this type of syntax, the XML document can be kept independent of the HTML page, which allows for easier updating of the document's data.

Using Data-Bound Controls

Internet Explorer supports binding XML data islands directly to certain types of HTML constructs, such as tables. This is accomplished by using the `dataSrc` and `dataFld` attributes of the HTML element that you want to bind the data to. The `dataSrc` attribute refers to the data island's ID attribute, preceded by a hash symbol (#). For example, to bind an HTML table to the XML data island myDataIsland, the syntax would be as follows:

```
<table dataSrc="#myDataIsland">
... table contents ...
</table>
```

NOTE

This only works on the Windows version of Internet Explorer. Data-bound controls do not work in the Macintosh version of IE.

To refer to a specific field of the data within the table, you use the `dataFld` attribute. For example, to create a span of text containing the value of a certain field within the XML, the syntax is as follows:

```
<span dataFld="name"></span>
```

When the two are put together, IE generates some basic HTML output containing the data for the island. Listing 10-8 shows Listing 10-7 modified to include a data-bound table.

Listing 10-8   *Binding XML Data to an HTML Table*

```
<html>
<head>
     <title>Inline XML Sample Document</title>
</head>
<body bgcolor="#FFFFFF">
<!-- The XML data for the page -->
<xml id="myDataIsland">
<people>
     <person>
          <name>John</name>
     </person>
     <person>
          <name>Paul</name>
     </person>
     <person>
          <name>George</name>
     </person>
     <person>
          <name>Ringo</name>
     </person>
</people>
</xml>
<table width="50%" dataSrc="#myDataIsland" border="1">
     <tr>
          <td><span dataFld="name"></span></td>
     </tr>
</table>
</body>
</html>
```

The table tag in the body section binds itself to the data island using this ID attribute as the value of a dataSrc attribute, preceded by a # character. The dataSrc attribute is available on a variety of HTML constructs within IE, such as tables, select lists, frames, layers, and so on.

Once the table has been bound to a data source, it is populated by using an HTML element that supports the dataFld property, which refers to an individual field within the XML data. In this example, the XML data island has the <people> tag as its document element because it is the root node. Under the root node, there are several <person> tags, each of which represent the series of data "records" within the data island. Each of these records has one field, <name>, which represents the person's name. Thus, to fill the table with the names of the people, the TD of the table must refer to the name field of each record. However, TDs cannot be bound directly to data because they don't support the dataFld property, so an element that does must be enclosed within the TD, such as a SPAN. Each TD will then be looped over using each successive record in the XML island to fill out the table with data.

When this document is viewed in Internet Explorer, the table is populated with all of the data records for the XML data island, as shown in Figure 10-6.

More information on using XML data islands within Internet Explorer can be found on Microsoft's developer network website at http://msdn.microsoft.com/ (search on the term "XML Data Islands"—it will provide more than enough hits to start with).

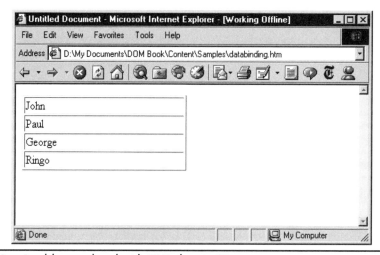

Figure 10-6   *A table populated with XML data in IE*

Data Islands in Netscape Navigator

Unfortunately, Netscape Navigator does not provide native support for data islands the same way that Internet Explorer does. However, you can emulate much of the same functionality in Netscape by using a few tricks and some custom JavaScript code.

Inline Data Islands

Let's take a look at what happens when you try to view the document in Figure 10-7 inside Netscape 6.2.

Although Netscape correctly parses the contents of the XML tag, it also renders the contents of the tag directly into the page instead of ignoring them. To prevent this from happening, you can enclose the XML data island inside an invisible DIV tag, as shown in Listing 10-9.

Listing 10-9 *Hiding a Data Island Inside an Invisible DIV*

```
<div id="xmlLayer1" style="position:absolute; width:0px; height:0px;
     z-index:1; visibility: hidden">
<xml id="myDataIsland">
<people>
     <person>
          <name>John</name>
     </person>
     ... more XML tags ...
</people>
</xml>
</div>
```

Now, when you view the file in Netscape 6, the XML data island will be invisible, hidden within the DIV layer. This technique does not interfere with Internet Explorer, which still correctly finds the data island when bound to an HTML element.

External Data Islands

Netscape also does not provide any native support for external data islands the way the IE does. However, you can use the DOM's createDocument() method along with the Document object's load() function to simulate this behavior. The

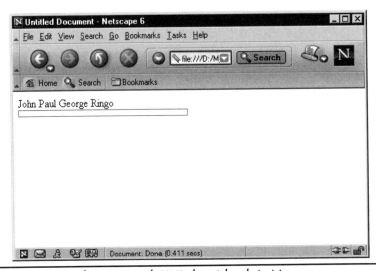

Figure 10-7   *Viewing a document with XML data islands in Netscape*

load() method of the document object was added by Netscape for compatibility with Microsoft. It takes a single argument, a URL to a document to be loaded. The load() method is asynchronous; that is, it will return control back to your script before the document has finished loading. To detect when the document has finished loading, you must use an event listener to listen for the load event.

The loading process is done in two steps. First, your script creates the document using the createDocument() method, which is found on the DOMImplementation interface (note that createDocument is a DOM Level 2 method). After the document has been created, you can call the load() method on it. When the load event listener fires, the document has been loaded into memory, and your script can begin processing it. The following code fragment illustrates the whole process:

```
// create the document
var myXMLDoc = document.implementation.createDocument("","myDoc",null);
// attach a "load" event listener
myXMLDoc.addEventListener("load",docLoaded,false);
// now load the document
myXMLDoc.load("myxmldoc.xml");

function docLoaded(evt)
{
    // do whatever processing is required
    alert(doc.documentElement.nodeName);
}
```

Example: Joe's Cafe Menu Application

In this example, we'll take what you've learned so far in this chapter and put it to use in a simple but practical application. You'll develop a web page for a fictional restaurant, Joe's Café, that displays the restaurant's menu and provides a variety of functions for the user. The web page visitor can view menu items from which to order and select items from the menu to find out what a hypothetical order would cost. In addition, the user can highlight items that are suitable for vegetarians.

The Menu Page

Figure 10-8 shows the HTML page that the user is presented with when using the Joe's Café Menu application.

The menu page allows the user to calculate what the total would be for a hypothetical meal before they even set foot in the restaurant. The tip calculator uses the bill total to figure a tip based on a user-selectable tip percentage. The content filter allows the user to highlight dishes that are suitable for people who are vegetarians. Listing 10-10 shows the code for the HTML portion of the page.

Listing 10-10   *HTML Source for the Menu Page*

```html
<html>
<head>
<title>Joe's Cafe Menu</title>
<meta http-equiv="Content-Type" content="text/html; charset=iso-8859-1">
<style type="text/css">
<!--
th.Title {
   font-family: Georgia, "Times New Roman", Times, serif;
   font-size: 24px; color: #663300 }
th.Column {
   font-family: Georgia, "Times New Roman", Times, serif;
   font-size: 14px; color: #663300 }
td {  font-family: Georgia, "Times New Roman", Times, serif;
   font-size: 14px; color: #000000 }
-->
</style>
<script language="JavaScript" src="MenuApp.js">
</script>
</head>
<body bgcolor="#FFFFFF" text="#000000"
     onLoad="initialize('menuTable','cafeMenuXML');
```

```
            document.forms[0].txtBillAmt.value=calculateBill('menuTable');
            ">
<!-- ( XML Code within invisible DIV tag goes here ...) -->
<h1>Welcome to Joe's Cafe</h1>
<p>Select your entrees from the menu below. To calculate the amount
      of the bill, click the Calculate Bill button. Check the
      &quot;Highlight Vegetarian meals&quot; box to highlight
      vegetarian dishes.</p>
<table id="menuTable" width="75%" border="1">
      <thead>
      <tr>
      <th colspan="3" class="Title">Joe's Cafe Menu</th>
      </tr>
      <tr>
      <th class="Column"> </th>
      <th class="Column">Item</th>
      <th class="Column">Price</th>
      </tr>
</thead>
<tbody>
</tbody>
</table>
<form>
<p>
<input type="button" name="btnCalcBill" value="Calculate Bill"
   onClick="document.forms[0].txtBillAmt.value=calculateBill('menuTable');">
Total: $<input type="text" name="txtBillAmt">
<input type="checkbox" name="cbOpts" value="isVeg"
      onClick="highlightVegetarian('menuTable',this.checked)">
Highlight Vegetarian Meals
</p>
</form>
</body>
</html>
```

The structure of the page is pretty basic. There are a couple of CSS styles to define the appearance of the menu, some text in the document to direct the user what to do, and some controls at the bottom of the page that allow the user to interact with the menu. The main centerpiece of the code is the <TABLE> tag with the ID "menuTable." This is the element that will hold the HTML code for the menu generated from the XML. The comment just below the body tag indicates where the DIV tag with the embedded XML code should go.

Figure 10-8   *The menu page for Joe's Cafe*

The Menu XML Code

Listing 10-11 shows the XML code that comprises the menu for Joe's Café. Note that the XML data island is contained within an invisible `<DIV>` tag.

Listing 10-11   *The XML Code for the Menu*

```
<div id="xmlLayer" style="position:absolute; width:0px;
      height:0px; z-index:1; visibility: hidden">
<xml id="cafeMenuXML">
<cafemenu>
      <section name="Breakfast">
            <entree>
                  <item>Two Eggs, any style</item>
                  <price>2.99</price>
            </entree>
            <entree>
                  <item>Joe's Famous Peppers and Eggs</item>
                  <price>6.29</price>
            </entree>
            <entree vegetarian="true">
                  <item>Bowl of fruit</item>
                  <price>4.99</price>
            </entree>
            <entree vegetarian="true">
                  <item>French toast</item>
                  <price>3.25</price>
            </entree>
      </section>
      <section name="Lunch">
            <entree>
                  <item>Grilled Chicken Sandwich</item>
                  <price>5.99</price>
            </entree>
            <entree>
                  <item>Tuna Melt</item>
                  <price>4.99</price>
            </entree>
            <entree vegetarian="true">
                  <item>Pasta Salad</item>
                  <price>5.39</price>
            </entree>
      </section>
      <section name="Dinner">
            <entree>
                  <item>New York Steak</item>
                  <price>8.99</price>
```

```
            </entree>
            <entree>
                  <item>Chilean Sea Bass</item>
                  <price>10.99</price>
            </entree>
            <entree vegetarian="true">
                  <item>Linguini with Porcini Mushrooms</item>
                  <price>7.79</price>
            </entree>
      </section>
</cafemenu>
</xml>
</div>
```

This XML structure is fairly straightforward, although it's obviously a simplified example. The menu is organized into sections, each delimited by a `<section>` tag. Each `<section>` tag defines a set of entrées for a particular type of meal: breakfast, lunch, or dinner, which is delimited by an `<entree>` tag. Each `<entree>` tag has an optional attribute, `vegetarian`, which indicates whether the entrée is vegetarian. If no `vegetarian` attribute is present, then the item is assumed to be not vegetarian. Each `<entree>` tag in a section contains child tags that describe the name of the item and its price. The `<item>` and `<price>` tags each contain a single text node that describes the item name and the price for the item.

From this XML structure, your DOM code generates the appropriate HTML and fills out the table in the page body with the results.

Generating the Menu HTML

Once the menu XML code has been embedded in the page, the HTML needs to be generated and displayed to the user. There are several good methods for doing this, based upon how much control you want to have over the display of the HTML, how much coding work you want to do yourself, what kinds of special features you want to provide, and which browser you expect the user to be viewing the page in.

If you're using Internet Explorer as the target browser, the available options are varied: you can bind the XML directly to a table control and have the table populate automatically, you can use XPath and XSLT to transform the XML code directly into HTML, or you can use the DOM to generate the page. In Netscape, you give up the data-bound controls, but you can still use the DOM and XSLT.

Binding the XML to an HTML table provides a direct solution in IE, but you want to provide some fairly advanced features without redesigning the XML structure of the code. In addition, Netscape doesn't directly support data-bound controls, although you could write some custom JavaScript to get it to behave properly and work acceptably. Still, this would be a daunting task, and if you're going to write JavaScript code to get it to work in one browser, you might as well use JavaScript for the entire solution. Therefore, for the requirements in this example, data-bound controls are out.

Using XSLT to transform the XML into displayable HTML would be a straightforward, elegant solution because that's what it is designed to do. XSLT is a standard also defined by the W3C that describes how to transform XML documents into other types of documents, such as XML, HTML, PDF, text, and so on. It works by applying templates to sections of the source XML file to produce the output file. The XSLT support provided by Internet Explorer and Netscape would be enough to perform the necessary transformation of the sample document if it were a stand-alone XML file that was being displayed by a browser. In addition, IE provides native XSLT transform support for individual document nodes via the `transformNode()` method, but Netscape lacks this feature as of version 6.2.2, so it won't work for the embedded XML data island example. In addition, you'll want more control over the generation of your document during processing than XSLT might allow. Because a full introduction to XSLT is beyond our scope, for now we'll put it aside.

That leaves using the DOM to directly manipulate the XML content, which will work in both Netscape and IE because both provide excellent support the DOM. You also can be sure that it will continue to work down the road as new DOM-compliant browsers are introduced because you're using an API that is independent of any particular vendor's implementation.

Listing 10-12 lists the JavaScript code that creates and handles the menu.

Listing 10-12   *JavaScript for Generating the Menu*

```
var gEntreeCount = 0;
function initialize(idTheTable,idXMLData)
{
      var oTheTable = document.getElementById(idTheTable);
      // if the table already has a TBODY, remove it
      var theTBODY = oTheTable.getElementsByTagName('TBODY');
      if (theTBODY.length > 0)
          oTheTable.removeChild(theTBODY[0]);

      // now create the menu content
      theTBODY = generateMenuContent(idXMLData);
      // and add it to the table
```

```
      oTheTable.appendChild(theTBODY);
}


function generateMenuContent(idXMLData)
{
    var i=0,j=0;
    var theTBODYNode = document.createElement('TBODY');
    var oXMLDoc = document.getElementById(idXMLData);
    var aMenuSections = oXMLDoc.getElementsByTagName('section');
    for (i=0; i < aMenuSections.length; i++)
    {
        // each <section> tag starts a new Menu section, so create
        // a table row for the section with the value of the
        // section's 'name' attribute
        var sName = aMenuSections.item(i).getAttribute('name');
        var oTR = document.createElement('TR');
        var oTD = document.createElement('TD');
        oTD.setAttribute('colspan','3');
        oTD.appendChild(document.createTextNode(sName));
        oTR.appendChild(oTD);
        theTBODYNode.appendChild(oTR);

        // now create each menu item. The child nodes of each
        // <section> tag represent an individual entree.
        var aEntrees = aMenuSections.item(i).getElementsByTagName('entree');
        for (j=0; j < aEntrees.length; j++)
        {
            oTR = document.createElement('TR');
            // create a custom attribute on the TR tag called "vegetarian"
            // to indicate whether the item is vegetarian or not. This
            // will save us a lot of effort later when we're trying to
            // highlight the vegetarian items.
            if (aEntrees.item(j).getAttribute("vegetarian"))
                oTR.setAttribute("vegetarian",
                    aEntrees.item(j).getAttribute("vegetarian")
                );

            // create the TD for the checkbox
            oTD = document.createElement('TD');
            oTD.setAttribute('align','center');
            var oCB = document.createElement('INPUT');
            oCB.setAttribute('name','item'+gEntreeCount++);
            oCB.setAttribute('type','checkbox');
            oTD.appendChild(oCB);
            oTR.appendChild(oTD);

            // create the TD for the item name
            oTD = document.createElement('TD');
```

```
        var oItemNode =
           aEntrees.item(j).getElementsByTagName('item')[0];
        // just copy the item node's text child to the TD
        oTD.appendChild(
           document.createTextNode(oItemNode.firstChild.data)
        );
        oTR.appendChild(oTD);

        // create the TD for the price
        oTD = document.createElement('TD');
        // align the prices to the right so they line up
        // over the decimal point
        oTD.setAttribute('align','right');
        var oPriceNode =
           aEntrees.item(j).getElementsByTagName('price')[0];
        // just copy the price node's text child to the TD
        oTD.appendChild(
           document.createTextNode(oPriceNode.firstChild.data));
        oTR.appendChild(oTD);

        // add the row to the table body
        theTBODYNode.appendChild(oTR);
      }
   }
   return theTBODYNode;
}

function calculateBill(idMenuTable)
{
     var fBillTotal = 0.0;
     var i=0;

     var oTable = document.getElementById(idMenuTable);

     // go through the table and add up the prices of all
     // the selected items. The code takes advantage of the
     // fact that each checkbox has a corresponding row in
     // the table, and the only INPUT tags are the checkboxes.
     var aCBTags = oTable.getElementsByTagName('INPUT');
     for (i=0; i < aCBTags.length; i++)
     {
          if (aCBTags[i].checked)
          {
               // get the checkbox' parent TR
               var oTR = getParentTag(aCBTags[i],'TR');

               // retrieve the price from the TD
               var oTDPrice = oTR.getElementsByTagName('TD')[2];
               // the child text node contains the price
```

```
                    fBillTotal += parseFloat(oTDPrice.firstChild.data);
              }
        }
        return Math.round(fBillTotal*100.0)/100.0;
}

function highlightVegetarian(idTable,bShowVeg)
{
        // if bShowVeg is true, then we're highlighting vegetarian
        //      meals, otherwise we're unhighlighting them.
        var i=0;
        var oTable = document.getElementById(idTable);
        // start by getting all of the TR elements in the TBODY
        var oTBODY = oTable.getElementsByTagName('TBODY')[0];
        var aTRs = oTBODY.getElementsByTagName('TR');
        for (i=0; i < aTRs.length; i++)
        {
              if (aTRs[i].getAttribute('vegetarian'))
              {
                    if (bShowVeg)
                          aTRs[i].style.backgroundColor = "lightGreen";
                    else
                          aTRs[i].style.backgroundColor = "";
              }
        }
}

function getParentTag(oNode, sParentType)
{
        var oParent = oNode.parentNode;
        while (oParent)
        {
              if (oParent.nodeName == sParentType)
                    return oParent;
              oParent = oParent.parentNode;
        }
        return oParent;
}
```

Initializing the Page

The menu page's <BODY> tag contains an onLoad event handler that handles the
details of the page initialization:

```
<body bgcolor="#FFFFFF" text="#000000"
      onLoad="initialize('menuTable','cafeMenuXML');
      document.forms[0].txtBillAmt.value=calculateBill('menuTable');
      ">
```

The `initialize()` function takes two arguments: the ID of the table that will hold the menu and the ID of the XML data island that will be used to generate the HTML. The function begins by locating the table represented by the given ID:

```
function initialize(idTheTable,idXMLData)
{
    var oTheTable = document.getElementById(idTheTable);
```

Next, the code removes any existing TBODY that it finds from the table. This will make it easier to add a new one later on.

```
    // if the table already has a TBODY, remove it
    var theTBODY = oTheTable.getElementsByTagName('TBODY');
    if (theTBODY.length > 0)
        oTheTable.removeChild(theTBODY[0]);
```

Once the table is ready for the HTML code, the `generateMenuContent()` function is called with the ID of the XML data island. This function returns a TBODY node populated with rows and columns representing the XML data for the menu:

```
    // now create the menu content
    theTBODY = generateMenuContent(idXMLData);
```

Now, the new TBODY node is appended to the table element using the `appendChild()` method:

```
    // and add it to the table
    oTheTable.appendChild(theTBODY);
}
```

Building the Table

The `generateMenuContent()` function is the workhorse of the menu page. This function is responsible for transforming the HTML code into a fully formed TBODY node with all of the child nodes in place to represent each section, item, and price in the menu XML code.

The `generateMenuContent()` function begins by creating a new TBODY element, which will hold the resulting <TR> and <TD> tags for the generated menu:

```
function generateMenuContent(idXMLData)
{
    var i=0,j=0;
    var theTBODYNode = document.createElement('TBODY');
```

Once the TBODY is created, the function locates the XML data island represented by the idXMLData argument:

```
var oXMLDoc = document.getElementById(idXMLData);
```

Next, the list of <SECTION> tags is generated. The function loops over each section tag in the XML structure and processes all of the child <ENTREE> tags:

```
var aMenuSections = oXMLDoc.getElementsByTagName('section');
for (i=0; i < aMenuSections.length; i++)
{
```

Each section tag corresponds to a table row that contains the name of the menu section:

```
var sName = aMenuSections.item(i).getAttribute('name');
var oTR = document.createElement('TR');
var oTD = document.createElement('TD');
oTD.setAttribute('colspan','3');
oTD.appendChild(document.createTextNode(sName));
oTR.appendChild(oTD);
theTBODYNode.appendChild(oTR);
```

Once the row for the section name is created, the rows for the entrées in the section need to be created and added to the table body. The function gets the list of <ENTREE> tags and loops over each one, processing the <ITEM> and <PRICE> tags:

```
var aEntrees =
    aMenuSections.item(i).getElementsByTagName('entree');
for (j=0; j < aEntrees.length; j++)
{
```

Each <ENTREE> tag corresponds to its own table row, so a new <TR> tag is created for the entrée:

```
oTR = document.createElement('TR');
```

If the entrée is vegetarian, you create a vegetarian attribute for the table row so it will be easier to find later. Both IE and Netscape allow you to attach custom-defined attributes to a tag using the setAttribute() DOM method.

NOTE

In IE, you can also set custom attributes in JavaScript by using the name of the attribute on the object, for example, `oTR.vegetarian="true"`. *This doesn't work in Netscape for some reason — instead, you need to use* `setAttribute()`.

```
if (aEntrees.item(j).getAttribute("vegetarian"))
    oTR.setAttribute("vegetarian",
      aEntrees.item(j).getAttribute("vegetarian")
    );
```

Now the function creates the contents of each table row. The row contains three columns: a check box that allows the user to "select" the menu item, the name of the entrée, and its price.

```
// create the TD for the checkbox
oTD = document.createElement('TD');
oTD.setAttribute('align','center');
var oCB = document.createElement('INPUT');
oCB.setAttribute('name','item'+gEntreeCount++);
oCB.setAttribute('type','checkbox');
oTD.appendChild(oCB);
oTR.appendChild(oTD);

// create the TD for the item name
oTD = document.createElement('TD');
var oItemNode =
    aEntrees.item(j).getElementsByTagName('item')[0];
// just copy the item node's text child to the TD
oTD.appendChild(
    document.createTextNode(oItemNode.firstChild.data)
    );
oTR.appendChild(oTD);

// create the TD for the price
oTD = document.createElement('TD');
// align the prices to the right so they line up
// over the decimal point
oTD.setAttribute('align','right');
var oPriceNode =
```

```
        aEntrees.item(j).getElementsByTagName('price')[0];
  // just copy the price node's text child to the TD
  oTD.appendChild(
        document.createTextNode(oPriceNode.firstChild.data));
  oTR.appendChild(oTD);
```

Once the row is created, it is appended to the <TBODY> tag, and the loop goes on to process the next entrée. When all of the entrées and sections are finished, the loops terminate.

```
        // add the row to the table body
        theTBODYNode.appendChild(oTR);
    }
}
```

That's it! Now the code returns the completed TBODY to the caller, and it is appended to its parent table element:

```
    return theTBODYNode;
}
```

Handling User Interaction

This menu page provides several ways in which the user can interact with the menu. Users can select items from the menu, calculate the total bill, and highlight items that are suitable for vegetarians. When the user performs each action, the menu page takes an appropriate response to the action by updating part of the page.

Selecting Items from the Menu

The user can choose items from the menu by clicking the check boxes in each row for each entrée item. No action is performed when the check box is actually checked— the code performs the bill calculation when the Calculate Bill button is clicked. This could be automated by having the bill update when each check box was checked by calling the calculateBill() function each time a check box was clicked.

Calculating the Bill

If the user wants to see how much money they can expect to spend on a meal before they even get to the restaurant, they can select items from the menu, and the page will display a running total of the items that have been selected. When the Calculate Bill button is clicked, the `calculateBill()` function examines all of the checked items, adds their prices up, and displays the result in the form below the table.

The function accepts one argument, the ID of the table, and returns a floating-point number representing the bill amount. The function first retrieves the table node with the given ID and then collects all of the <INPUT> tags in the table:

```
function calculateBill(idMenuTable)
{
      var fBillTotal = 0.0;
      var i=0;

      var oTable = document.getElementById(idMenuTable);

      // go through the table and add up the prices of all
      // the selected items. The code takes advantage of the
      // fact that each checkbox has a corresponding row in
      // the table, and the only INPUT tags are the checkboxes.
      var aCBTags = oTable.getElementsByTagName('INPUT');
```

Because the only <INPUT>tags within the table are the check boxes themselves, and they are only present within the TBODY, the code can take advantage of this fact to work backward to find the corresponding TR for the menu item. The function loops over each check box tag, gets its parent <TR> tag using the `getParentTag()` method, and then retrieves the child <TD> tag corresponding to where the price information is kept. The text string within the <TD> tag is always formatted as a floating-point number, so the code can call the `parseFloat()` function on the child text node's `data` property to get a floating-point number (this, of course, is usually not the case in real life, and the text would probably require some further processing to get the numerical representation):

```
for (i=0; i < aCBTags.length; i++)
{
    if (aCBTags[i].checked)
    {
        // get the checkbox' parent TR
        var oTR = getParentTag(aCBTags[i],'TR');

        // retrieve the price from the TD
        var oTDPrice = oTR.getElementsByTagName('TD')[2];
        // the child text node contains the price
```

```
                    fBillTotal += parseFloat(oTDPrice.firstChild.data);
        }
    }
    return Math.round(fBillTotal*100.0)/100.0;
}
```

The code for the getParentTag() function retrieves the indicated parent type for a given node, if one exists. The function takes two arguments: the node for which the ancestor is to be returned, and the name of the node type to find. The function then walks upward through the node's parent nodes until it finds a parent of the given type, or the top of the document is reached, in which case NULL is returned:

```
function getParentTag(oNode, sParentType)
{
    var oParent = oNode.parentNode;
    while (oParent)
    {
        if (oParent.nodeName == sParentType)
            return oParent;
        oParent = oParent.parentNode;
    }
    return oParent;
}
```

Highlighting Vegetarian Meals

One of the features that the menu page provides to users is the ability to highlight certain dishes in the menu based upon a vegetarian dietary restriction. When the user clicks the check box that highlights vegetarian entrées, the onClick handler for the check box calls the highlightVegetarian() method, which modifies the background color of the vegetarian items in the table to make them stand out more.

The highlightVegetarian() function accepts two arguments: the ID of the table and a Boolean value indicating whether the items should be highlighted or not. The function first retrieves the table with the given ID and then collects all of the <TR> tags in the table's TBODY section:

```
function highlightVegetarian(idTable,bShowVeg)
{
    // if bShowVeg is true, then we're highlighting vegetarian
    //      meals, otherwise we're unhighlighting them.
    var i=0;
    var oTable = document.getElementById(idTable);
```

```
// start by getting all of the TR elements in the TBODY
var oTBODY = oTable.getElementsByTagName('TBODY')[0];
var aTRs = oTBODY.getElementsByTagName('TR');
```

For each tag, the function checks for the presence of the vegetarian attribute on the <TR> tag. If it is present, the <TR>'s backgroundColor style selector is changed to the named color "lightGreen," otherwise it is set to the empty string value (which effectively removes it):

```
for (i=0; i < aTRs.length; i++)
{
      if (aTRs[i].getAttribute('vegetarian'))
      {
            if (bShowVeg)
                  aTRs[i].style.backgroundColor = "lightGreen";
            else
                  aTRs[i].style.backgroundColor = "";
      }
}
}
```

Adding New Items to the Menu

The data for the page has now been isolated to the XML data island fragment, so adding new sections to the menu is as simple as adding new XML tags—the changes are automatically picked up by the processing script and handled accordingly. For example, if a new section were added, such as Side Dishes, Listing 10-13 shows what the XML code might look like.

Listing 10-13   *A New Section Added to the Menu XML*

```
<!-- New section here: side dishes -->
<section name="Side Dishes">
      <entree vegetarian="true">
            <item>Potato Salad</item>
            <price>2.95</price>
      </entree>
      <entree>
            <item>French Fries</item>
            <price>2.50</price>
      </entree>
```

```
</section>
<section name="Lunch">
      <entree>
            <item>Grilled Chicken Sandwich</item>
            <price>5.99</price>
      </entree>
      <entree>
            <item>Tuna Melt</item>
            <price>4.99</price>
      </entree>
      <entree vegetarian="true">
            <item>Pasta Salad</item>
            <price>5.39</price>
      </entree>
</section>
... more section tags follow ...
```

Now, when the page is reloaded in the browser, the changes are automatically incorporated into the HTML table, as shown in Figure 10-9.

The page automatically handles all of the menu selection, bill calculation, and highlighting of the vegetarian options.

Conclusion

In this chapter, we examined various ways of building and processing data-driven documents directly on the client without having to make round-trips to the server. First, you saw how to sort data using the DOM and the built-in JavaScript classes, and you built scripts that allowed users to sort HTML lists and tables directly in the browser.

Next, you looked at an example of using "screen-scraping" techniques to extract data from a web page that was dynamically generated on the server to provide the user with some additional client-side post-processing.

Finally, you looked at XML data islands, what they are, and how they can be used to present and manipulate data on the client. You also built a functioning example that transformed an XML document into an interactive HTML page.

The advantages of client-side data processing are clear: by offloading document processing to the client where possible, the load on the server diminishes significantly, and the user experiences a more responsive, interactive application.

In the next chapter, we'll take a look at some possible future directions for the DOM and examine the new types of functionality being considered for DOM Level 3.

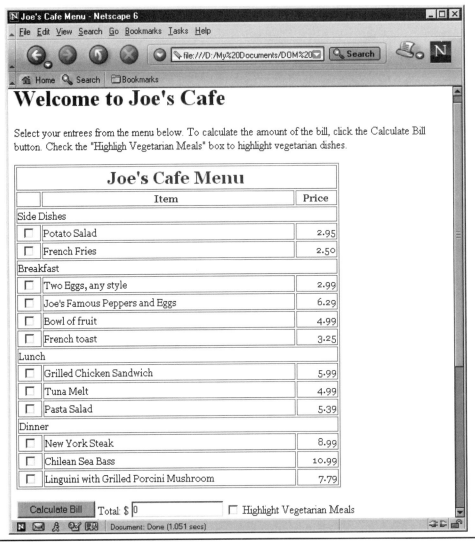

Figure 10-9   *Updated XML in the browser*

Future Directions for the DOM

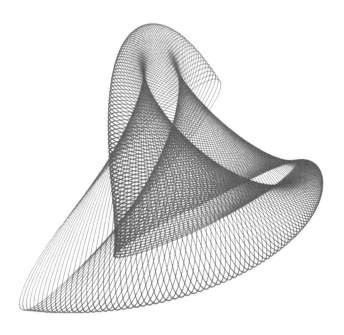

T he W3C DOM is an evolving standard, designed from the beginning to be improved upon with time. The currently published version of the DOM is Level 2, which was adopted as a W3C Recommendation on November 13, 2000 (except for Level 2 HTML, which is currently in last call status as of April 2002). The DOM Working Group is currently working on Level 3, which is available as a set of working draft publications on the W3C web site (www.w3.org/DOM). One of the major changes in the way that the DOM has been published since Level 2 is that separate DOM modules can now be put forth as recommendations on an individual basis to speed up the adoption process.

This chapter takes a look at some of the new additions and changes to the DOM that are being developed for Level 3, along with some other trends and technologies that are shaping and influencing the development of the next version of the DOM standard. Some of these efforts are well underway, while some others are still ideas that are just now being discussed for possible future implementation in the DOM.

NOTE

The information in this chapter is based on working draft publications and other in-progress work from the W3C and other sources, which may change before being officially adopted as W3C recommendations or other accepted standards. Some of the information in this chapter may not become part of the standard at all. This information should be used only as a high-level guide to where the DOM API may be going in future releases. Readers are encouraged to check the W3C DOM website for the most up-to-date information.

Where Is the DOM Headed?

When DOM Level 1 was published, it provided a base reference for implementing a set of functionality that allowed applications to manipulate the contents of structured documents. Level 1 only allowed certain basic document operations, such as creating and deleting nodes, working with their contents, and traversing the document tree. Everything else was left to be implementation specific, even operations that might be considered obvious, such as loading and saving documents.

DOM Level 2 included support for more types of document operations and content, such as events and styles. These additions gave developers standardized ways of handling user events and working with Cascading Style Sheets (CSS) information within XML documents.

Currently, the DOM's future is taking shape as the Level 3 specification, parts of which are now in "last call" phase (such as DOM XPath) and parts of which are still under development. In addition, there are other standards under development that are not officially part of the DOM, but directly or indirectly affect how developers use it and may be considered for inclusion in the DOM at a later date. In the Level 3 version of the DOM, more attention is being paid to some of the things that were left out of earlier versions, such as loading and saving files. In addition, the DOM is beginning to consider the use of other W3C recommendations within DOM documents, such as XPath expression handling.

In the following sections, I'll summarize the changes and additions that are being developed for DOM Level 3 and examine some of the new modules that will be included. We'll also take a look at some developing technologies and trends that are not yet being considered for inclusion in the DOM but probably will be at some later date.

Proposed Changes in DOM Level 3

The working drafts of the Level 3 DOM modules incorporate several changes and additions to the specification that have been requested by developers. The size and scope of the changes range from relatively small, such as new data types and methods, to entirely new modules, such as Load and Save, Abstract Schemas, and XPath support. In this section, I'll summarize the more important changes made to the existing modules and take a look at some of the new modules that will be included in Level 3.

General Changes

Some of the more general changes in the Level 3 version of the DOM specification include new data types, new methods and properties for various interfaces, and modifications to existing interfaces and properties. In addition, Level 3 introduces some entirely new concepts to the DOM, such as mixed DOM implementations.

New Data Types

DOM Level 3 introduces two new data types. The first is DOMObject, which represents an arbitrary memory object. The second is DOMUserData, which represents an interface to an arbitrary block of data in a DOM application.

The DOMObject type has the following IDL specification:

```
typedef Object DOMObject;
```

The DOMUserData type has the following IDL specification:

```
typedef Object DOMUserData;
```

NOTE

The DOM Level 3 specification uses the DOMObject and DOMUserData types in its interfaces, though actual implementations may use different bindings. In Java, for example, the DOMObject and DOMUserData types are bound to the Java's Object type. In C++, they may be specified as void pointers (void *), as in the Xerces-C implementation. In JavaScript, they can be bound to any type.

Currently, the Level 3 specification uses DOMObject and DOMUserData types in the interfaces for handling user data on document nodes (discussed later).

New and Modified Interface Methods

Several of the DOM interfaces have added new methods in the Level 3 specification. In this section, we'll review the more notable additions to the DOM interfaces.

The Node interface is slated to receive a fair number of additions, allowing developers to compare the document tree positions of nodes, test for node equality, retrieve the text content of nodes, and attach application-defined data to nodes.

Comparing the tree positions of nodes is done via the `compareTreeNode()` method, which returns the position of a given node relative to the node it is called on. Application-specific data can now be attached to nodes using the `setUserData()` and `getUserData()` methods. Each of these new capabilities is discussed more fully later in this chapter in the section "Attaching Application-Specific Data to Nodes."

Two new methods, `isSameNode()` and `isEqualNode()`, have been added to allow applications to test two nodes for sameness and equality, respectively. Two node references are said to be the *same* if both node references refer to the same underlying node in memory. When two node references are the same, DOM operations on either reference will behave as if the same operation had been performed on the other reference.

Two nodes are considered to be *equal* if *all* of the following conditions are met:

▶ The two nodes are the same type (Element, Comment, and so on).

▶ The `nodeName`, `localName`, `namespaceURI`, `prefix`, `nodeValue`, and `baseURI` properties on one node are all equal to the corresponding property on the other node. That is, they are both `null`, or they both have the same string value.

▶ All of the two nodes' attribute nodes are equal. Either the `attributes` NamedNodeMap properties of the nodes are both `null`, or they both have the same length, and an attribute that exists in one of the NamedNodeMaps also exists in the `attributes` NamedNodeMap property of the other node, and they are equal to each other (although they don't have to be at the same index).

▶ The `childNodes` lists are equal on both nodes. Either they are both `null`, or they contain the same number of child nodes and each one is equal to the other and is at the same index. Note that the process of normalizing, or concatenating adjacent text nodes, can affect node equality, so normalization should be done before tests for equality are performed.

In addition to the preceding, the following conditions must be met for two DocumentType nodes to be equal:

▶ The `publicID`, `systemID`, and `internalSubset` properties are equal.

▶ The `entities` NamedNodeMap structures are equal.

▶ The `notations` NamedNodeMap structures are equal.

For example, consider the following document fragment:

```
<myNode attr1="first attr" attr2="second attr"/>
<myNode attr2="second attr" attr1="first attr"/>
```

Both of these nodes are equal because they are both Element nodes, they have the same `nodeName`, and their attributes are equal, even though they are at different indexes. On the other hand, consider this example:

```
<myNode attr1="first attr" attr2="second attr">
Hello World!</myNode>
<myNode attr2="second attr" attr1="first attr"/>
```

Here, the two nodes are not equal because one of them has a text child node while the other does not. Even though everything else about the two nodes match up, they fail the equality test because of their child node content. This is an important consideration to remember when comparing two nodes: you're not just comparing the nodes themselves; in some cases, you're comparing two subtrees of the document.

To retrieve the text content of a node, applications can now use the `textContent` property. This property returns the text content of a node and its descendant nodes, depending on the node type. It can also be set to a string, in which case all of the descendants of the node are removed and replaced with a single Text node containing the string value that this property is set to. When this property is read, the string returned does not contain any markup at all, and no extra whitespace is removed from the string. Table 11-1 lists the value of the `textContent` property that is returned for the different types of nodes.

The Document interface also received a good dose of new methods and properties. Among the more important ones are the `actualEncoding`, `encoding`, `standalone`, and `version` properties that represent the corresponding values provided in the `<?xml?>` statement declaration at the top of the XML file. There is also a new `errorHandler` property, which allows developers to set a `DOMErrorHandler` object on the document to handle errors (discussed in depth later in the "Error Handling" section).

Among the new methods, there is now an `adoptNode()` method, which changes the `ownerDocument` of a given node along with its child and attribute nodes, if there are any. This method was added to allow the moving of a document subtree to another document.

The `insertBefore()`, `removeChild()`, and `replaceChild()` methods have been changed to raise a new DOMException, VALIDATION_ERROR, if the requested operation would leave the node in an invalid state.

For a full list of the additions and changes to the DOM 3 interfaces, consult the appropriate module specification at the W3C DOM website.

Mixed DOM Implementations

Over the past few years, specialized vocabularies of XML have started to become prevalent, and they are targeted at specific tasks or markets. As a result, the developers of these new vocabularies have begun extending the DOM to provide specialized services to developers that need to perform certain operations frequently. Examples of this can be seen in the MathML and Scalable Vector Graphics (SVG)

Node Type	TextContent Value
Element, Entity, EntityReference, DocumentFragment	The concatenated value of the `textContent` property for all of the child nodes, except for Comment and ProcessingInstruction nodes.
Attribute, Text, CDATA, Comment, ProcessingInstruction	`nodeValue`
Document, DocumentType, Notation	`null`

Table 11-1   `textContent` *Values for Individual Node Types*

specifications, where those specifications have started providing DOM extension methods and properties to their respective developers. This becomes an issue when fragments of one type of XML document (SVG, for example) are embedded within an XML document that follows a different schema (such as XHTML). The DOM Working Group realized that Level 2 didn't provide enough functionality to cover all of the instances that come up when working with documents that can contain two or more different types of XML fragments.

DOM Level 3 tries to remedy this by allowing DOM implementations to make specialized interfaces available when needed by an application to perform special processing on certain parts of the document that contain specialized node types. The solution takes the form of the new `getInterface()` method on the DOMImplementation interface, which has this IDL definition:

```
DOMImplementation getInterface(DOMString feature);
```

An application can request a specialized DOM implementation by passing in the name of the feature that it wishes to support. If there is no alternative implementation that supports the requested feature, the return value is `null`.

Abstract Schema Support

DOM Level 3 includes the new Abstract Schemas module, which is intended to provide support for working with Document Type Definition (DTD) files, XML Schemas, and other nonspecific schema types. The DOM Working Group realized early on that such support would one day be a necessity in the DOM. In fact, the 1997 DOM requirements document explicitly refers to the ability "to determine the presence of a DTD" and "to add, remove, and change declarations in the underlying DTD (if available)." However, the spec notes that this work was intentionally delayed beyond DOM Level 2 because XML Schemas were still being defined, and they hoped that any support provided for working with DTDs would be extended to work with XML Schemas as well as any other abstract schemas that came along later.

The Abstract Schema module formalizes the API provided to address these issues, as well as some other specific use cases, such as changing the abstract schema associated with a document, validating the document against the schema, and loading a schema independently from a document. Implementations can provide read-only access to abstract schemas, editing access to schemas, and document-editing access to schemas. Each of these capabilities can be discovered by a DOM application by calling the `hasFeature()` method on the DOMImplementation interface with the "AS-READ," "AS-WRITE," and "AS-DOC" feature strings.

The Abstract Schema module is included in the module for Load and Save because the two are intended to interact closely with each other. For example, the Load and Save module will have to read and write any abstract schema associated with a particular document and may be required to load an abstract schema independent of a document.

The subject of abstract schemas is beyond the scope of this section. If you would like to read more about them, see the Abstract Schema module working draft of the DOM Level 3 for more information. The current working draft can be found at www.w3.org/TR/DOM-Level-3-ASLS.

Error Handling

The DOM introduces new error-handling interfaces in Level 3: DOMError, DOMErrorHandler, and DOMLocator. The DOMError interface describes an error condition that occurred while processing a document or performing some other document operation (such as validating the document). It has the following IDL definition:

```
interface DOMError {
    const unsigned short      SEVERITY_WARNING      = 0;
    const unsigned short      SEVERITY_ERROR        = 1;
    const unsigned short      SEVERITY_FATAL_ERROR = 2;
    readonly attribute unsigned short severity;
    readonly attribute DOMString message;
    readonly attribute Object relatedException;
    readonly attribute DOMLocator location;
}
```

The three severity constants describe the severity of an error, indicating whether it is a warning, an error, or a fatal error. Warnings and some errors may be ignorable or recoverable; fatal errors always terminate the attempted operation. These values are reported in the severity field.

The message field contains an implementation-supplied error message that can be displayed to the user describing the error. If the platform on which the implementation is running supports exceptions, the relatedException field will contain the platform-specific exception for the error, if there is any. The location field represents a DOMLocator object that describes the location of the error in the document.

The DOMLocator interface has the following IDL definition:

```
interface DOMLocator {
    readonly attribute long           lineNumber;
    readonly attribute long           columnNumber;
```

```
    readonly attribute long         offset;
    readonly attribute Node         errorNode;
    readonly attribute DOMString    uri;
}
```

When an error occurs and a DOMError object is available to describe it, the location property will contain a DOMLocator object that describes the location of the error. The lineNumber and columnNumber fields indicate the line and column in the text where the error was caught. If this information is not available, these fields will be −1. The offset field represents the byte or character offset into the input source where the error occurred, or −1 if this information is not available. The errorNode field indicates the node where the error occurred or `null` if no node is available. The uri field will be the URI where the error occurred or `null` if there is no URI available.

Errors are reported by means of a DOMErrorHandler, which represents a callback interface that an implementation will call when reporting errors. The DOMErrorHandler has the following interface:

```
interface DOMErrorHandler {
    boolean    handleError(in DOMError error);
}
```

The `handleError()` method is called when the DOM implementation needs to report an error. The method returns a boolean value indicating what the implementation should do after reporting the error. If the method returns true, the implementation should try to continue as if the error didn't happen (the spec notes that this may not always be possible). If the method returns false, the implementation should stop any further processing (again, the spec notes that this may not always be possible).

Loading and Saving DOM Documents

It may be hard to believe, but Levels 1 and 2 of the DOM specification did not provide a way to load or save documents to or from a DOM implementation. This was intentionally left as an implementation-dependent function, and several DOM implementers such as Macromedia, Apache, Microsoft, and Netscape went ahead and defined their own interfaces and methods for loading and saving documents. The result, of course, was that not all DOM implementations used the same methods for document persistence. For example, loading a document in Macromedia's Dreamweaver DOM implementation is done via a method called `openDocument()`, whereas in Microsoft Internet Explorer the method is named `load()`.

The DOM Level 3 Load and Save module aims to standardize the methods used for performing these types of document persistence functions. The good news here is that the Load and Save module interfaces and methods are modeled on many of the already existing load and save implementations in use today in DOM applications such as Apache Xerces, Microsoft Internet Explorer 6, and Netscape Navigator 6, so learning the new interfaces should be a relatively straightforward task.

The Document Load and Save Module defines nine new major interfaces and a few smaller, ancillary interfaces for use when saving and loading XML documents. Table 11-2 lists the major interfaces and describes each.

Load and Save Interface	Description
DOMImplementationLS	Provides the factory methods that are necessary for creating the objects used for loading and saving documents.
DOMBuilder	An interface to an object that is capable of building a DOM document tree by reading data from a variety of input sources, such as files, URLs, and strings of text.
DOMInputSource	Specifies a single source of data from which the application can read data.
DOMEntityResolver	Provides an interface through which applications can redirect references to any external entities.
DOMBuilderFilter	Allows an application to examine document nodes as they are built when the document is being parsed.
DOMWriter	Provides an API for writing a document out to an XML file.
DOMWriterFilter	Allows an application to examine document nodes as they are being written to the output. The application can use this interface to affect which nodes get written out.
DocumentLS	Extends the base Document interface with methods that allow loading and saving of an existing document's contents.
ParserErrorEvent	Specifies the type of error event that is fired if an error is encountered when the document is being parsed.

Table 11-2   *The DOM Level 3 Load and Save Module Interfaces*

After reading through Table 11-2, you're probably asking the obvious question: why are there so many interfaces for loading and saving documents? The simple answer is that loading and saving DOM documents is not always as easy as it may seem at first blush. Consider, for example, the seemingly simple task of loading an XML file and creating a document tree from it.

Recall from Chapter 6 the process of using the Xerces parser to load a document from a file; that is the closest analogy to the way the new DOM interfaces work. First, there has to be a way to get the necessary interfaces for creating the objects to do the loading and parsing of the data. This is usually done by a "factory method" that creates an object that represents the input source. Once the proper factory method has been called to create the object that reads or writes the data source, an object needs to be created that parses the input and builds a document. Because the document source might refer to an external entity, such as a DTD or other Abstract Schema, an object will be needed to find the schema and cause it to be loaded. If an error occurs during the loading or parsing process, there needs to be an error handler object to report the errors. Suddenly, simply loading a document doesn't seem so simple!

In fact, most of the DOM Level 3 Load and Save interfaces are provided to serve the same functions that the ones in standalone DOM implementations such as Xerces already provide. For example, the DOMBuilder, DOMInputSource, DOMEntityResolver, and ParserErrorEvent interfaces in Level 3 are formalized versions of the Xerces API's DOMParser, InputSource, EntityResolver, and ErrorHandler interfaces. Implementations that allow creating and loading documents from scratch will need to provide these interfaces to their applications.

Fortunately, there are many common instances in which loading and saving XML is, in fact, a simple process. Because most browser-centric DOM applications already have a document created and available to them, along with a built-in way of reading data from a URL, they will usually only need to deal with the simplest of the interfaces, DocumentLS. The DocumentLS interface provides four methods for loading and saving content from an existing document. According to the W3C specification, it is expected that each DOM implementation will have a way of using a binding-specific casting mechanism to cast the regular Document interface to a DocumentLS interface to use these methods. It has the following IDL specification:

```
interface DocumentLS {
   attribute boolean  async; //raises DOMException on setting
   void               abort();
   boolean            load(in DOMString URI);
   boolean            loadXML(in DOMString source);
   DOMString          saveXML(in Node snode) raises (DOMException);
}
```

The `async` attribute specifies whether the document is loaded synchronously or asynchronously. When a document is loaded asynchronously, it means that control of the application is given back to the calling function before the `load()` function actually completes loading the document. In this case, your application should define an event handler for the document's `load` event, which will fire when it has finished loading. On the other hand, when loading a document synchronously, everything stops until the `load()` function finishes loading the document and returns control to the caller. This attribute defaults to false, meaning that documents are loaded synchronously by default.

The `abort()` method immediately interrupts the loading process of the document (if it is being loaded asynchronously). The document is cleared of any partial parsing result that may have taken place up to the point where `abort()` was called and all the document content is discarded.

The `load()` method will replace all of the current contents of the document with the result of parsing the given URI. If the value of the `async` attribute is false, the function immediately returns control to the caller. The document will fire off a `load` event when it has finished loading, or a ParserErrorEvent if the load fails. If this method is called on a document that is already loading, that loading process is aborted and a new loading process is started with the new URI.

The `loadXML()` method replaces the contents of the document with the parsed result of the XML string given by the source argument. This method is always called synchronously, and it always returns a UTF-16 encoded DOMString. The source argument must contain a legal, fully formed XML document. The method returns true if the source string was successfully parsed, or false if there was a parsing error.

The `saveXML()` method saves the contents of the document to a DOMString. If the `snode` argument is `null`, the whole document is serialized. If `snode` represents a node in the document, the given node is written to the string.

Both Internet Explorer 6 and Netscape Navigator 6 currently support the `load()` method; however, only IE supports the `async` attribute (the W3C Level 3 spec says that supporting asynchronous loading is optional). Interestingly, even though the `async` attribute is not present in Netscape 6, the application loads documents asynchronously by default. IE6 also supports the `loadXML()` method for creating a document from a string of XML code. Neither application supports the `saveXML()` method, though IE6 does have an `xml` property on the document object that contains a string of XML code that represents the entire document contents.

Even though Netscape 6 doesn't support the `loadXML()` or `saveXML()` methods, you can emulate them with some JavaScript code. To implement the `saveXML()` method, you need to create an XMLSerializer instance and then use it to serialize the document to a string, as in the following code.

```
// emulate the saveXML method
Document.prototype.saveXML = doc__saveXML;
function doc__saveXML()
{
   var s = new XMLSerializer();
   var xmlStr = s.serializeToString(this);
   return xmlStr;
}
```

The `loadXML()` method can be implemented by using a DOMParser object to parse a document source from a string:

```
// emulate the loadXML() method
Document.prototype.loadXML = doc__loadXML;
function doc__loadXML(xmlStr)
{
   var domParser = new DOMParser();
   var newDoc = domParser.parseFromString(xmlStr,"text/xml");
   // the current document needs to have all of its nodes replaced
   while (this.childNodes.length > 0)
      this.removeChild(this.firstChild);
   // now all of the new child nodes need to be appended
   // to the existing document.
   this.appendChild(this.importNode(newDoc.documentElement, true));
}
```

You can find more information on this subject on Microsoft's MSDN website (http://msdn.microsoft.com) or on the Mozilla site (www.mozilla.org).

Attaching Application-Specific Data to Nodes

Developers often find it useful to be able to attach application-defined data to a document's nodes. For example, some legacy applications may use an XML file to represent certain types of internal data that are computationally expensive to construct. To avoid the performance hit, they can build the complex data structure once and then attach it to the corresponding node in the DOM document tree. In addition, developers might choose to use this functionality as an alternative to subclassing the DOM interfaces in their particular implementation because it might just be easier to define a data structure and attach it to a node rather than write a new node subclass.

Levels 1 and 2 of the DOM did not provide an official way to do this, though certain DOM implementations did allow applications to take arbitrary data pointers and store them within a specially provided "slot" on the Node interface, such as the Apache Xerces implementation. The Xerces DOM implementation provides two Node interface methods for working with data objects attached to document nodes: setUserData() and getUserData(), which (for Xerces-C) have the following function definitions:

```
// Xerces-J setUserData and getUserData interfaces
public void setUserData(java.lang.Object data);
public java.lang.Object getUserData();

// Xerces-C setUserData and getUserData interfaces
void setUserData(void *p);
void *getUserData(void);
```

These methods allow a Xerces-based application to attach an arbitrary block of data to a given node in a document (see the Xerces section of Chapter 6). The Xerces implementation does have a few drawbacks, however. First, when that node is cloned, the Xerces parser explicitly does *not* clone the data along with it, preferring instead to leave this as something the application should take care of. Second, there can be only one data block attached to a node at any given time, so if an application wants to attach more than one piece of data to the node, it has to come up with its own management scheme to get and set the correct data blocks. For example, in the Java version of Xerces, the application might choose to store a Vector object on the node and then use it to manage an array of other data objects.

DOM Level 3 seeks to remedy these shortcomings and officially add the setUserData() and getUserData() methods to the Node interface. The new methods have the following proposed IDL definition:

```
DOMUserData    setUserData( in DOMString key, in DOMUserData data,
                            in UserDataHandler handler );
DOMUserData    getUserData( in DOMString key );
```

The DOM solution differs from the Xerces-style solution in two important ways. First, it allows more than one piece of user-defined data to be associated with a node by using a key-value approach. Each piece of data is associated with a key, which is used to identify a particular piece of data. When the data is stored in the node via the setUserData() method, the key is used as an indexing mechanism to locate it, much the same way that associative arrays work in JavaScript. When the data needs to be retrieved, the key is supplied to the getUserData() method and the data object is returned. Figure 11-1 illustrates how the data is stored within the node.

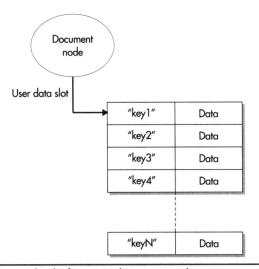

Figure 11-1 *Key-value method of storing data in a node*

The second major difference is in the behavior of nodes that are cloned or imported into another document. Whereas Xerces does not perform any special processing on nodes that are cloned, deleted, renamed, or imported, the DOM solution allows an application to supply a UserDataHandler that will be called when one of these operations is performed on a node. The UserDataHandler has the following IDL definition:

```
interface UserDataHandler {
const unsigned short    NODE_CLONED    = 1;
const unsigned short    NODE_IMPORTED  = 2;
const unsigned short    NODE_DELETED   = 3;
const unsigned short    NODE_RENAMED   = 4;

void  handle( in unsigned short operation,
              in DOMString key,
              in DOMObject data,
              in Node src,
              in Node dst);
}
```

The first four constants represent the four Node operations that a UserDataHandler can be informed about. There is a single method, `handle()`, which is called when one of the operations is being performed on the node. The first argument, operation, indicates the type of operation being performed. The key argument specifies the key for the handler that is being called. The data argument contains the data object for which the handler is being called. The src argument specifies the node that the data object is attached to (when the node is being deleted, this argument is null). If a new node is being created as part of the operation (that is, it is being cloned), then the dst argument specifies the newly created node. The handle() method has no return value.

Determining Relative Document Positions of Nodes

One of the new features that DOM Level 3 will allow applications to take advantage of is the concept of a node's "tree position" relative to other nodes in the document. In Chapter 4 we discussed the concept of *document order*—that is, the order in which nodes appear in the document when they are parsed. The Level 3 DOM API provides a new method on the Node interface called compareTreePosition(), which takes a node as an argument. The return value of the function is the position in the document tree of the given node relative to the node that this method was called on (also referred to as the "reference" node). The possible return values from compareTreePosition() are as follows:

Return Value	Meaning
TREE_POSITION_ANCESTOR	The given node is an ancestor of the reference node.
TREE_POSITION_DESCENDANT	The given node is a descendant of the reference node.
TREE_POSITION_DISCONNECTED	The two nodes do not have a relationship to each other. This occurs when the two nodes are in separate documents.
TREE_POSITION_EQUIVALENT	The two nodes have an equivalent position. This is the case when comparing two attribute nodes that are on the same element.
TREE_POSITION_FOLLOWING	The given node follows the reference node in the document.
TREE_POSITION_PRECEDING	The given node comes before the reference node in the document.
TREE_POSITION_SAME_NODE	The two nodes are the same. When two nodes are the same, they also have an equivalent position.

As an example, consider the document tree in Figure 11-2.

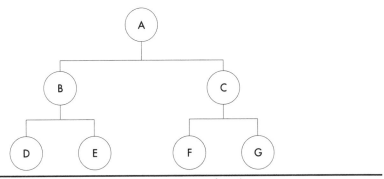

Figure 11-2   *Sample document illustrating tree positions of nodes*

This document can be described by the following XML code:

```
<NodeA>
   <NodeB>
       <NodeD/>
       <NodeE/>
   </NodeB>
   <NodeC>
       <NodeF/>
       <NodeG/>
   </NodeC>
</NodeA>
```

Suppose you currently had a reference to node F and wanted to know what the relative position of node B was to it. The call to compareTreePosition() would be written as

```
var nodeF, nodeB; // contain references to nodes F and B
// nodeF is the reference node, nodeB is the given node
nodeF.compareTreePosition(nodeB);
```

In this example, the return value of compareTreePosition() would be TREE_POSITION_PRECEDING because node B precedes node F (the reference node, in this case) in the document order. If the same function were called where the given node was nodeC, the return value would be TREE_POSITION_ANCESTOR.

NOTE

The functionality provided by the `compareTreePosition()` *method can also be achieved by using the DOM Level 1 methods and properties. This method is provided as a convenience for applications.*

XPath Support

Recently, a lot of activity has been occurring around XPath, which is a W3C Recommendation describing how to declaratively address nodes in an XML file using path-like syntax. XPath is finding its way into several W3C specifications, such as XSLT, XPointer, XML Query, and so on. DOM Level 3's XPath module introduces new interfaces for allowing XPath to be used in DOM applications. Although it is beyond the scope of this book to provide a full section on XPath, it is worth a brief discussion here to note the functionality available to developers today in certain DOM implementations and to provide an introduction for the support that will be available down the road in the DOM. The full XPath specification is available on the W3C website at www.w3.org/TR/1999/REC-xpath-19991116.html.

What Is XPath?

Basically, XPath is a way of addressing parts of an XML document. In fact, the name "XPath" is derived from the way that the language uses non-XML path structures to navigate through the structure of an XML document, similar to the way paths are used in regular URLs in Internet addresses.

For example, consider the following sample XML document, which models what a typical book structure might look like:

```
<book title="My Book">
   <toc />
   <chapter name="Chapter 1">
      <section>text</section>
      <section>text</section>
   </chapter>
   <chapter name="Chapter 2">
      <section>text</section>
      <section>text</section>
   </chapter>
   <chapter name="Chapter 3">
      <section>text</section>
      <section>text</section>
   </chapter>
```

```
    <appendix name="Appendix A">
        <section>text</section>
        <section>text</section>
    </appendix>
</book>
```

XPath provides a way of describing the location of each node or a set of nodes using a path-like syntax. Technically, these are called "expressions," which, when evaluated, represent a node set, a boolean value, a number, or a string. One of the most important types of expressions is called the LocationPath, which is the syntax used to describe a node's location in a document relative to another node. Because XML documents are organized as hierarchical tree structures, much like the directories on a computer's file system, you can think of LocationPaths the same way you would think of a directory path to a file on a computer system. For example, just as a directory path can be absolute, starting from the very top of the hard drive, an XPath expression can start from the root of the document tree. On a computer system, directory paths can also be evaluated as "relative" paths—that is, relative to the current "working directory" on the computer. Likewise, XPath expressions are also evaluated relative to what is called the "context node" in the XML document.

There is a major difference between directory paths and XPaths, however. In a computer's file system, all of the files in a particular directory must have unique names. This is not the case in XML, where the child nodes of a given node may all have the same name—witness the book example just shown, where the book node has several chapter child nodes. As a result, XPath must be able to represent not just one node per path, but multiple nodes. In this sense, XPath expressions can be thought of as patterns in addition to just regular paths.

A basic XPath LocationPath describes a path through the XML hierarchy and uses forward-slash characters to separate the names of the elements. So, to refer to the chapter elements in our book example, the following path could be used:

```
book/chapter
```

Note that this LocationPath matches *all* of the chapter elements in the book, not just the first one that it encounters. In addition to specifying actual element names within the path expression, XPath allows wildcard characters such as the * to be used in place of element names. So, a LocationPath specified as

```
book/*/section
```

would refer to all the section elements in the document, as long as they are grandchildren of the book node, though they do not have to be child nodes of a chapter element. In this case, all of the section elements in our example document would be returned as a result, both in the chapter elements and the appendix element.

XPath can also be used to take the values of attributes into account when evaluating the path expression. For example, to get chapter elements that have a particular title, you can use a LocationPath expression such as

```
book/chapter[@name="Chapter 1"]
```

Using the @ character indicates the name of an attribute of the given element. The preceding example retrieves the chapter elements that have a name attribute whose value is Chapter 1.

XPath also provides a core set of functions that can be used when selecting nodes in a document. For example, the following XPath expression uses the `position()` function to select the first chapter child node of the book node:

```
book/chapter[position()=1]
```

Of course, the full XPath language supports far more than can be shown here in just a simple introduction. In addition to regular path specifiers and functions, XPath supports comparison operators, branching, and filters. XPath is a very flexible way of working with nodes in a document, and it can often be more convenient to address nodes in a document using XPath than writing the corresponding application logic using standard DOM methods. This helps explain its growing popularity and support in real-world DOM implementations.

XPath Support in DOM Level 3

The DOM XPath Module specifies six interfaces for working with XPath expressions within DOM documents. Table 11-3 lists the interfaces and their purpose.

The main interfaces used in evaluating XPath expressions are the XPathEvaluator, XPathExpression, and XPathResult. To evaluate a DOM XPath expression relative to a given node, applications use the XPathEvaluator interface to create a parsed and compiled XPathExpression either by calling `createExpression()` or by calling the `evaluate()` method directly to evaluate an XPath expression contained within a DOMString. According to the DOM spec, the XPathEvaluator interface is expected to be available on the same object that provides the Document interface for a given implementation. The result of the expression is returned as an XPathResult.

Interface	Purpose
XpathException	Defines new exception codes for exceptions raised when working with XPath expressions.
XpathEvaluator	Provides evaluation of XPath expressions.
XpathExpression	Represents both parsed and resolved XPath expressions.
XPathNSResolver	Resolves namespaces by permitting prefix strings to be bound to namespaceURI strings.
XpathResult	Represents the result of the evaluation of an XPath expression when it has been evaluated within the context of a certain node.
XpathNamespace	Because the DOM does not provide the necessary namespace nodes that XPath requires, this interface is returned by the XPathResult interface to represent such a namespace node. For more information, see the DOM Level 3 XPath module specification.

Table 11-3 *The DOM XPath Interfaces*

The XPathEvaluator interface has the following IDL definition:

```
interface XPathEvaluator {
  XPathExpression createExpression(in DOMString expression,
                             in XPathNSResolver resolver)
                    raises(XPathException, DOMException);
  XPathNSResolver createNSResolver(in Node nodeResolver);
  XPathResult evaluate(in DOMString expression,
                  in Node contextNode,
                  in XPathNSResolver resolver,
                  in unsigned short type,
                  in XPathResult result)
                  raises(XPathException, dom::DOMException);
};
```

The `evaluate()` method is used to directly evaluate XPath expressions given in string form. The `expression` argument contains the XPath expression to be evaluated. The `contextNode` argument represents the document node that will serve as the context node with respect to which the expression will be evaluated. The `resolver` argument translates any prefixes within the XPath expression into appropriate namespace URIs (this argument can be specified as `null` if no namespaces are to be used). The `type` argument allows the caller to specify the type of result desired. If possible, the XPath result will be coerced into the specified type, which should be one of the type codes listed in the XPathResult interface. The `result` argument is provided so that any previously returned XPathResult may be reused.

The `createNSResolver()` method uses the node in the given `nodeResolver` argument to resolve namespaces by calling the `lookupNamespacePrefix()` method on the node.

Sometimes, it is more convenient for performance reasons to compile an XPath expression that will be reused within an application because the expression can be compiled into a more efficient internal representation. In addition, any needed namespace resolution can be done at this point. The `createExpression()` method allows an application to create an XPathExpression object that represents a compiled expression.

The XPathExpression interface has the following IDL definition:

```
interface XPathExpression {
  XPathResult evaluate(in Node contextNode,
                       in unsigned short type,
                       in XPathResult result)
                       raises(XPathException, dom::DOMException);
};
```

The XPathExpression interface contains one method, `evaluate()`, which performs the same function as the `evaluate()` method in the XPathEvaluator interface.

The XPathResult interface represents the result of an evaluated XPath expression. It has the following IDL definition:

```
interface XPathResult {
  // XPathResultType
  const unsigned short   ANY_TYPE                        = 0;
  const unsigned short   NUMBER_TYPE                     = 1;
  const unsigned short   STRING_TYPE                     = 2;
  const unsigned short   BOOLEAN_TYPE                    = 3;
  const unsigned short   UNORDERED_NODE_ITERATOR_TYPE    = 4;
  const unsigned short   ORDERED_NODE_ITERATOR_TYPE      = 5;
  const unsigned short   UNORDERED_NODE_SNAPSHOT_TYPE    = 6;
  const unsigned short   ORDERED_NODE_SNAPSHOT_TYPE      = 7;
  const unsigned short   ANY_UNORDERED_NODE_TYPE         = 8;
  const unsigned short   FIRST_ORDERED_NODE_TYPE         = 9;

  readonly attribute unsigned short   resultType;
  readonly attribute double           numberValue;
```

```
                        // raises(XPathException) on retrieval
    readonly attribute DOMString        stringValue;
                        // raises(XPathException) on retrieval
    readonly attribute boolean          booleanValue;
                        // raises(XPathException) on retrieval
    readonly attribute Node             singleNodeValue;
                        // raises(XPathException) on retrieval
    readonly attribute boolean          invalidIteratorState;
    readonly attribute unsigned long    snapshotLength;
                        // raises(XPathException) on retrieval
    Node            iterateNext()
                        raises(XPathException, dom::DOMException);
    Node            snapshotItem(in unsigned long index)
                        raises(XPathException);
};
```

The first ten constant values represent the possible types of an XPathResult, which can be accessed via the `resultType` property. Table 11-4 lists the possible constant values along with the meaning of each.

Result Type Constant	Meaning
ANY_TYPE	Does not represent any specific type. This value will never be returned by an evaluated expression; but if this type is requested, the evaluation returns whatever type naturally results from evaluation of the expression.
NUMBER_TYPE	Returns a number result. Modifying the document doesn't invalidate the result, but reevaluating the expression might not return the same number value.
STRING_TYPE	Returns a string result. Modifying the document doesn't invalidate the result, but reevaluating the expression might not return the same string value.
BOOLEAN_TYPE	Returns a boolean result. Modifying the document doesn't invalidate the result, but reevaluating the expression might not return the same boolean value.
UNORDERED_NODE_ITERATOR_TYPE	Returns a node set that will be accessed iteratively using the `iterateNext()` method. The nodes in the set may not be in any particular order. Modifying the document will invalidate the node set.

Table 11-4   *XPath Result Codes and Meanings*

Result Type Constant	Meaning
ORDERED_NODE_ ITERATOR_TYPE	Returns a node set that will be accessed iteratively using the iterateNext() method. The nodes in the set will be ordered in document order. Modifying the document will invalidate the node set.
UNORDERED_NODE_ SNAPSHOT_TYPE	Returns a node set that will be accessed as a snapshot list of nodes using the snapshotItem() method. The nodes in the set will be returned in no particular order. Modifying the document will not necessarily invalidate the snapshot list, but it does mean that reevaluating the expression might not produce the same list, and any nodes already in the list may have been removed, relocated, or altered.
ORDERED_NODE_ SNAPSHOT_TYPE	Returns a node set that will be accessed as a snapshot list of nodes using the snapshotItem() method. The nodes in the set will be returned in document order. Modifying the document will not necessarily invalidate the snapshot list, but it does mean that reevaluating the expression might not produce the same list, and any nodes already in the list may have been removed, relocated, or altered.
ANY_UNORDERED_ NODE_TYPE	Returns a node set that will be accessed as a single node value using the singleNodeValue property. If the document is modified, the node may no longer correspond to the current document. If more than one node fits the expression, the returned node may not be the first one in the document order.
FIRST_ORDERED_ NODE_TYPE	Returns a node set that will be accessed as a single node value using the singleNodeValue property. If the document is modified, the node may no longer correspond to the current document. If more than one node fits the expression, the returned node will be the first one in the document order.

Table 11-4   *XPath Result Codes and Meanings* (continued)

The numberValue property retrieves the value of the number type result. If the result is not NUMBER_TYPE, a TYPE_ERR exception is raised. The stringValue property returns the value of the string type result. This raises a TYPE_ERR if the result is not STRING_TYPE. The booleanValue property contains the value of the boolean type result. If the result is not BOOLEAN_TYPE, a TYPE_ERR exception is raised. The singleNodeValue property contains the value of a single node result. If the result is not a FIRST_ORDERED_NODE_TYPE or ANY_UNORDERED_NODE_TYPE, a TYPE_ERR exception is raised.

The invalidIteratorState property is true if the node iterator has become invalid due to the document being modified since the iterator was last returned. This will only be relevant when the result type is UNORDERED_NODE_ITERATOR_TYPE or ORDERED_NODE_ITERATOR_TYPE.

The `snapshotLength` property returns the number of nodes in the result snapshot. This is only relevant when the result type is UNORDERED_NODE_SNAPSHOT_ TYPE or ORDERED_NODE_SNAPSHOT_TYPE.

The `iterateNext()` method returns the next node in the node iterator and advances the iterator position to the next node. The method returns `null` if there are no more nodes. This method will raise a TYPE_ERR exception if the result type is not UNORDERED_NODE_ITERATOR_TYPE or ORDERED_NODE_ ITERATOR_TYPE. In addition, if the document has been modified since the result was returned, an INVALID_STATE_ERR exception will be raised.

The `snapshotItem()` method returns the item in the snapshot list specified by the given index. If the index is larger than the number of nodes in the index, `null` is returned. Snapshots do not automatically become invalid like the iterator when the document is modified, but the nodes in the snapshot may no longer correspond to the document. If the result type is not UNORDERED_NODE_SNAPSHOT_TYPE or ORDERED_NODE_SNAPSHOT_TYPE, a TYPE_ERR exception will be raised when this method is called.

XPath Support in Today's Applications

Microsoft Internet Explorer 6 supports XPath operations in XML documents and XML data islands through the use of the `selectSingleNode()` and `selectNodes()` methods, which are proprietary Microsoft DOM extension methods available on the Node interface. To evaluate an expression relative to a particular node (the context node), your application calls one of these methods with an appropriate XPath expression. The `selectNodes()` method returns a NodeList containing the nodes that match the given XPath expression. It has the following IDL definition:

```
NodeList selectNodes(in DOMString queryStr);
```

The `selectSingleNode()` method returns a single document node that matches the given XPath expression. If more than one node match the given pattern, then only the first matching node is returned. It has the following IDL definition:

```
Node selectSingleNode(in DOMString queryStr);
```

For example, assuming you have a web page with an embedded XML data island named myXMLDataIsland, the following script will return a NodeList containing all of the child chapter elements of the root book element in the data island.

```
// assume an embedded XML data island named "myXMLDataIsland"
var xmlDoc = document.getElementById('myXMLDataIsland');
var myNodeList = xmlDoc.selectNodes('book/chapter');
```

The Apache Xerces Java version has a minimal XPath implementation. The C++ version of Xerces does not directly support XPath, though there are third-party solutions that do, such as Pathan from DecisionSoft. In addition, the Apache Xalan implementation does support XPath because it is needed to support XSLT (discussed in the upcoming section). The Apache Xalan package can be downloaded at http://xml.apache.org, and the Pathan package is available at http://software.decisionsoft.com.

Currently, Netscape 6 does not support programmatic XPath expression evaluation from within DOM applications, though it does support XPath notation when using XSLT transforms.

Other Potential Future DOM Enhancements

In this section, we'll take a look at some technologies and concepts that haven't officially found their way into the DOM yet but may be considered for inclusion at some point. Specifically, we'll examine the XSL Transformation language (XSLT) and the concepts behind transaction-oriented processing.

XSLT Support in the DOM

Extensible Style Language Transformation (XSLT) is fast becoming a rapidly accepted standard for transforming XML documents into other types of documents. It is being used primarily as a bridge language to take data-centric XML documents and give them a visible appearance, such as HTML. XSLT is a W3C Recommendation currently in version 1.0, which was adopted on November 16, 1999 (and is available online at www.w3.org/TR/xslt). In this section, we'll take a look at what XSLT is, how it works, and the level of XSLT support available in today's applications. Note that this isn't intended to be a full introduction to XSLT. I encourage you to check out the XSLT specification on the W3C website and other good tutorials available on the web. The purpose here is to provide a brief introduction to XSLT concepts and examine some implementations at a high level.

What Is XSLT?

In a nutshell, XSLT provides the ability to take a source XML document tree, apply a transformation to it, and produce a result tree. The result document can be of almost any type: text, XML, HTML, and so on. Figure 11-3 illustrates this process.

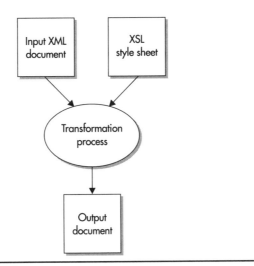

Figure 11-3   *XSLT transformations*

Why would you want to do this? Increasingly, XML is being used as a format for data storage and representation, and there is a clear need for being able to take XML data and present it in a human-consumable form. Often, in fact, it is desirable to be able to present the same data in several forms, such as HTML for web pages, WML for mobile phones, PDF for print versions, CSV for importing into spreadsheets, and so on. This is essentially what XSLT allows developers to do: create transformations that can produce multiple versions of output for a single input document.

How XSLT Works

XSLT works by applying a series of template rules to the source document tree to produce the result document tree. Each template rule consists of two parts: a pattern, which is used to determine which portions of the source tree are affected, and a template, which is used to produce a portion of the output tree.

The rules are described in a construct called an XML style sheet using XSL (Extensible Style Language). XSL describes how the data contained within an XML document should be presented—whether the presentation medium is a web page, handheld device, piece of paper, and so on.

The style sheet is then associated with the XML document, typically by using the `<?xml-stylesheet?>` processing instruction defined in the W3C's XML style sheet specification. To see how it all works, let's look at a simple example.

Consider the following simple XML document:

```
<?xml version="1.0"?>
<hello>Hello there, world!</hello>
```

Suppose you had the task of taking this XML document and transforming it into an HTML document that looked like this:

```
<HTML>
<HEAD>
  <TITLE>Transformed Document</TITLE>
</HEAD>
<BODY>
<H1>Hello there, world!</H1>
</BODY>
</HTML>
```

In other words, you want the text contained in the <hello> tag to be displayed inside an <H1> tag in the resulting HTML document. To perform this in XSLT requires a couple of steps.

First, you need to define the XSL style sheet that will be responsible for generating the output. This means that an HTML document must be created with some kind of "holding slot" where the <hello> tag's text will go. If you name the style sheet "hello.xsl," in XSL parlance, the style sheet would look like this:

```
<xsl:stylesheet xmlns:xsl="http://www.w3.org/1999/XSL/Transform">
<xsl:template match="/">
<HTML>
<HEAD>
  <TITLE>Transformed Document</TITLE>
</HEAD>
<BODY>
<H1><xsl:value-of select="hello"/></H1>
</BODY>
</HTML>
</xsl:template>
</xsl:stylesheet>
```

The <xsl:stylesheet> tag indicates that this file defines an XSL style sheet. The <xsl:template> tag defines an XSLT template. Its match attribute is an XPath expression indicating what part of the source document this template will match up to. The value of / means that the template will be used to match the root element of the source document.

Contained within the template is some literal HTML code that will be included in the output document, along with the `<xsl:value-of>` tag. This XSLT tag means "take the value of the tag that matches my select attribute and insert it here." The `select` attribute uses an XPath expression to determine which node in the source document will supply the value. Here, the node is the `<hello>` tag.

Now, you need to associate the XSL style sheet file "hello.xsl" with the source XML document. This is done by using the `<?xml-stylesheet?>` instruction, which looks like this:

```
<?xml-stylesheet type="text/xsl" href="hello.xsl"?>
```

The `type` attribute indicates to the processor that this is an XSL document, and the `href` attribute contains the relative path to the XSL file. In your finished XML document, it all comes together like this:

```
<?xml version="1.0"?>
<?xml-stylesheet type="text/xsl" href="hello.xsl"?>
<hello>Hello there, world!</hello>
```

When run through an XSLT processor, the resulting HTML file contains the value of the `<hello>` tag where the `<xsl:value-of>` tag was in the XSL file:

```
<HTML>
<HEAD>
  <TITLE>Transformed Document</TITLE>
</HEAD>
<BODY>
  <H1>Hello there, world!</H1>
</BODY>
</HTML>
```

Of course, this example shows just a fraction of the capability provided by XSLT. For further reading, check out the XSLT specification on the W3C website. There are also several good XSLT tutorials on the web; a recent search on the term "XSLT Tutorial" yielded several good starting points.

XSLT Support in Today's Browsers

Both Netscape 6 and Internet Explorer 6 support XSLT, though of the two only IE6 supports programmatically triggering a transformation from within a web page.

That is, IE6 lets you dynamically load and transform XML documents using XSL style sheets from within a script in an HTML page.

Internet Explorer supports the `transformNode()` and `transformNodeToObject()` methods on the Node interface, which perform XSLT transformations on XML data. The `transformNode()` method actually performs the transformation in-place, and will replace the target node with the transformed contents of the XML data. The `transformNodeToObject()` method performs the same kind of transformation but stores the results in a supplied XML document object. These two methods have the following IDL definitions:

```
DOMString transformNode(in Node stylesheet);
void transformNodeToObject(in Node stylesheet, in Node target);
```

Using these methods from within a web page requires that you create a new XML document for the source XML file and source XSL file, load the two documents, and then perform the transformation. Listing 11-1 demonstrates this process using sample HTML, XML, and XSL documents.

Listing 11-1 *Transforming an XML Document Within an HTML Page*

```
// File 1: helloworld.xml
<?xml version="1.0"?>
<?xml-stylesheet type="text/xsl" href="helloworld.xsl"?>
<hello>
  Hello there, world!
</hello>

// file 2: helloworld.xsl
<?xml version="1.0"?>
<xsl:stylesheet
     xmlns:xsl=http://www.w3.org/1999/XSL/Transform
     version="1.0">
  <xsl:template match="/">
      <HTML>
        <HEAD>
          <TITLE></TITLE>
        </HEAD>
        <BODY>
          <H1><xsl:value-of select="hello"/></H1>
        </BODY>
      </HTML>
  </xsl:template>
```

```
</xsl:stylesheet>

// file 3: helloworld.html
<HTML>
<HEAD>
  <TITLE>Programmatic Transform Sample</TITLE>
  <SCRIPT>
     function transformContent ()
     {
         var srcXML = new ActiveXObject("Msxml2.DOMDocument.4.0");
         srcXML.async=false;
         srcXML.load("helloworld.xml");

         var xsltTree= new ActiveXObject("Msxml2.DOMDocument.4.0");
         xsltTree.async = false;
         xsltTree.load("helloworld.xsl");

         var resNode = document.getElementById("theResult");
         resNode.innerHTML = srcXML.transformNode(xsltTree);
     }
  </SCRIPT>
</HEAD>
<BODY onload = "transformContent()" >
<div id="theResult"></div>
</BODY>
</HTML>
```

This example code loads two documents, the source XML and the XSL style sheet, and then calls the `transformNode()` method to transform the DIV element in the document's body into the resulting HTML code.

In this example, you're doing something a little differently than you've done before. You're creating new XML and XSL documents by calling the ActiveXObject constructor function to return empty documents, and then loading them using the documents' load functions. For this example to work, you must have the MSXML4 parser installed on your computer, which can be downloaded from Microsoft's developer site (http://msdn.microsoft.com). The MSXML4 package contains all the documentation necessary for creating new XML documents in IE using the supplied API.

The `transformNode()` method returns a string as its result, so you can store it directly into the `innerHTML` property of the `DIV` element to replace its content with the transformed HTML code. Figure 11-4 shows the web page that results from the transformation.

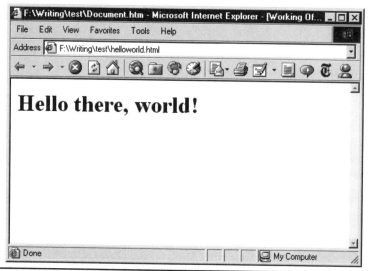

Figure 11-4   *The transformed web page*

XSLT in Other Applications

Among standalone implementations, Apache's Xalan package is a free, open-source implementation of the XSLT specification, and it includes its own copy of the Xerces parser for manipulating XML documents. It also includes its own support for using XSLT on Xerces DOM structures and an XPath implementation used for selecting nodes to transform in the source document. Microsoft's MSXML4 parser also supports XSLT transformations.

There are also several XSLT authoring applications that support XSLT development, such as Xselerator from MarrowSoft; XMLSpy from Altova, Inc.; and XMetaL from SoftQuad. All of these applications are available in downloadable demonstration form from their respective company's web site.

Transaction-Oriented Processing

Transaction-based processing is a term used to describe a type of processing where several small actions can be grouped together to form a single large, logical action. For example, consider the common task of doing a search-and-replace operation on a document in a word processor. When performing one search-and-replace operation at a time, each change to the document can be considered an individual action. If you were to stop making replacements and start using the application's "undo" command, each change you had made to the document would be individually undone.

However, if you were to use the "change all" function, in which the program automatically searches the entire document and replaces all of the matches that it finds, each one of those changes would no longer be considered one individual change. If you were to use the undo command after a "change all" operation, all of the individual changes that were made to the document's content would be undone all at once. In this case, all of the singular changes would be grouped together into one transaction.

Another benefit of transactions is that they lock out other changes while the underlying data is being modified. If an application allows concurrent processes access to a shared piece of data, such as a document, and each of those processes tries to modify the document at the same time, the results can quickly become chaotic unless some type of control mechanism is employed. Transactions can prevent this from happening by ensuring that only one pending transaction can be active at any one time.

NOTE

The Level 3 DOM does not yet address transactions, although it is an idea that might find its way into future versions of the specification.

Though it is beyond the scope of this section to provide an in-depth discussion of how transactions work and all their nuances, it is worth a brief exploration to see how transactions might be applied in the DOM.

Wrapping a Series of Edits as a Transaction

To create a single transaction, it is necessary to indicate the beginning and end of the range of edits that will comprise the transaction. This can be done in several ways, but one way is to use explicit function calls to wrap each transaction. The following JavaScript pseudocode illustrates one example of what this might look like:

```
DOMImplementation impl = document.implementation;
DOMTransaction tID = impl.beginTransaction();
// perform some edits to the document
var text = document.createTextNode("Some Text");
document.documentElement.appendChild(text);
// end the transaction
impl.endTransaction(tID);
```

This code explicitly wraps the beginning and ending of a transaction with calls to two made-up functions called `beginTransaction()` and `endTransaction()`.

The `beginTransaction()` call also returns an identifier token that can be used to identify the transaction.

In addition, it may be useful for an application to be able to discover whether a transaction is currently taking place. This can be accomplished by calling a method like `isInsideTransaction()`, which would return the identifier of the current transaction ID or −1 if no transaction is underway:

```
var tID = impl.isInsideTransaction();
```

Rolling Back a Transaction

One of the nice things about transactions is that once completed, they can be recorded and "rolled back," or undone on an individual basis. For example, an application may keep a list of completed transactions on a document and expose this to the user when implementing a "multiple undo" feature, or a history-like list of past operations that show all of the operations on a document. To roll a transaction back, the developer might use a function like `rollBackTransaction()`, which returns true if the transaction was able to be rolled back:

```
var bResult = rollBackTransaction(tID);
```

Conclusion

In this chapter, we examined the changes proposed in the latest working drafts of the DOM Level 3 modules and investigated some other trends and technologies that are affecting the development of the DOM, though they are not yet part of the official standard.

We started off by examining the latest proposed changes in DOM Level 3, beginning with the additions and changes to the existing interfaces. We looked at the new data types and methods added to the DOM to support such concepts as testing nodes for sameness and equality, extracting text content from nodes, attaching application-specific data to document nodes, and determining the positions of nodes in the document tree relative to other nodes.

Next, we investigated some entirely new interfaces proposed for the latest specification to support document loading and saving, error handling, working with and editing DTDs and other abstract schemas, and working with XPath expressions—all very useful functionality that has been noticeably absent from prior DOM levels.

Finally, we investigated XSLT and transaction-oriented processing and how they might be used in future DOM implementations. In the case of XSLT, some DOM implementers have already started adding support without waiting for the W3C Working Group, such as Microsoft and Apache.

When DOM Level 3 is released, it will substantially increase the DOM's capabilities and types of operations available to developers. Level 3 will finally address many of the limitations of earlier DOM levels and will allow developers to create even richer, standardized applications than are possible today.

DOM Core Level 1 API Reference

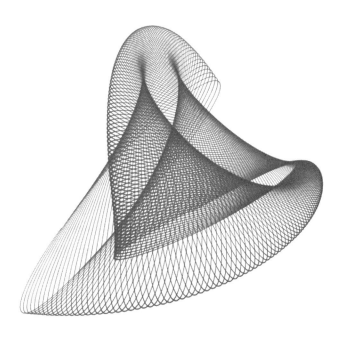

his appendix lists the methods and properties of the interfaces that make up the Core Level 1 DOM API. Each interface entry lists the constants (if any) for that interface, along with the properties and methods that the interface provides.

DOM Interface Inheritance Tree

Figure A-1 shows the inheritance relationships among the various Core DOM Level 1 interfaces.

Interface Attr

The Attr interface represents an attribute node on an Element node. Typically, the permissible values for an attribute are specified by a Document Type Definition (DTD) file. Attributes inherit from the Node interface, but they are not actually children of the Element node that they are attached to, and they are not considered part of the Document tree by the DOM. For this reason, their `previousSibling`, `nextSibling`, and `parentNode` properties are always `null`.

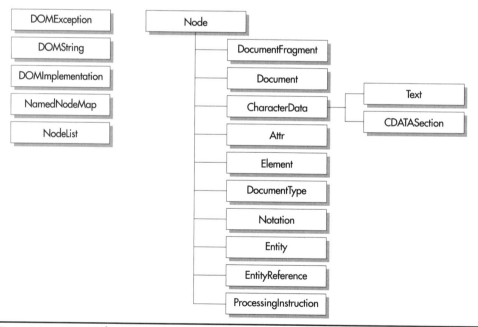

Figure A-1 *DOM inheritance diagram*

Attribute values are determined as follows: if a value has been explicitly assigned to an attribute, it has that value. Otherwise, if the DTD specifies a default value for the attribute, that default value is the attribute's effective value. If neither condition is true, the attribute has no value and does not exist on the element until explicitly created.

Properties

name (read-only)

Type: DOMString
Description: Represents the name of the attribute.
Exceptions: None

specified (read-only)

Type: Boolean
Description: Indicates whether the attribute was explicitly assigned a value in the source document.
Exceptions: None

value

Type: DOMString
Description: When retrieved, returns the value of the attribute as a string. When set, a new Text node is created for the attribute containing the unparsed text content of the string.
Exceptions: None

Methods

No methods other than those inherited from the Node interface.

Interface CDATA

CDATA sections are used to escape blocks of text containing characters that would otherwise be processed by the XML parser as markup. CDATA sections cannot be nested, and they do not have any child nodes. According to the DOM specification, the primary purpose of a CDATA section is for including material such as XML fragments without needing to escape all the delimiters.

Properties

No properties other than those inherited from the Text interface.

Methods

No methods other than those inherited from the Text interface.

Interface CharacterData

The CharacterData interface provides methods and properties for working with character data in the DOM. The CharacterData interface is provided only as an interface from which others inherit, such as Text. There are never any objects in the DOM document tree that correspond directly to CharacterData.

The CharacterData interface provides properties for directly accessing the text content of a node and its length, and it provides methods for appending, inserting, replacing, deleting, and extracting substrings of text.

Properties

data

Type: DOMString
Description: Indicates whether the attribute was explicitly assigned a value in the source document.
Exceptions:
   NO_MODIFICATION_ALLOWED_ERR   Raised when set if the node is read-only
   DOMSTRING_SIZE_ERR   Raised when retrieving if it would return more characters than fit in a DOMString variable on the implementation platform

length (read-only)

Type: unsigned long
Description: Indicates whether the attribute was explicitly assigned a value in the source document.
Exceptions: None

Methods

substringData

Syntax:

```
DOMString substringData(in unsigned long offset,
                        in unsigned long count)
raises(DOMException);
```

offset: Offset at which to start the substring

count: Number of characters to extract

Description: Extracts a substring of data from the node.

Returns: The requested substring

Exceptions:

INDEX_SIZE_ERR   Raised if the specified offset is negative or greater than the number of characters in data, or if the specified count is negative

DOMSTRING_SIZE_ERR   Raised if the specified range of text does not fit into a DOMString

appendData

Syntax:

```
void appendData(in DOMString arg)
raises(DOMException);
```

arg: The string to append to the node data

Description: Append the given string to the end of the character data of the node.

Returns: Nothing

Exceptions:

NO_MODIFICATION_ALLOWED_ERR   Raised if this node is read-only

deleteData

Syntax:

```
void deleteData(in unsigned long offset,in unsigned long count)
raises(DOMException);
```

offset: Offset at which to delete characters

count: Number of characters to delete

Description: Deletes characters from the node's text data.
Returns: Nothing
Exceptions:

INDEX_SIZE_ERR   Raised if the specified offset is negative or greater than the number of characters in data or if the specified count is negative

NO_MODIFICATION_ALLOWED_ERR   Raised if this node is read-only

insertData

Syntax:
```
void insertData(in unsigned long offset,in DOMString arg)
raises(DOMException);
```
offset: Offset at which to insert the new string
arg: The new string to be inserted
Description: Inserts the given string into the node's text data at the given offset.
Returns: Nothing
Exceptions:

INDEX_SIZE_ERR   Raised if the specified offset is negative or greater than the number of characters in data

NO_MODIFICATION_ALLOWED_ERR   Raised if this node is read-only

replaceData

Syntax:
```
void replaceData(in unsigned long offset, in unsigned long count,
                 in DOMString arg)
raises(DOMException);
```
offset: Offset at which to begin replacing characters
count: Number of characters to replace
arg: String to replace characters with
Returns: Nothing
Description: Replaces the characters starting at the given character offset with the given string.
Exceptions:

INDEX_SIZE_ERR   Raised if the specified offset is negative or greater than the number of characters in data, or if the specified count is negative

NO_MODIFICATION_ALLOWED_ERR   Raised if this node is read-only

Interface Comment

This represents the content of a comment, that is, all the characters between the starting < ! - - and ending - ->.

Properties

See CharacterData interface.

Methods

See CharacterData interface.

Interface Document

The Document interface represents the entire XML or HTML document and is conceptually the "root" of the document. The Document interface also provides the factory methods for creating new document nodes because they cannot exist outside of the context of a document.

Properties

docType (read-only)

Type: DocumentType
Description: Represents the Document Type Declaration (DTD) for this document. When the document has no DTD, this will return `null`. Note that DOM Level 1 does not support editing DTDs, thus the `docType` cannot be altered.
Exceptions: None

documentElement (read-only)

Type: Node
Description: Refers to first child node of the document root. In HTML documents, this corresponds to the <HTML> tag.
Exceptions: None

implementation (read-only)

Type: DOMImplementation
Description: The corresponding DOMImplementation that handles this document. DOM applications are not limited to using documents from a single implementation.
Exceptions: None

Methods

createElement

Syntax:
```
Element createElement(in DOMString tagName)
raises (DOMException);
```
tagName: The type of element to create
Description: Creates an Element node of the specified type. Note that in XML, this is case sensitive. In HTML, the string provided may be in any case, but will be mapped to uppercase by the application.
Returns: The newly created Element node
Exceptions:
   INVALID_CHARACTER_ERR   Raised if the specified name contains an invalid character

createDocumentFragment

Syntax:
```
DocumentFragment createDocumentFragment();
```
Description: Creates an empty DocumentFragment object to which child nodes can then be appended.
Exceptions: None

createTextNode

Syntax:
```
Text createTextNode(in DOMString data);
```
data: The content for the newly created Text node

Description: Creates a new Text node whose data is the given string.
Returns: The newly created Text node
Exceptions: None

createComment

Syntax:
```
Comment createComment(in DOMString data);
```
data: The content for the newly created Comment node
Description: Creates a Comment node whose data is the given string.
Returns: The new Comment node
Exceptions: None

createCDATASection

Syntax:
```
CDATASection createCDATASection(in DOMString data);
raises (DOMException);
```
data: The content for the newly created CDATASection node
Description: Creates a CDATASection node whose data is the given string.
Returns: The new CDATASection node
Exceptions:
   NOT_SUPPORTED_ERR   Raised if this document does not support
CDATASection nodes (for example, the document is an HTML document)

createProcessingInstruction

Syntax:
```
ProcessingInstruction createProcessingInstruction(in DOMString target,
                                            in DOMString data)
raises(DOMException);
```
target: The target for the ProcessingInstruction
data: The data for the node
Description: Creates a ProcessingInstruction node given the specified name and
data strings.

Returns: The new ProcessingInstruction node
Exceptions:
    INVALID_CHARACTER_ERR   Raised if an invalid character is specified
    NOT_SUPPORTED_ERR   Raised if this document does not support
CDATASection nodes (for example, the document is an HTML document)

createAttribute

Syntax:
```
Attr createAttribute(in DOMString name)
raises (DOMException);
```
name: The name of the attribute node to create
Description: Creates a new Attr node of the given name.
Returns: The new attribute node
Exceptions:
    INVALID_CHARACTER_ERR   Raised if the specified name contains an
invalid character

createEntityReference

Syntax:
```
EntityReference createEntityReference(in DOMString name)
raises(DOMException);
```
name: The name of the Entity to create a reference to
Description: Creates a new EntityReference node.
Returns: The new EntityReference node
Exceptions:
    INVALID_CHARACTER_ERR   Raised if the specified name contains an
invalid character
    NOT_SUPPORTED_ERR   Raised if this document does not support
CDATASection nodes (for example, the document is an HTML document)

getElementsByTagName

Syntax:
```
NodeList getElementsByTagName(in DOMString tagName);
```
tagName: The tag name of the elements to match. The special tagName * will
match all elements in the tree.

Description: Returns a NodeList containing all the Element nodes with a given tag name in the order in which they would be encountered in a preorder traversal of the Document tree.
Returns: A NodeList containing the matching Element nodes
Exceptions: None

Interface DocumentFragment

The DocumentFragment interface was added as a lightweight way of extracting a portion of a document tree and manipulating it without having to construct and populate a whole new Document object because this might be an expensive operation in some implementations. For this reason, the DocumentFragment inherits directly from the Node interface.

There are several methods in the DOM API that take Nodes as arguments that also allow DocumentFragments to be passed. Doing so operates on all of the child nodes in the DocumentFragment (but not the DocumentFragment node itself).

DocumentFragments are not required to be well-formed XML documents (although they do need to follow the rules imposed upon well-formed XML parsed entities, which can have multiple top nodes). For example, a DocumentFragment node may have a Comment node as its only child.

Properties

No properties other than those inherited from the Node interface.

Methods

No methods other than those inherited from the Node interface.

Interface DocumentType

The DocumentType interface in the DOM Level 1 Core provides an interface to the list of entities that are defined for the document. DOM Level 1 defines these properties to be read-only, recognizing that a future level of the DOM will specify how to read and write these settings.

Properties

name (read-only)

Type: DOMString
Description: The name of DTD for this document. That is, the name immediately following the DOCTYPE keyword.
Exceptions: None

entities (read-only)

Type: NamedNodeMap
Description: A NamedNodeMap containing the general entities, both external and internal, declared in the DTD, with duplicates discarded. DOM Level 1 does not provide a way to edit these entities.
Exceptions: None

notations (read-only)

Type: NamedNodeMap
Description: A NamedNodeMap containing the notations declared in the DTD, with duplicates discarded. Every node in this map also implements the Notation interface. DOM Level 1 does not provide a way to edit these notations.
Exceptions: None

Methods

No methods other than those inherited from the Node interface.

Interface DOMImplementation

The DOMImplementation interface is intended to provide methods that are independent of any particular document instance. DOM Level 1 does not specify a way of obtaining a DOMImplementation interface, leaving it as an implementation-dependent operation. For example, in the browsers, you refer to the DOMImplementation by using the implementation object on the document interface (document.implementation).

Properties

No properties.

Methods

hasFeature

Syntax:
```
boolean hasFeature (in DOMString feature, in DOMString version)
                    raises(DOMException);
```
feature: The package name of the requested feature

version: The version number of the package name to test. If not specified, supporting any version of the requested feature will cause the method to return true.

Description: Test if the DOM implementation implements a specific feature.

Returns: Returns true if the feature is implemented in the specified version, false otherwise.

Exceptions: None

Interface DOMException

The DOMException interface is used by an implementation to report exceptions raised in the process of working with a document. Some implementations do not support exceptions, so the codes provided by the DOMException interface may be reported using other standard error reporting mechanisms used natively by that implementation.

Constants

```
const unsigned short INDEX_SIZE_ERR = 1;
const unsigned short DOMSTRING_SIZE_ERR = 2;
const unsigned short HIERARCHY_REQUEST_ERR = 3;
const unsigned short WRONG_DOCUMENT_ERR = 4;
const unsigned short INVALID_CHARACTER_ERR = 5;
const unsigned short NO_DATA_ALLOWED_ERR = 6;
const unsigned short NO_MODIFICATION_ALLOWED_ERR = 7;
const unsigned short NOT_FOUND_ERR = 8;
```

```
const unsigned short NOT_SUPPORTED_ERR = 9;
const unsigned short INUSE_ATTRIBUTE_ERR = 10;
```

Properties

code
Type: unsigned short
Description: Contains the exception code representing the exception.
Exceptions: None

Methods

No methods

Interface Element

Element nodes represent the majority of node types that a DOM application will encounter in any given document. They correspond to what are commonly called the tags in XML and HTML documents.

Properties

tagName (read-only)
Type: DOMString
Description: The tag name for this element. This is equivalent to the Node interface's nodeName.
Exceptions: None

Methods

getAttribute
Syntax:
```
DOMString getAttribute(in DOMString name);
```
name: Name of the attribute to retrieve

Description: Retrieves the value of the given attribute.
Returns: The string content of the requested attribute
Exceptions: None

getAttributeNode

Syntax:
```
Attr getAttributeNode(in DOMString name);
```
name: The name of the attribute to retrieve
Description: Retrieves the requested attribute as an Attr node. If there is no such attribute, returns `null`.
Returns: An Attr node corresponding to the requested attribute, or `null` if there is no attribute by the given name.
Exceptions: None

getElementsByTagName

Syntax:
```
NodeList getElementsByTagName(in DOMString name);
```
name: Tag name of the elements to match
Description: Returns a NodeList of all descendant elements with a given tag name, in the order in which they would be encountered in a preorder traversal of the Element subtree.
Returns: A NodeList containing the child element nodes matching the given name. The special tagName * matches all elements.
Exceptions: None

normalize

Syntax:
```
void normalize();
```
Description: Collapses all of the adjacent Text nodes in the full depth of the subtree under this Element into singular text nodes. This has the same effect as if the document were saved and then reloaded.
Returns: Nothing
Exceptions: None

removeAttribute

Syntax:
```
void removeAttribute(in DOMString name)
raises(DOMException);
```
name: The name of the attribute to remove

Description: Removes an attribute by name. If the removed attribute has a default value in the DTD it is immediately replaced.

Returns: Nothing

Exceptions:

NO_MODIFICATION_ALLOWED_ERR   Raised if this node is read-only

removeAttributeNode

Syntax:
```
Attr removeAttributeNode(in Attr oldAttr)
raises(DOMException);
```
Description: Removes the specified attribute.

Returns: The Attr node of the removed attribute

Exceptions:

NO_MODIFICATION_ALLOWED_ERR   Raised if this node is read-only

NOT_FOUND_ERR   Raised if oldAttr is not an attribute of the element

setAttribute

Syntax:
```
void setAttribute(in DOMString name,in DOMString value)
raises(DOMException);
```
name: The name of the attribute to create or change

value: New value for the attribute

Description: Adds a new attribute. If an attribute with that name is already present in the element, its value is changed to be that of the value parameter. Note that the value is a simple string and is not parsed when it is set. Applications must escape the appropriate markup characters when writing out the attribute.

Returns: Nothing

Exceptions:
    INVALID_CHARACTER_ERR   Raised if the specified name contains an invalid character
    NO_MODIFICATION_ALLOWED_ERR   Raised if this node is read-only

setAttributeNode

Syntax:
```
Attr setAttributeNode(in Attr newAttr)
raises(DOMException);
```
Description: Adds a new attribute. If an attribute with that name is already present in the element, it is replaced by the new one.
Returns: If the given attribute node replaces an existing one, the replaced node is returned; otherwise `null` is returned.
Exceptions:
    WRONG_DOCUMENT_ERR   Raised if `newAttr` was created from a different document than the one that created the element.
    NO_MODIFICATION_ALLOWED_ERR   Raised if this node is read-only.
    INUSE_ATTRIBUTE_ERR   Raised if the given attribute node is already an attribute of another Element object. The DOM user must explicitly clone Attr nodes to reuse them in other elements.

Interface Entity

This interface represents an entity, either parsed or unparsed, in an XML document. The nodeName attribute that is inherited from the Node interface contains the name of the entity.

Properties

publicID (read-only)

Type: DOMString
Description: The public identifier associated with the entity, if specified. If the public identifier was not specified, this is `null`.
Exceptions: None

systemID (read-only)

Type: DOMString
Description: The system identifier associated with the entity, if specified.
If the system identifier was not specified, this is `null`.
Exceptions: None

notationName (read-only)

Type: DOMString
Description: For unparsed entities, the name of the notation for the entity.
For parsed entities, this is `null`.
Exceptions: None

Methods

No methods other than those inherited from the Node interface.

Interface EntityReference

Represents an EntityReference node in the document.

Properties

No properties other than those inherited from the Node interface.

Methods

No methods other than those inherited from the Node interface.

Interface NamedNodeMap

The NamedNodeMap interface is used to represent collections of nodes that can be accessed by name. NamedNodeMaps are not maintained in any particular order.

Properties

length (read-only)

Type: unsigned long
Description: The number of nodes in the map
Exceptions: None

Methods

getNamedItem

Syntax:
```
Node getNamedItem(in DOMString name);
```
name: Name of the node in the NamedNodeMap to return
Description: Retrieves a node in the map, given its name.
Returns: The requested node, or `null` if it does not exist in the map
Exceptions: None

setNamedItem

Syntax:
```
Node setNamedItem(in Node arg)
raises(DOMException);
```
arg: Name of the node to add to the NamedNodeMap
Description: Stores a node in the map using its `nodeName`. If another node by the same name is already in the map, it is replaced by the new node.
Returns: If the new node replaces an existing node with the same name the previously existing node is returned, otherwise `null` is returned.
Exceptions:

WRONG_DOCUMENT_ERR   Raised if `arg` was created from a different document than the one that created the NamedNodeMap.

NO_MODIFICATION_ALLOWED_ERR   Raised if this NamedNodeMap is read-only.

INUSE_ATTRIBUTE_ERR   Raised if `arg` is an Attr that is already an attribute of another Element object. The application must explicitly clone Attr nodes to reuse them in other elements.

removeNamedItem

Syntax:

```
Node removeNamedItem(in DOMString name)
raises(DOMException);
```

name: Name of the node in the NamedNodeMap to remove

Description: Removes a node specified by name. If the removed node is an Attr with a default value it is immediately replaced.

Returns: The node removed from the map or `null` if no node with such a name exists

Exceptions:

  NOT_FOUND_ERR   Raised if there is no node with the given name in the map

item

Syntax:

```
Node item(in unsigned long index);
```

index: Index of the node in the NamedNodeMap to return

Description: Returns the node at the given index in the NamedNodeMap. Note that even though NamedNodeMaps allow retrieval by index, this does not imply any ordering of the nodes.

Returns: The node at the given index in the NamedNodeMap, or `null` if it is not a valid index

Exceptions: None

Interface Node

The Node interface represents the primary, basic type of object present in DOM documents. All of the specific node types such as Elements, Attrs, and so on derive from the Node interface. However, even though the Node interface exposes properties and methods for working with child nodes, not all node types support children.

Constants

```
const unsigned short ELEMENT_NODE = 1;
const unsigned short ATTRIBUTE_NODE = 2;
const unsigned short TEXT_NODE = 3;
const unsigned short CDATA_SECTION_NODE = 4;
const unsigned short ENTITY_REFERENCE_NODE = 5;
const unsigned short ENTITY_NODE = 6;
const unsigned short PROCESSING_INSTRUCTION_NODE = 7;
const unsigned short COMMENT_NODE = 8;
const unsigned short DOCUMENT_NODE = 9;
const unsigned short DOCUMENT_TYPE_NODE = 10;
const unsigned short DOCUMENT_FRAGMENT_NODE = 11;
const unsigned short NOTATION_NODE = 12;
```

Properties

nodeName (read-only)

Type: DOMString
Description: The name of this particular node, depending on its type
Exceptions: None

nodeValue

Type: DOMString
Description: Value of the node, depending on its type
Exceptions:
  NO_MODIFICATION_ALLOWED_ERR   Raised when setting if the node is read-only
  DOMSTRING_SIZE_ERR   Raised when retrieving if it would return more characters than fit in a DOMString variable on the implementation platform

nodeType (read-only)

Type: unsigned short
Description: A code number representing the node type; see the Constants section above for allowable values.
Exceptions: None

parentNode (read-only)

Type: Node
Description: The parent node of this node or `null` if it has no parent
Exceptions: None

childNodes (read-only)

Type: NodeList
Description: A NodeList containing all of the child nodes of this node. If the node has no children, the NodeList is empty.
Exceptions: None

firstChild (read-only)

Type: Node
Description: The first child of this node. If there is no such node, this returns `null`.
Exceptions: None

lastChild (read-only)

Type: Node
Description: The last child of this node. If there is no such node, this returns `null`.
Exceptions: None

previousSibling (read-only)

Type: Node
Description: The node immediately preceding this node. If there is no such node, this returns `null`.
Exceptions: None

nextSibling (read-only)

Type: Node
Description: The node immediately following this node. If there is no such node, this returns `null`.
Exceptions: None

attributes (read-only)

Type: NamedNodeMap
Description: If this node is an Element node, this property represents a NamedNodeMap containing the attributes of this node. Otherwise, it is `null`.

Exceptions: None

ownerDocument (read-only)

Type: Document
Description: The document that owns this node. This is also the Document object that creates new nodes. If this node is itself a Document, this property is `null`.
Exceptions: None

Methods

appendChild

Syntax:

```
Node appendChild(in Node newChild)
raises(DOMException);
```

newChild: The node to be appended
Description: Appends the given new child node to this node. If the given node already exists elsewhere in the document, it is first removed from its current position.
Returns: The appended node
Exceptions:
   HIERARCHY_REQUEST_ERR   Raised if this node is of a type that does not allow children of the type of the `newChild` node, or if the node to append is one of this node's ancestors
   WRONG_DOCUMENT_ERR   Raised if `newChild` was created from a different document than the one that created this node
   NO_MODIFICATION_ALLOWED_ERR   Raised if this node is read-only

cloneNode

Syntax:

```
Node cloneNode(in boolean deep);
```

deep: True if this should perform a deep clone
Description: Performs a copy of this node. If the `deep` argument is true, all child nodes are also copied.
Returns: The new copy of the node
Exceptions: None

hasChildNodes

Syntax:

```
boolean hasChildNodes();
```

Description: Returns true if this node has any child nodes.
Returns: True if this node has child nodes, false otherwise
Exceptions: None

insertBefore

Syntax:

```
Node insertBefore(in Node newChild,in Node refChild)
raises(DOMException);
```

newChild: The node to be inserted
refChild: The node to insert the new node before
Description: Inserts the `newChild` node before the existing child node represented by `refChild`. If `refChild` is `null`, the new node is inserted at the end of the list of children.
Returns: The newly inserted node
Exceptions:

HIERARCHY_REQUEST_ERR   Raised if this node is of a type that does not allow children of the type of the newChild node, or if the node to insert is one of this node's ancestors

WRONG_DOCUMENT_ERR   Raised if `newChild` was created from a different document than the one that created this node

NO_MODIFICATION_ALLOWED_ERR   Raised if this node is read-only

NOT_FOUND_ERR   Raised if `refChild` is not a child of this node

removeChild

Syntax:

```
Node removeChild(in Node oldChild)
raises(DOMException);
```

oldChild: The child node to be removed

Description: Removes the given child node from the list of children.

Returns: The removed node

Exceptions:

NO_MODIFICATION_ALLOWED_ERR   Raised if this node is read-only

NOT_FOUND_ERR   Raised if `oldChild` is not a child of this node

replaceChild

Syntax:

```
Node replaceChild(in Node newChild, in Node oldChild)
raises(DOMException);
```

newChild: The new node to insert

oldChild: The node to be replaced

Description: Replaces the given child node `oldChild` with the new node `newChild`.

Returns: The old, replaced child node

Exceptions:

HIERARCHY_REQUEST_ERR   Raised if this node is of a type that does not allow children of the type of the `newChild` node, or it the node to put in is one of this node's ancestors

WRONG_DOCUMENT_ERR   Raised if `newChild` was created from a different document than the one that created this node

NO_MODIFICATION_ALLOWED_ERR   Raised if this node is read-only

NOT_FOUND_ERR   Raised if `oldChild` is not a child of this node

Interface NodeList

The NodeList interface provides a way of accessing an ordered collection of nodes, without defining or constraining how this collection is implemented.

Properties

length (read-only)

Type: unsigned long

Description: The number of nodes in the list

Exceptions: None

Methods

item

Syntax:

```
Node item(in unsigned long index);
```

index: Index of the node in the NodeList to return

Description: Retrieves the node in the collection at the given index.

Returns: The node at the given index in the NodeList, or `null` of the given index is out of range

Exceptions: None

Interface Notation

This interface represents a notation declared in the DTD. A notation either declares by name the format of an unparsed entity, or is used for formal declaration of Processing Instruction targets. The `nodeName` attribute inherited from the Node interface is set to the declared name of the notation. The DOM Level 1 does not support editing Notation nodes, so all properties therefore read-only. Notation nodes do not have parent nodes.

Properties

publicID

Type: DOMString

Description: The public identifier of this notation. If the public identifier was not specified, this is `null`.

Exceptions: None

systemID

Type: DOMString

Description: The system identifier of this notation. If the system identifier was not specified, this is `null`.

Exceptions: None

Methods

No methods other than those inherited from the Node interface.

Interface ProcessingInstruction

Represents a *processing instruction,* which is used in XML as a way to keep processor-specific information stored in the document content.

Properties

data

Type: DOMString
Description: Represents the content of this processing instruction. This is from the first non-whitespace character after the target to the character immediately preceding the ?>.
Exceptions:
   NO_MODIFICATION_ALLOWED_ERR   Raised if the ProcessingInstruction node is read-only

target (read-only)

Type: DOMString
Description: The target of this processing instruction. XML defines this as being the first token following the markup that begins the processing instruction.
Exceptions: None

Methods

The ProcessingInstruction interface has no methods other than those inherited from the Node interface.

Interface Text

The Text interface represents the textual content of an Element or Attr node. If there is no markup inside an element's content, the text is contained in a single object implementing the Text interface that is the only child of the element. If there is markup, it is parsed into a list of elements and Text nodes that form the list of children of the element.

Properties

See CharacterData interface.

Methods

splitText

Syntax:

```
Text splitText(in unsigned long offset) raises(DOMException);
```

offset: Character offset at which to split the text content of the node

Description: Breaks this Text node into two Text nodes at the specified offset, keeping both in the tree as siblings. This node then only contains all the content up to the offset point. A new Text node, which is inserted as the next sibling of this node, contains all the content at and after the offset point.

Returns: The newly created Text node

Exceptions:

INDEX_SIZE_ERR   Raised if the specified offset is negative or greater than the number of characters in data

NO_MODIFICATION_ALLOWED_ERR   Raised if this node is read-only

Index

INTERNATIONAL CONTACT INFORMATION

AUSTRALIA
McGraw-Hill Book Company Australia Pty. Ltd.
TEL +61-2-9415-9899
FAX +61-2-9415-5687
http://www.mcgraw-hill.com.au
books-it_sydney@mcgraw-hill.com

CANADA
McGraw-Hill Ryerson Ltd.
TEL +905-430-5000
FAX +905-430-5020
http://www.mcgrawhill.ca

GREECE, MIDDLE EAST, NORTHERN AFRICA
McGraw-Hill Hellas
TEL +30-1-656-0990-3-4
FAX +30-1-654-5525

MEXICO (Also serving Latin America)
McGraw-Hill Interamericana Editores S.A. de C.V.
TEL +525-117-1583
FAX +525-117-1589
http://www.mcgraw-hill.com.mx
fernando_castellanos@mcgraw-hill.com

SINGAPORE (Serving Asia)
McGraw-Hill Book Company
TEL +65-863-1580
FAX +65-862-3354
http://www.mcgraw-hill.com.sg
mghasia@mcgraw-hill.com

SOUTH AFRICA
McGraw-Hill South Africa
TEL +27-11-622-7512
FAX +27-11-622-9045
robyn_swanepoel@mcgraw-hill.com

UNITED KINGDOM & EUROPE (Excluding Southern Europe)
McGraw-Hill Education Europe
TEL +44-1-628-502500
FAX +44-1-628-770224
http://www.mcgraw-hill.co.uk
computing_neurope@mcgraw-hill.com

ALL OTHER INQUIRIES Contact:
Osborne/McGraw-Hill
TEL +1-510-549-6600
FAX +1-510-883-7600
http://www.osborne.com
omg_international@mcgraw-hill.com